"Crucial reading for anyone interested in the political history of New York, *Boss of Black Brooklyn* provides us with a deep understanding of ethnic and racial urban politics of the early and mid–twentieth century. Howell skillfully traces the life of Brooklyn's first black elected official following Bertram Baker's start in politics, to his election to the New York state Assembly, to his appointment as chairman of the state Assembly's Education Committee, Waiting for Stuyvesant. An inspiration for the next generation of black politicians."
—**Clarence Taylor, Baruch College, The City University of New York**

"This warm, insightful, and deeply researched study of Bertram Baker, arguably the most important black political leader in Brooklyn's history, reveals how Afro-Caribbeans contributed centrally in the rise of black political influence in New York City. Both a biography of the author's grandfather and an autobiography of growing up as a third-generation immigrant in Brooklyn today, Howell's book is a brilliant contribution to understanding how our city came to be as it is."
—**John Mollenkopf, Director, Center for Urban Research, The Graduate Center, CUNY**

"*Boss of Black Brooklyn* is a story of hope. Howell sheds light on Freudian conflicts that have wreaked havoc on black families over the course of the black presence in the American hemisphere. Bertram Baker is a contradictory model for how to live and how not to live. Although he has been dead for more than three decades, Baker's story shows us that we can achieve great things despite our weaknesses. We can claim to be righteous and bold, but we must learn that compromise is one of life's most valuable skills."
—**Raymond T. Diamond, James Carville Alumni Professor; Jules F. & Frances L. Landry Distinguished Professor, Louisiana State University Law Center**

"*Boss of Black Brooklyn: The Life and Times of Bertram L. Baker* is a great treat for lovers of twentieth-century Brooklyn history. Part biography and part family memoir, longtime New York City journalist Ron Howell's book traces his family's lineage back to the islands of Nevis and Barbados. Ambitious from an early age, Bertram Baker emigrated from Nevis to Brooklyn at the age of sixteen. He arrived with other aspiring West Indian immigrants during World War I and began a journey that took him from the stockroom floor of the cavernous Abraham & Straus department store on Fulton Street to the heights of New York state politics to become one of the historic power brokers of New York City and Brooklyn."
—**Julie A. Gallagher, author of *Black Women and Politics in New York City***

"Bertram Baker's story is about Brooklyn politics in the early 1900s. But it's also about how blacks fought to break down barriers keeping them out of all-white tennis competitions in the early twentieth century. During the Great Depression, and all the way through the 1960s, Baker headed the American Tennis Association, the all-black organization that nurtured Althea Gibson and Arthur Ashe. Baker helped make history when, in the 1950s, he negotiated to have Althea accepted into white tennis matches like Wimbledon and what's now known as the U.S. Open. Baker believed that something in sports strengthened the character. And something about Baker helped Althea focus on winning while navigating racial and gender issues on and off the court. He not only encouraged blacks to play tennis, but he also started baseball leagues for boys in his Bedford Stuyvesant neighborhood. As Baker's grandson and biographer, Ron Howell, reports, Bertram Baker believed that life itself was a game."
—**Yanick Rice Lamb, author of *Born to Win: The Authorized Biography of Althea Gibson***

"Today generations and children from now on will know that it was Bertram Baker who broke the color line in Brooklyn.... Let the record of history show that I owe a debt of gratitude to Bertram Baker and that I acknowledge Bertram Baker for his greatness and his vision. May today be, not only a recognition of his greatness, but a sign that we will try our best to memorialize those who opened doors for me and others to take seats in legislative bodies and other offices, in Brooklyn and throughout New York state. May God bless him. May he rest in peace."

—Letitia James, former Brooklyn city councilwoman; first black woman to hold any citywide office when she became New York City public advocate; candidate to be the first black and first woman New York state attorney general

"A gift from the island of Nevis to Brooklyn and the rest of America. Howell tells the story of Bertram L. Baker, who emigrated from Nevis in 1915 and became Brooklyn's first black elected official in 1948. Later, Baker served in the New York state Assembly and continually paid tribute to another Nevisian who had served before him—Alexander Hamilton."

—Everson W. Hull, Ph.D., ambassador for St. Kitts and Nevis to the Organization of American States

"*Boss of Black Brooklyn* is a story about politics in early-twentieth-century Brooklyn, but it is much more than that. It is also a story about the hearts, minds, and spirits of the Caribbean people."

—Kirkley C. Sands, Ph.D., dean of faculty at Codrington College, Barbados

"*Boss of Black Brooklyn* is a story about an extraordinary man. Bertram Baker, an immigrant from the then-British island of Nevis, had joined other West Indians, and American blacks, in the 'Great Migration.' Baker became the first black elected to political office in Brooklyn. In Baker's era, blacks began demanding their fair share of the patronage pie, such as civil service jobs. Baker had weaknesses and high ambitions. Part memoir and part history, Howell's book tells the story of both Baker's wins and losses, crafting a unique story of the American dream."

—Jerome Krase, Ph.D., author of *Race, Class, and Gentrification in Brooklyn: A View from the Street*

"A fascinating book on Bertram L. Baker, the first black representative elected to the state Assembly from Brooklyn, New York, in 1948. As an author of New York's first housing anti-discrimination bill, Baker became one of New York's most important legislators. However, Baker's and Howell's intermingled lives revealed generational divides that cleaved through American society during that pivotal decade of the 1960s. Baker, the immigrant striver, embodied respectability and rectitude. His grandson Howell, the American-born, Ivy League–educated militant, embodied rebellion and resistance. These tensions remain important aspects of African Americans' and the entire nation's history. Howell's strengths as a journalist, his honesty, care, and humor, mix memoir and biography, personal reflection and scholarship into a book that is informative and exciting."

—Brian Purnell, author of *Fighting Jim Crow in the County of Kings: The Congress of Racial Equality in Brooklyn*

"We, the Brooklyn Oldtimers Foundation, held our first meetings half a century ago, when Bertram Baker was leaving the political stage. We are retired police officers, firefighters, social workers, and teachers. We are proud of Ron Howell for writing this book about his grandfather: *Boss of Black Brooklyn: The Life and Times of Bertram L. Baker.* In December 2016, we gave Ron a plaque that said, 'A son of Bed-Stuy, you never forgot your roots. Your outstanding journalistic skills have been a breath of fresh air, shown in your published articles.' Using Ron's book, we will teach our youngsters what it means to be from black Brooklyn and how they should be faithful to it. Over the years we have given hundreds of thousands of dollars to college-bound students from our community. 'Bed-Stuy, do or die,' we used to say back in the day. We will fight today's onslaughts and try to keep black Brooklyn breathing. The Boss would want us to do it."

—The Brooklyn Oldtimers Foundation

BOSS OF
BLACK BROOKLYN

BOSS OF
BLACK BROOKLYN

THE LIFE AND TIMES
OF BERTRAM L. BAKER

RON HOWELL

Empire State Editions

An imprint of Fordham University Press

ESE New York 2019

Visit us online
www.empirestateeditions.com
www.fordhampress.com

Library of Congress Control Number: 2018950286

Printed in the United States of America

21 20 19   5 4 3 2 1
First edition

Contents

Foreword
Former Mass. Gov. Deval Patrick Reminisces

Deval L. Patrick

I never knew Bertram Baker as the "Boss of Brooklyn." I never knew him as the Majority Whip of the New York state Assembly, or as the patron of the borough's tennis league, or the lion of Democratic Party politics in Bedford Stuyvesant. I knew Bertram Baker long after he had stepped aside from an active career in politics, long after an upstart called Shirley Chisholm challenged his decades-long hold on his Assembly seat, "accusing" him of being a Negro when the world had moved on to Black Power.

I met Bertram Baker in 1983 as just "Daddy B," the grandfather of my then-fiancée—now-wife, Diane Bemus Whiting, when I was first introduced to the family. Fifteen years out of public life, soft-spoken and slightly deaf, he still dressed every morning in a three-piece blue serge suit with a starched white shirt and conservative tie. He wore garters to hold his socks in place. He never went outside without a fedora. He greeted me as he greeted every day—formally, properly, and with a certain studied gravity. He expected the same in return. Warmth and wit were left to his amazing wife and partner, Irene, or "Mommy I." Daddy B was all about decorum.

Diane was the youngest of his grandchildren. We had in common an upbringing in a multi-generational household. With her parents, sister, and brother, Diane had spent her early years in the same Bed-Stuy brownstone with Daddy B and Mommy I, some of that time with her Aunt Marian and her son Ron Howell, the author of this book, as well. Daddy B presided. Everyone seemed to know his rules, when and with what he could be disturbed, which decisions were his alone to make. After years of political leadership, he seemed to be accustomed to deference, from his family as well as from everyone else. I picked up that scent and complied. He seemed to like me, but frankly I could never really tell.

By the time Daddy B and I met, he was an elderly man in retirement. Not quite two years later, he would be dead. But he lived long enough to inquire about my upbringing and schooling, and my plans to practice civil rights law in New York. He appeared to approve of my marriage to Diane, or at least he did not make any objections apparent. I gathered from the family that approval was imminent when he toured me through the library in his home, pointer in hand, explaining the provenance of the many awards and citations displayed there of his life's work. I was and still am genuinely impressed. But the man I met was by then less Bertram Baker than Daddy B.

Diane and I were trying to figure out how to get a mortgage to buy a house we had come to love in Brooklyn. Daddy B offered to introduce us to the manager at his bank. On the appointed day, we met at his house and piled into the car to drive over to the bank. Daddy B was probably never a good driver. If ever he had been, he was no longer. There was nothing smooth about the ride. He drove with a fitful style, first over-accelerating and then slamming on the brakes. It was maddening to Diane and me. Of course, New Yorkers are famously impatient on the roads, so the honking and rude gesturing from other drivers was incessant. Daddy B's response was placid. He waved at them breezily, explaining to us, "They know me."

Not long after Diane and I married in May 1984, we attended a special convocation at St. John's University at which Daddy B received an honorary degree. New York Governor Mario Cuomo and California Governor George Deukmejian were also honorees, and the whole family was present for the occasion. Daddy B was the first to be honored and presented with a beautiful citation. He was to sit on one of three large armchairs at the center of the stage through the remaining presentations and a brief address by Governor Cuomo at the end. To the horror of the family seated in the close-up rows, he fell asleep, in full view of the whole auditorium. But when Governor Cuomo acknowledged him at the beginning of his address, Daddy B bolted awake, stood, and bowed to the audience. Ever the pro, the man never missed his cue.

Ten months after our wedding, Daddy B passed away. We learned on that very same day that our first daughter was coming. The concentric circles of our lives continued, with a second daughter, a move to Boston, a grandson, Diane's successful career as a lawyer and managing partner at Ropes & Gray in Boston, my own career as a lawyer, business executive, and ultimately Governor myself of Massachusetts. I've come to understand more fully and to appreciate Bertram Baker's political and public stature in those years: his rise from the life of a humble West Indian immigrant to become the first black person elected to office in the long history of Brooklyn; his sponsorship of the first housing nondiscrimination legislation in America; his firm control of borough politics; his encouragement of so many local organizers and politically ambitious young people; his close working partnership with New York Governor Nelson Rockefeller. I came to know his history as the lion of Brooklyn politics, but oddly I value my early memories of Daddy B more. The diminished public figure, the great man whose greatness was overtaken by time, the old man growing old just like other old men, has probably done more to keep me grounded, focused on what each of us must do with the little time we have to leave things better for those who come behind us.

Bert Baker was a pioneer and a giant, especially for a black man in his time. His story has not been fully told. This book undertakes to do so. That's important—because great men become great by building a legacy. It's up to others to preserve it.

For this we have the author and journalist Ron Howell to thank. Ron is Daddy B's grandson. He is the right person to write this memoir, but I will venture that he has not always realized that. A child of the 1960s, Ronnie was an activist undergraduate at Yale College, rejecting the very traditions that the university—and Daddy B—embraced. Daddy B was resentful and angry with Ronnie for his choices back then. Now, after a life of parenthood and partnership of his own, Ron has through this book found his own way of reconciling, of appreciating that Daddy B had his own insurgent history, every bit as challenging and important in his time as Ronnie's was in his.

Preface
A Grandson Learns His Duty

Lucky I was, for sure, that I didn't get blasted when Chris shot off that rifle as he clumsily tried to clean it. Fortunate, too, that no one outside heard it. We were in the old Chapel Street building that housed the Black Student Alliance at Yale, or Afro House, as some began calling it.

It was the spring of 1970. Black Panther leader Bobby Seale was on trial and the whole city was on edge. We had guns all over the place. Guys had pistols tucked into their belts as they walked around Afro House. I kept a 12 gauge shotgun in my room in Trumbull College, one of Yale's resort-like residential complexes. Local members of the Panther Party had told us the New Haven "pigs" and white motorcycle gangs would be coming after us.

On a résumé, I would have seemed the last person to be doing all that. I had gone to a Jesuit high school, studied Latin and Greek. I was a twenty-one-year-old Yale senior, several weeks away from graduation. The only thing missing was my senior essay in history, which I hadn't begun to write yet.

I had gotten sucked into the gun thing by Chris. He knew I had a new Volvo and that I was a chump for a brother in need of help in a good cause. I took Chris to a gun shop outside New Haven and we bought a carload's worth of weapons, some automatic. Chris told me I could keep the Mossberg shotgun.

As for the Volvo, I had purchased it with money left from the sale of a Cadillac, bequeathed to me by a godfather who had recently died. The godfather's name was J. Daniel Diggs, and he had been a New York City

Councilman, the first black one from Brooklyn, New York. He had been elected back in the 1950s, eons ago to me. Danny Diggs wore pinstriped blue suits, with a vest, and a fedora that sat to the right side. He owed his seat on the City Council to my maternal grandfather, Bertram Baker.

Daddy B, as I called my grandfather, had been the political boss of black Brooklyn since the 1930s. I grew up in his Bedford Stuyvesant brownstone home and was planning to return there in a few weeks— I mean, if I graduated. I would cast a thought Daddy B's way from time to time, though I tried not to think about him. I was, at bottom, a jittery type of guy. When he got angry he could make grown men, even judges, shiver.

By the grace of a higher power, the Yale revolution, such as it was, fizzled. I didn't get shot, arrested, or even threatened with expulsion. No one outside the group learned about the guns. I nervously got down to doing my senior thesis, titled "The West Indian Negro in the United States Between World War I and World War II."

My grandfather dwelled at the foundation of that project, even though his name barely came up. I know now that he was at the root of it because I'm wiser and more honest. Bertram Llewellyn Baker immigrated to the United States in 1915 from the (then) British Caribbean island of Nevis, and he climbed the ladder of political power in Brooklyn over the coming decades. During my college years of chanting "Black Power" and taking all kinds of drugs, I grew increasingly distant from my grandfather. I was dumbly unmindful of the crises he was living through at the time: His young protégés had been deserting him for greener pastures of rival Democratic clubs. He was at the end of a span that had taken him to signature moments of glory.

In November 1948 Bertram L. Baker had put his name on a page of Brooklyn history. That was when he was elected to the New York state Assembly, representing the growing central Brooklyn neighborhood of Bedford Stuyvesant, becoming the first black person ever elected to office in Brooklyn, a place that by the end of the twentieth century came to be called the capital of the Black Diaspora. For several decades Daddy B had also been the chief executive officer of the all-black American Tennis Association, and in that capacity he negotiated with white tennis administrators to have them accept Althea Gibson into white competitions. That led to her historic Wimbledon victory in 1957 and opened doors for Arthur Ashe and Venus and Serena Williams.

In my May Days of 1970, my grandfather was living his final days as the the boss of black Brooklyn. On April 18, 1970, the *Amsterdam News*

ran a front-page story headlined "Bert Baker to Quit Post After 22 Years."
It said: "A bombshell was dropped in the Assembly here, Monday, when
Bertram Baker, Assembly representative of the 56th Assembly District,
Brooklyn, announced that he is concluding his 22-year-old career and
will not seek re-election this year."

The leader of the Democrats, Stanley Steingut, was quoted as saying
that Bert Baker "will live on in our history" as a fighter against discrimination in housing and education. The *Amsterdam News* called Baker a
"pioneer" and a man of many "firsts" in the Empire State. The newspaper
also noted he was called "the Chief" throughout central Brooklyn.

This meant very little to me at the time, in large part because my
grandfather and I had been barely speaking. Having heard that I would
not be wearing a cap and gown to my graduation, but rather a mere suit
with an armband protesting the Vietnam War, Daddy B did not come to
my graduation; being a dutiful West Indian wife, neither did my beloved
grandmother, my Mommy I.

After graduation, I went back to my grandparents' brownstone home
on Jefferson Avenue. And in short order there came a day of reckon-
ing. I was lying in my seven-by-six-foot room on the top floor when
my grandfather, now in retirement, called me down. Even at the age of
twenty-one, I fairly shook every time he bellowed my name. Those who
had known me since childhood called me Ronnie. Others called me by
what I thought was the adult name I deserved, Ron. My grandfather
always called me Ronald. At that point in our lives, toward the end of
1970, he was seventy-two years old. Five-foot-seven, pot-bellied, and
slope-shouldered, he could still inspire fear with that look and that voice.
A foreboding tugged at my stomach. I sat down opposite him at the dinner table in front of the old marble fireplace.

"I saw you had a book on guns," he said, with no evident emotion in
his voice. "I said to myself, if he has a book on guns, he must have a gun.
So I went into your room and found a rifle in the closet." He told me he
didn't want a weapon in his house and that besides, it was time for me to
be on my own. "There's just not room in this house for the two of us."
He lifted one hand up from his lap in a gesture of finality.

Today, four-and-a-half decades after being kicked out of my granddad's home, and thirty years after his death, I feel nothing but gratitude
when the name of Bertram Baker is mentioned. A higher power blessed
me with a gift that had my grandfather's name on it, a gift of being

forgiven and seeing the blessings inherent in one's past honestly assessed. My grandfather and I had begun speaking to each other again by the late 1970s and we even enjoyed our time together. He remained a little suspicious of my motives in becoming a journalist. (And, yes, the Freud in me did come to believe, over time, that the decision to join that power-challenging craft was due to an upbringing in the home of an old-time politician.)

I owe my grandfather and grandmother my life. You see, in the early 1950s my father had fallen into a trap of alcoholism that kept him out of the apartment he shared then with me and my mom, Marian Baker Howell. My mother then developed polio. That's when her parents, Bertram and Irene Baker, took us into their brownstone home in Bed-Stuy. Mom became one of the lucky ones who recovered from polio. Dad eventually overcame his alcoholism. But he never again lived with me and Mom, as she and I stayed there in Bed-Stuy over the decades with my grandfolks.

In my college years, I did not see black Brooklyn as my grandfather did. I saw Bed-Stuy (which was the focal point of black Brooklyn) as a ghetto. He, on the other hand, saw it as a work in progress. Over the course of my grandparents' years in Brooklyn, almost a century, the percentage of blacks in Brooklyn went from 1 percent to 34 percent, a wondrous thing to behold. And my grandfather, rest his soul, played a role in ameliorating the burdens placed on black residents by *de facto* discrimination that was accepted policy in housing and education. In the mid-1950s, he pushed through the state legislature one of the nation's first bills outlawing discrimination in the sale or rental of housing. It was called the Metcalf–Baker law, co-named after George Metcalf, his senate partner in the writing and defense of that bill, which was signed by then-Governor Averell Harriman. Hopes for an end to housing discrimination rose. But look where we are now. Developers and realtors are all but conspiring to push blacks out of the city and take the percentage back down to 1, where it was in 1901, when my grandmother was born in an apartment off Fulton Street.

Knowing whence we came can help us figure out where to go. When I ask myself who I am and what I should do with my remaining time, ancestry inevitably presents itself in the rising answer. I hear a now-softened voice that once screamed to set me on a path. I will listen and try to be true, processing what I hear and passing it along to those who come behind, my son and his family, and all those who love Brooklyn for what it was and will be.

BOSS OF BLACK BROOKLYN

Introduction
An Ancestor Speaks from Beyond

Bertram Baker never spent money on art. Like other immigrants who came through Ellis Island a century ago, he set his sights on practical things. When he started finally to find his spot in Brooklyn politics in the 1940s, he filled his home/office with simple trappings, like books about public speaking, about the power of positive thinking, and about the history of the Caribbean isles he'd left behind in 1915. He didn't read with the consuming spirit of a scholar but rather put 90 percent of his waking hours into the attainment of influence—not the rich man's kind, but the handshake deals that led to jobs as city clerks or as an office manager with a state agency, or as an assistant prosecutor, or even a judge. He loved putting little quotations into pleasant-looking frames and hanging them on the walls of his office in the brownstone house he purchased just before World War I. One of those quotations was as trite as it was revealing of his character: "The Boss isn't always right, but he is always the Boss." It hung eye-high beside an entrance door, so family members could see it whenever they entered and left. Baker seemed always to believe he was the boss, though the flame burned low before he became an American citizen in 1924. His "Where's mine?" attitude got him fired from a couple of jobs. And the fire grew as he became a Democratic Party club captain, then a leader of his own Democratic club, and then a striver in hoity-toity government jobs. The Irish pols were impressed with his confident manner and even his accent, which was British enough to be proper and poised without seeming pompous. The wire-framed spectacles only added to this air of erudition. In the early 1940s, when his cute little niece, Arlene Dash, would visit the house, he'd ask her, "What's my name?" And she'd always answer, "Dabby B the Big Shot!" He would pull a quarter out of his pocket and hand it to her. His smile implied future rewards, as it did also with others who would stay in line and act as they were expected to act. His smile never seemed to say, on its own, "I love you." His love took form over time and without the tender words normally associated with that feeling.

I knew what it was like to be bossed by Bert Baker. Once, in 1960 or so, when I was sitting in the dining room chatting with a kid from my grammar school, Our Lady of Victory, my grandfather stormed down the stairs and bellowed, "Ronald, I need you up here—and your friend, too!" The kid and I marched up to the office and began moving pieces of furniture, as we'd been told to, then folding and stuffing letters into envelopes with names and addresses on them. When we were done, the boss said, "Okay" and waved his hand for us to go. We went back downstairs, my friend looking bullied and puzzled. "Your grandfather is mean," he said as he stepped beyond the front gate. I didn't say anything. I suppose I agreed.

It was only several years after graduation from college that I began to develop a fascination with my grandfather as a boss in that larger sphere where he frightened many Brooklyn lawyers, the same way he scared me and just about everybody else in the family and neighborhood, except for avowed enemies who didn't back then have much of a platform to make themselves heard. The word "boss," as I use it in the title of this book, refers to the American political personality that began revealing itself in New York City in the 1800s, lasting all the way through the 1930s, as Bertram Baker formed his United Action Democratic Association political club and began acquiring influence and power in central Brooklyn. The first significant one of the early city bosses was William M. Tweed, known as "Boss Tweed," who was a New York state Senator and managed to get himself onto commissions that handed out lucrative contracts and jobs. Like Bertram Baker, Tweed lived in a brownstone, Tweed's being on the West Side of Manhattan. Unlike Baker, he was white and had access to just about all the money and influence handled by government officials in his day. Tweed was eventually charged with corruption and died in prison in 1873. Thereafter came a series of reformers who changed the local political culture a bit. But following the reform came lapses, and that sequence has continued through to our time today, with "machine" and "boss" still used to refer to some influence-wielding officials. But the word "boss" is today nowhere as fraught as it was in Baker's time in politics or, as he used to say, "in the game."

This book is not about only the Democratic boss who became Brooklyn's first black elected official. It's about the man whom I and my cousins called "Daddy B" and my grandmother and others called "B." Although most of it reads as a biography, it is also a memoir-inspired story about fatherhood, marriage, and fidelity to asserted principles. To the extent that an arc can be seen in the telling of this story, it's formed from emotions I've suppressed and then freed, I hope, in fruit-bearing ways. Along the way, I mix exposition with commentary, as in the boldface ending of the chapter about Baker's search in the 1930s for a band of like-minded brothers in Brooklyn. Also, after the chronological end of Bertram Baker's story (i.e., his death), I've added a number of chapters that are born of him. One is about my other (paternal) grandfather, who was largely absent in my life. He was a man of superb character who, like Bertram Baker, hailed from the old British Caribbean and who, with poetic irony, was an Episcopal priest, the very calling in life that Baker once aspired to before giving it up for politics. I also include further reflections on the life and times of Bertram Baker.

My grandfather's story, on its own, illuminates a fascinating era when an early-twentieth-century cohort of West Indian families left their native islands and settled in Brooklyn. They entered through Ellis Island, that place of dreams that became embedded, lovingly, in the memories of countless immigrants from Europe, largely Italians and Jews arriving in that same wave between 1897 and 1924. Those white entrants shaped the city and, indeed, the post-industrial image of America as revealed in books, movies, and news stories over the following decades of the twentieth century. Their children became the movie stars, teachers, police officers, and politicians who were the recognizable face of America by midcentury, just before and after World War II, when virtually everyone around the globe believed the United States was the greatest destination of the modern era.

The darker foreigners had their own distinct impact. Although West Indians made up less than 1 percent of the black population of America in the earliest decades of the twentieth century, they were the first in the black communities of New York City to gain positions of political power as elected officials and as the bosses of the city's political parties. They were also successful in the black community as realtors and set paths not only in established political parties but also as radical activists, forming organizations such as the African Blood Brotherhood and agitating on the street corners of Harlem. "Without them the genuinely radical movement among New York Negroes would be unworthy of attention," Jamaica-born W. A. Domingo, an early Caribbean activist, boasted in a 1925 article titled "The Tropics in New York."[1]

But until recently historians paid attention only to the early black immigrant politicians in Harlem. That's because for a long while in the twentieth century, Harlem was the best known and most politically powerful of the black communities of New York City and, indeed, the whole country. The tales of Harlem's West Indian political pioneers have been recounted in biographies and memoirs. For instance, there was Hulan Jack, the St. Lucia–born immigrant who became Manhattan's (and New York City's) first black borough president. There was J. Raymond Jones, born on the island of St. Thomas in the Danish West Indies, who would make history as the first black to head the powerful Democratic machine organization known as Tammany Hall. And there was Constance Baker Motley, the first female borough president of Manhattan (and the first, in fact, of any of the boroughs in the history of New York City). Motley then broke through another ceiling as the first black female federal judge. Her parents, like the Bakers, came from the island of Nevis. A blood relationship was never established through DNA testing, or even St. Kitts and Nevis birth records, many of which were destroyed in a nineteenth-century fire, but the families of Bertram Baker and the younger "Connie" Baker assumed they had common family roots going back to the early 1800s, and they called each other "cousin."

Baker has been sitting in the dustbin of history, even though black Brooklyn overtook Harlem in population size and political clout more than three decades ago. Two developments explain why he has been ignored. One is that, as an early-century Democratic machine boss, Baker fell out of favor with so-called reformers and black nationalists (like my associates when I was in college at Yale), who began entering the realm of activism and electoral politics in Brooklyn in the 1960s. The second reason he has been forgotten is that someone else rose to prominence and took a strong presence on the stage and in so doing helped to obliterate Baker from local memory. That person was Shirley Chisholm, who in 1972, two years after Baker's retirement, became the first woman ever to mount a serious campaign for the presidency of the United States of America. Chisholm, the first black woman in the country to gain a seat in Congress, became the subject of documentaries and books, including her autobiography, *Unbought and Unbossed*. Baker accepted her popularity, even if he quietly resented it.

Dying Before He Could Tell His Story

In the late 1970s, when I was working as a reporter at the *Baltimore Evening Sun*, my grandfather sent out invitations announcing he would be appearing at the Long Island Historical Society[2] to give a talk about the origins of black political power in Brooklyn. I was excited about it. The fact was that, while I had majored in history at Yale, I knew very little about my grandfather's experiences in politics, the struggles he had dealt with.

The audience was a mix of black and white, some of them history-loving seniors from the fashionable Brooklyn Heights neighborhood where the Historical Society was located. Baker went out of his way to carefully introduce all of his family members in attendance, the first one being his wife, Irene. (That was notable because, for one thing, in his politically active years she generally didn't attend the functions where he was featured, and, for another thing, on that night he seemed to show a genuine affection and deference, both of which had been missing in their half-century of marriage.) I have to say it was tender. Then he said something that went toward the heart of the differences that, several years back, he and I had had. He said, "You will pardon me if during my talk I used the word Negro instead of black. I do that by choice. I am old-fashioned and I prefer to use the word Negro." Whatever. I was developing a bond that had everything to do with the survival of those who had spawned me and those I was spawning. My wife, Marilyn, and I were there with our then year-old son, Damani.

Baker's hour-long talk was a play-by-play, name-by-name account, from 1900 onward to the 1960s, about blacks—excuse me, Negroes—who fought for political power and the accompanying patronage (though he didn't use the word) that other groups—Irish, Italians, and Jews—had attained before. Much of that chronology, edited and laced with judgment, shows up in the pages that follow.

In his remarks at the end, he fired a zinger at the press. I'm not sure it was with me in mind. He had told me a few times that he didn't like journalists. I could hear Sigmund Freud humming.

Reading from the index cards that he held comfortably in both hands, grabbing one card and shifting it to his other hand as he finished with the thoughts thereon, Baker appeared very much at ease; in fact, he seemed more at ease than he had been all the prior years at home since his retirement. He spoke of how he'd tried and failed to win elective offices before his locally historic 1948 victory, when he won a seat in the state assembly representing Bedford Stuyvesant. He spoke of how before that, in 1941, he'd thrown his hat into the ring for a seat on the City Council, losing, and how he tried again in 1944, losing once more. He ended with a gentle reflection on what he called the craft of serving the people, saying that politics in those post-Watergate days was unfairly looked down upon. He said, "I'm asking of the young people who are here today, interest yourself in politics, to be assured of good government for yourselves and for posterity."

His years after that presentation were like previous ones following his retirement—buying books, getting together with family on special occasions, and often looking out that front window with a wistfulness and hurt he would never acknowledge. Once, in about 1982, he went to the corner to buy a newspaper, and when he got back to his front gate to enter, a man holding a gun said, "You got money! I seen you! I seen you!" Once the power broker of black Brooklyn, Bert Baker was by then a slow-walking, slightly hunched-over octogenarian. He handed over the money in his pocket, which couldn't have been more than $10. By the grace of God, the thug, likely a junkie, did not ask my grandfather for the key to the house, and the former boss of the neighborhood entered his brownstone, called the police, who did nothing, and reflected on the ignominy of what he had just been through.

Several times between September 1984 and January 1985 I pulled out an old tape recorder and sat with my grandfather, asking him questions about himself, the work he had done, and his thoughts about life. By grace, it was ending as a good life, like returning to the womb. He had even reestablished his connections to his birthplace, the beautiful island of Nevis, going there twice in the previous decade. Of special note was visiting the gravesite of his mother, who had died in 1900. But he had also become fascinated with Alexander Hamilton and gave a speech outside Hamilton's Nevis birthplace in 1983, on the occasion of St. Kitts and Nevis's becoming an independent nation, no longer a colony of Great Britain. Baker proudly told anyone he could that he had been the second Nevisian to serve in the New York state assembly, the first having been, yes, Hamilton in 1787. One of the most heartwarming honors bestowed upon him in his final years was the honorary doctorate St. John's University gave him in 1983. My grandmother Irene; my mother, Marian;

and I were with him the morning of his death on March 8, 1985, at his brownstone home in Bedford Stuyvesant. Weeks before, on his deathbed, he had asked me whimsically whether I thought he could finish the book he had so much wanted to write, about the black men of his day who were "firsts" to attain positions in "various fields of endeavor." He had hoped to call it *Breaking Down Barriers*. So, overwhelmed with my newspaper deadlines, I answered with silence and he nodded, knowing it was another dream deferred.

In addition to me, Bertram L. Baker left behind three other grandchildren: my three first cousins, Jay, Lynn, and Diane (born Bemus). He would have been so proud to know that Diane—whose wedding he had happily attended the year before his death—would go on to be a prominent lawyer in Massachusetts, and that the guy she married, Deval Patrick, would in 2006 become the first black Governor of Massachusetts.

My grandmother Irene Baker, whom the family lovingly called Mommy I, survived her husband, Bertram, by fifteen good years and remained a trusty link of connection to the past for me. We would chat and I even interviewed her on tape, which she seemed to enjoy. Her death came in January 2001, two months shy of her one-hundredth birthday. Journalists at a certain point in their lives often suffer guilt. We spend so much of our lives learning about others and neglect the people who made us who we are. As I learned more about my grandfather, I wanted to share in the way that journalists do.

In 2003, I approached editors at *African American Lives*[3] about doing an article about Bertram L. Baker. Their first question was, of course, Who was he? When I explained, they were very interested, and I ended up doing an entry—about 2,000 words—on Brooklyn's black pioneer. As I worked over the years, I would go to the Schomburg Center for Research in Black Culture and do research at the Central Branch of the Brooklyn Public Library and the Brooklyn Historical Society (once called the Long Island Historical Society). And though my journalism work was once focused on Latin America and the Caribbean, I found myself writing more about black Brooklyn and my feelings about it.

Over on Jefferson Avenue, residents took note of the articles that appeared in the *New York Daily News* and other papers. And as Jefferson Avenue, along with other streets in Bed-Stuy, became home to increasing numbers of gentrifying "pioneers," the outside world seemed to care more about the neighborhood. There came a time, blessedly, in 2011, when the city, pushed by then–City Councilman Al Vann, passed a resolution giving a new name to Jefferson Avenue between Tompkins and

Throop avenues. Signs saying "Bertram L. Baker Way" were hung from all the corners. What a fun day it was.

Among the special guests were the First Lady and Governor of Massachusetts, in other words the granddaughter and grandson-in-law of Bertram Baker. I may have spent considerably more time than the other three grandchildren of Bertram Baker looking at his life, and I in fact spent more time in his house than they did. But there's no doubt in my mind that my grandfather would be most proud of Diane, a tough and successful labor lawyer. Diane, now retired, was known in political circles as the ideal political spouse because she was such a great speaker on the stump. I had worked in Deval's 2006 campaign and saw up close how Diane was in continual demand for speaking. She became especially appreciated for her openness about the abuse she was subjected to in her first marriage. There were times, as I traveled around Massachusetts, when I thought Diane was even more popular than Deval was.

Before the Bertram L. Baker Way street naming event, I wrote a press release/article that ran in several community newspapers. It noted that Governor Deval Patrick had "always said he owes a special debt to Bertram L. Baker" and that when he ran for his first term as Governor his "website was laced with photos of Baker."

At her turn, Diane spoke about living there on Jefferson Avenue in the mid- and late 1950s with her maternal grandparents—Bertram and Irene Baker—plus her sister and brother, her parents, and me and my mom.[4] I was struck perhaps most of all by her concession that while growing up and even into adulthood, she knew very little about what Bertram Baker did, who he really was. In truth, I felt that way also.

"I did have this sense that Daddy B was larger than life . . . but I really didn't know what he did. I knew he was somebody important. I knew people admired him. I knew he spent a lot of time up there in Albany, and he took us there a couple of times and we met Governor [Nelson] Rockefeller. But it wasn't until much later in my life that I came to understand and appreciate really who Bert Baker was.

"This was a man who was a West Indian immigrant, who came here and adopted this city, this block, this neighborhood, this state as his own. And he served with such dignity, and showed such ethical values, and he worked hard and tirelessly and in a committed way to make life better for the people of this state and this city and particularly this community that he loved.

"And it took me a long time to appreciate—it was probably just over the last five years, since I've been the wife of an elected official—what my grandmother contributed as well. I always knew she was the best per-son in the world, the best grandmother, just the most wonderful person. But I never knew the kind of sacrifice really that a spouse of an elected official has to make in order to enable that person to do what they do. And I realize that this dedication today is to my grandmother as well, and I just want to make sure that we don't forget that legacy as well."

Diane was right. We, his four grandkids, were living there in Bertram Baker's house and we had little idea of what he did on the outside. It was our grandmother Irene Baker who meant the most to us. This was be-cause we always saw her. She cooked for us, sometimes roast beef with corn meal and okra, or maybe roasted chicken with white rice and string beans. In the evenings, as we rollicked like maniacs through the dining room and adjoining kitchen, she would sit peacefully, sketching beach scenes, or reading a newspaper, or writing a letter to a family member back on the island of Nevis. It was only in 2018, as I was finishing this book, that I learned how fittingly she had been named, that Irene was the ancient Greek word for peace.

Our grandfather, on the other hand, could be belligerent even when circumstances were otherwise warm and friendly. The B in Daddy B's name was linguistically appropriate, a hard-stopping of the breath, fol-lowed by forced projection of it, suggesting power, sometimes provoking fear. Bertram Baker. The boss.

Images of our grandfather as a needy little boy never entered our minds.

1

The Lasting Anger of an Abandoned Son

Bertram L. Baker was born on the tiny island of Nevis in the eastern Caribbean on January 10, 1898.

Americans, especially those in the aborning city of gaslights called New York, to which the Bakers and other globe riders were casting star-seeking eyes, knew that year as a time of expanding opportunities and new horizons. Just nine days before baby Bertram's first wails, New York City had annexed the growing borough of Brooklyn and three other boroughs, making them together a grand metropolis that would, in the coming years, become the rival of ancient Rome in the cultural and intellectual impact it would have on the known world. Dreams were being planted and nurtured in that new land, as immigrants from southern and eastern Europe entered it through the final docking point of Ellis Island, where they would wait for hours or days, their hearts beating nervously as they were examined for contagious diseases and questioned before being allowed to settle into lodgings in the city. Off the radar screen of most demographers and the conveyors of popular American history, a cohort of pioneers from the Caribbean was also beginning to settle in New York City, notably in Brooklyn, also entering through Ellis Island, that now mythic portal close to the Statue of Liberty in New York harbor.

Southward, a stomach-churning week's ship ride away on the Atlantic waters, there on the island of Nevis, the year 1898 was a time of strife, of painful transition.[1]

Through the 1700s and much of the 1800s, the sugar economy had given Nevis a level of prosperity that was the envy of the other isles of the Caribbean, including its sister island, St. Kitts, sitting half an hour's ferry ride across the peaceful waters between them. Today, twenty-first-century Nevis, a plot of hills and dirt roads, and the larger St. Kitts form the smallest independent nation in the Western hemisphere, united now as St. Kitts and Nevis.

For the better part of its colonial history, Nevis had been called the "gem" of the Caribbean because of its healing spring waters and its heart-pleasing ocean air. It was, then as today, the tiniest of places, with winding narrow roads leading to various parishes known by the names of saints denominating the local Anglican churches. In the center of the island stands a soaring mountain, Mount Nevis, site of a dormant volcano, ringed with white clouds that give it a mystical quality. The clouds are said to have appeared to Christopher Columbus as the snows of the Alps, as he approached them slightly more than five hundred years ago from a visible distance in the sea. Thus the Spanish word *nieves*, or snows, was applied to the new land by its visitors, *nieves* eventually being corrupted to Nevis. As births have counterbalanced outmigration from Nevis, the population has remained notably steady over the past century, between 10,000 and 13,000.

It was often said that Nevisians, even compared with their sisters and brothers on St. Kitts, were notable for gentility (though it should be noted that no one ever described Bertram Baker as gentle). The vast majority of the island's residents, as was true throughout the British Caribbean, were of African descent, offspring of the slaves who had worked the sugar and cotton plantations through the 1700s and the first decades of the nineteenth century. Slavery had ended in the British Caribbean in 1832, a full generation before it ended in the United States, and without the national trauma of a bloody civil war such as the one that defined the United States socially and politically for generations, into the present time. Be warned: Though less stark than in the United States, slavery was the foundation of all that Nevisian society was and all that it came to be; violence was endemic to its history, though it was subtler and had all but vanished from the national memory over the next century and a half.[2]

On November 24, 1900, Bertram Llewellyn Baker was two months shy of his third birthday and suffered one of the biggest blows a child can endure. His mother, Lilian, died that day from the complications of tuberculosis.[3] Years later Bertram would remember the sadness that overwhelmed him as friends and relatives from around the little island of Nevis came to the Baker enclave in Brown Pasture and paid their respects. He sat alone under the shade of a tree on the day of his mother's funeral, watching as the horse-drawn carriages came and then departed for the services at the nearby Anglican Church.[4] For the rest of his life he held his mother close to him in his heart. Lilian de Grasse Baker was lithesome, gay in the old sense of the word, laughing easily and nimble on the dance floor. She had coffee-with-milk skin, braidable hair, and mixed features. Later in life, in 1920, a year after his marriage in Brooklyn, Bertram must have considered it a blessing from his still-loving mother when his first child, a daughter, was born on November 24, the very date, twenty years earlier, of his mom's death. He named that child Lilian, and he would loudly correct anyone who made the mistake of writing the name with two l's between the i's rather than one.

At the age of three, little boys are beginning to construct within their minds the attitudes and views that shape their relations with the outside world. In later life Bertram would come to be considered quite the ladies' man, and it might be postulated that this sense of women as creatures who wanted his attention stemmed from his glorification of his departed mother. It was a love that, in the first years after Lilian's death, would be transferred to his maternal grandmother, Eliza de Grasse, who did all she could to make life comfortable for her grandchild.[5]

If there was a flip side to the attachment Bertram felt toward his mother and grandmother, it was the coldness he seemed to feel when reacting to his father. The Reverend Alfred Benjamin Blanchflower Baker, born in 1871, was a Methodist minister. Those who knew Rev. Baker through the Methodist Church in Nevis almost invariably described him as generous and gracious. But it seems there were tensions between him and Bertram's mother, Lilian, even at the time of their marriage, more than a year before Bertram's birth. It appears the father was not living in the household with Lilian and Bertram in the months before Lilian's death. He may have been on the preaching circuit at that time, but that is not certain. The fact that the funeral had taken place in an Anglican church, rather than a Methodist church, spoke volumes about the underlying problems in the relationship.

Faithful Methodists who had known Rev. Baker would recall what they saw as barriers between the husband and wife, even in the months before their marriage in 1897. It was said that Rev. Baker felt uncomfortable being with Lilian at parties because she was too quick to jump up and dance. This was according to Rupert Byron, a lay minister in the Nevisian Methodist Church, who spoke with me during a 1996 visit to Nevis. The unanimous opinion of those who had known Rev. Baker,

Byron said, was that his was not a good marriage.[6] Within a year after Lilian's death, on December 19, 1901, Alfred Baker, referred to as a "widower," married Evangeline ("Eva") O'Neill, "a spinster of full age," at the Charlestown Wesleyan (Methodist) Church.[7]

And so as little Bertram stayed with his de Grasse grandmother, his father ministered on nearby islands ("on the circuit," as they used to say) and then eventually decided to leave the Caribbean and go to Brooklyn, where a number of Nevisians and other West Indians were starting to settle. Among those who had emigrated previously were Rev. Baker's two brothers, Ned and Edwin, who lived in Downtown Brooklyn with their respective families. The two Baker brothers had joined forces with a growing number of Nevisians and other Caribbean immigrants in Brooklyn and incorporated the Ebenezer Wesleyan Methodist Church, which held its first services at various available locations downtown. Ned, a printer, born in 1863 and the oldest of the trio, and Edwin, a clerk with a shipping company, born in 1874, were listed as leaders of the new church, and they and the new church members invited Rev. Alfred Baker to be their first pastor.

One has to wonder what was on little Bertram's mind as his dad and stepmother were departing Nevis. It's possible that Bertram accompanied his dad and stepmom to the Nevisian shore for the boat ride to St. Kitts, whence they would be transported to the land of endless possibilities up north. Little Bertram was approaching an age of awareness then and surely felt, just as he felt his mother's death at an even younger age, the departure of his dad. Moreover, the lad surely had already been hearing about Brooklyn, that place of dreams, and an ambitious seven-year-old lad such as he might have intuitively felt it as his own.

Rev. Baker and Eva purchased their tickets and sailed northward on the ship called the *Parima*, and on August 7, 1905, they entered New York harbor. They went through the check-in procedures on Ellis Island and then made their way to an apartment at 235 Smith Street, in the downtown neighborhood, about ten blocks south from where his brothers, Ned and Edwin, were living with their families.

On August 14, just a week after his arrival, Rev. Baker officiated at the first Sunday service of the new Ebenezer Wesleyan Methodist Church. It took place at 114 Myrtle Avenue, about two blocks from Ned Baker's home on Lawrence Street.[8]

Over time, young Bertram came to take on the arrogance of those who considered the world around them to be their own and no one else's. This attitude was likely encouraged by his grandmother Eliza, whom

Bertram called "Nice Mammie." Bertram had a silver tongue, and his self-assurance would lead him to express himself with a directness that some often took as rudeness, a perception that grew annoying to many around him as he was entering his teens. Also, he seemed to intuit the impulses of self-interest he heard in the exchanges of his uncles, as they spoke about their businesses in Charlestown and elsewhere on the island.

The surrounding presence of water clearly had an impact on young Bertram, the ocean stretching along the piers just behind the Scotch House retail store, owned by the de Grasse family, and moving in waves also around the whole island. He no doubt spent time there as a child, and doing so must have given him a sense of the great possibilities that lay beyond, possibilities conveyed in the tales and chatter of his loquacious and success-loving de Grasse relatives. This was a place and time when men ruled the land, and his role models were the de Grasse men, who were having fair successes as owners of property around the island, in addition to the Scotch House.[9]

Records for Nevis, St. Kitts, and other Leeward Islands don't reach back beyond the mid-1800s, so what information there is about the names and ages of Bertram's de Grasse ancestors comes from his own notes and information entered in parish archives. What's intriguing and still, for me, full of mystery, is the French origin of the family. After all, it was the French admiral François Joseph Paul de Grasse who sailed onto St. Kitts in 1783 and engaged with British navy vessels in a battle that would determine the political future of the French and British Caribbean. De Grasse (who spelled his name as Bertram's maternal family did, with the small d and a space before the Grasse) had entered the U.S. history books just before his arrival at St. Kitts. He had cordoned off the bay around eastern Virginia for the Battle of Chesapeake, enabling George Washington's forces to whip the British soldiers and their allies, as de Grasse kept British fighting and transport ships away. De Grasse's defeat at the hands of the British in 1782 spelled the end of the strong French presence in parts of the Caribbean, including St. Kitts and Nevis, a presence that had dated back to the 1600s.

The legendary French warrior's defeat in the Caribbean brought his fighting career to a halt. He was compelled to sail to England, where he helped conduct negotiations that led to the Treaty of Paris, where victory was formally conceded to the British. But the de Grasse name continued to multiply in the Caribbean region in the late 1700s and 1800s, notably in Nevis. The de Grasses were not only the ancestors of Bertram Baker. They were forebears also of the famous New York City–born astrophysicist Neil deGrasse (no space) Tyson. Tyson's paternal grandmother, Altima Tyson, was born in Nevis in the 1890s with the surname de Grasse.[10] In an e-mail to me in the early 2000s, Tyson acknowledged his Nevisian roots but said he did not like to discuss ancestry. From my own research on Bertram Baker's family, I learned of a number of haughty de Grasse men from the turn of the nineteenth century who had outside-marriage relationships with employees and houseworkers. Ancestry regarding some de Grasse descendants became a touchy matter among some sensitive descendants. (In another book perhaps I'll look into the Tysons of Nevis, who presumably have ancestral connections to award-winning actress Cicely Tyson, whose roots are on the island. Names and relationships meant a lot to up-and-coming West Indians because they knew they had to take advantage of any connections afforded them if they were to have notable successes in this life.)

The de Grasses owned land throughout the islands of Nevis and St. Kitts, hiring workers to cultivate cotton on some of it, such as the strip called Kades (sometimes written as Cades) Bay. The de Grasses as well as the mulatto Bakers were listed in the British birth, marriage, and death registries, from the late 1800s into the 1900s, as "coloured," with the rest of the Nevisians, perhaps 95 percent of the total, designated as "black." The same was true of the Huggins sisters, who married Rev. Baker's brothers (Ned and Edwin) and were living in Brooklyn in the first years of the 1900s.

Little Bertram probably took some pride also in knowing about Alexander Hamilton, the American Founding Father. The de Grasse store, the Scotch House, was located on Main Street in Charlestown, about 150 yards from the old stone house where, in 1757, Hamilton was born.

Not much was known about Hamilton's father, and some believed that, while the mother was white, the father was of "mixed blood" and thus, in the categorical racial thinking of American racists, a Negro. Hamilton emigrated as a teenager with his mother to the Virgin Islands and went from there to New York, where he attended college, became a top aide to George Washington in the Revolutionary War, and went on to a uniquely successful life as a politician and man of his times.

Hamilton earned a seat in the New York state assembly in 1787, making laws for the state that had become his home. Then he was appointed the nation's first U.S. Secretary of the Treasury; he served in that capacity under President George Washington and came to be considered the father of the U.S. financial system.

Succeeders are dreamers. So what were the chances that little Bertram ever thought he might one day hold an office previously held by one of the Founding Fathers? I'd say fair to good. That is, of course, what happened in 1948, when Bertram L. Baker became the Honorable Bertram L. Baker, the second Nevisian-born person to hold a seat in the New York state legislature. All missives addressed to Baker from that time onward, to the days before his death in 1985, carried the ministerial abbreviation "Hon." before his name, a title that he found flattering and, given who he knew he was, appropriate.

When it came time for schooling, young Bertram initially received education from tutors on the island. Handwriting commanded quite a bit of attention in those days, and there was a stress on the beauty of flowing script.[11]

In 1911 or 1912 he went off for his secondary education to the St. Kitts Grammar School across the water in Basseterre, the capital city of St. Kitts, just a forty-minute boat ride from Nevis. There the education was classical, with rote memorization of lines from Caesar and Virgil, and formulaic writing of objective answers to very specific questions. The culmination was the so-called fifth form that led to the taking of the Oxford Preparatory examination, which in turn allowed one with adequate scores to attend a college elsewhere in the Caribbean or in England.[12]

A grammar school student typically finished at the age of seventeen. There are no papers showing that Bertram graduated from St. Kitts Grammar. What is known is that in mid- and late 1914, when he was sixteen, Bertram took on administrative duties at the Scotch House family store. In short order he began showing signs of irritation, even with his uncles, the owners. He felt he had been promised more money and a better position. His anger reached a point where he began "raising Cain," as family members in New York were told in letters. His tantrums caused unease among the elders in Nevis. The male de Grasse owners appealed to Bertram's grandmother to control the boy and talk some sense into him, but to no avail.

The grandmother, Bertram's Nice Mammie, sensed that her beloved and very spoiled grandchild was showing signs of frustration with the limited opportunities facing him. Even in school he would walk out of the classroom if he felt he wasn't learning anything of value. She knew, having heard about the experiences of the Bakers living in Brooklyn, that New York was a place of opportunity with doors at least ajar for someone like Bertram, who wanted to make his mark on the world around him and—perhaps more than anything else—to boss people around. There had been a little Nevisian enclave developing in Brooklyn. It was a world that was insular, in a metaphorical way, just like the tiny island the Nevisians had left behind. There were the Baker brothers—Ned (whose home-based printing business produced newsletters and brochures for local black organizations and even Irish community groups) and Edwin, who owned a typewriter and was a full-time clerk with a shipping company, even as he did superintendent work in successive apartments where he and his family stayed—and Bertram's father, Rev. Alfred Baker, who tended to the spiritual needs of the Caribbean Methodist community in Brooklyn.

Ned and Edwin were married to, respectively, Frances and Sarah, sisters with the maiden name of Huggins. They had been raised on a former sugar plantation on Nevis called Bucks Hill and likely had blood connections to the powerful eighteenth-century British merchants and slave-owners named Huggins.[13] Like their husbands, Frances and Sarah were well read and well spoken. They knew how to play piano. Like most West Indian women, they let the men rule the house. Edwin and Sarah had three daughters. Of twelve born, Ned and Frances had eight daughters and a son surviving into adulthood. The parents of both families stayed in touch with relatives back on Nevis, writing as frequently as they could.

One day in 1914 Bertram's grandmother Eliza sent a letter to Rev. Baker, who was pastoring one church up in Brooklyn and in the process of starting another in Harlem, saying that Bertram had reached a point in life where she could no longer control him and that he, as his father, must do something—come and get him.[14]

Emigrating from the Caribbean to the United States at that time was not terribly difficult, certainly not for one such as Bertram, who already had close family members there. In 1900, there were 20,336 foreign-born blacks among the 8.8 million blacks in the United States. By 1910 that figure had doubled to 40,339 while the total number of blacks in the country was 9.8 million. And in 1920 there were 73,803 immigrant blacks in the United States out of a total of 10.5 million blacks, according to U.S. Census Bureau figures cited by Ira De A. Reid, in a classic study on early black immigration to America.[15] World War I was causing death and destruction even as it opened job opportunities for black immigrants and their brothers and sisters seeking work as part of the Great Migration. A major result of the war, which had begun in 1914, was an increased demand for American products, which meant that American manufacturers and other businesses were looking for workers. Those workers came from the American South and, to a lesser extent, from the West Indies.

In Brooklyn, Rev. Baker must have had qualms about leaving to go to Nevis to get his son, and then bringing the young man back to the apartment he was sharing peacefully with his quiet, confrontation-hating wife, Eva. Without the duties of children, the couple had been living in a second-floor unit at 235 Smith Street, a quick ten-minute walk from the residences of Rev. Baker's relatives and friends in Downtown Brooklyn.[16] Rev. Baker was experiencing great successes in his ministry. In 1913 he had been called upon to pastor yet another new West Indian church, the Beulah Wesleyan Methodist Church, then on the West Side in what was then black Manhattan. (Beulah in later decades moved up to Harlem with the rest of the black population.) Ebenezer grew so quickly it had to stop conducting services out of the Myrtle Avenue home of the Bridgewater family, and it moved from location to location in Downtown Brooklyn, which half a century before had been a center of abolitionist activity.[17]

Rev. Baker boarded a ship back to the Caribbean and arrived in Nevis just after Christmas of 1914. He stayed on the island for a few months to reconnect with family and old friends. Sixteen-year-old Bertram at that time began keeping handwritten notes in a little brown booklet, two-and-a-half inches long and two inches wide. It was a diary in which he would make sporadic, dry, succinct, and strictly factual notations. All of the entries were in pencil—which fades quickly over time—written in flowing script of the era. "Dad arrived in Nevis on Dec. 30th 1914," the teenager wrote. The comments are notable for lacking expressions of feelings or descriptions, leaving one to guess about his thoughts. Some notations were cryptic. For example, written across one of the pages was this: "Dad came down to Scotch House to settle my matter." After that entry, several pages were torn out, leaving the imagination of one reading the notes ninety years later to run wild with speculation.

It is likely that "the matter" had to do with that thing Bertram saw later in life as so necessary when he was engaging in political contests (though he never seems to have let it be his main motivator): money. How much was involved is not known, but from his earliest years Bertram had been treated as heir to the de Grasse business and, according to the family tradition, was in line for the perquisites due the males in the line. And, although Bertram would never in his life become wealthy, he was not one to let a perk be yanked from his hand.

Nothing in the diary hinted at a seed of affection for the long-missing and now-returned father. A psychologist spending just a few minutes reading the entries would sense lingering tensions within the son. On Friday, January 15, Bertram wrote: "I slept with Dad again. Was very much disappointed in the evening." (Nothing was written on January 10, which was Bertram's birthday.)

On March 8, 1915, Bertram went with his father to St. Kitts to buy their tickets for the trip north.

The United States required that, before he could leave Nevis, Bertram have a physical examination, and he did. Bertram was thin and almost sickly looking. This was not because he did not have enough to eat. It was just his physique. He was never athletic. He was not a robust type, at least not in the physical way. He was robust in his manner, his speaking voice, and in his sense of himself.

A picture of Bertram from that time revealed a young man who fit tightly into his shirt and jacket, always a gentleman's jacket, and requisite tie. His stern expression made him appear erudite and wise beyond his years. But before leaving the island for the new home far north, Bertram made his required visit to a doctor, who examined him and, noting his frailty, told him: "Young man, you'll never survive a winter in New York City."[18] If the doctor's intention was to discourage Bertram from going to Brooklyn with his father, and from embarking up there on a path to success of one sort or other, he failed miserably. Bertram would end up surviving seventy winters in New York City.

The evening of March 12 must have been one of the most somber of Bertram's life until then. On the next day, he would be leaving the grandmother who up to that point meant more to him than anyone else in the world, and he would never see her again.

But on the departure day, March 13, 1915, as he traveled from Nevis to St. Kitts, there to board the ship that would take him on a seven-day trip north to the American dream, Bertram might have been pulled down in spirit by two things. One was leaving his grandmother. The other was being with his father, with whom he never seemed to have developed a relationship that had any warmth or shared energy.

On the voyage to Ellis Island, Bertram spent much of his time alone, relieving himself in vomiting fits caused by the wicked ups and downs of rolling seas.[19] Throughout his life his stomach would be the part of his body that caused him the most distress. Beyond that, one has to suspect that the son reacted with chilliness to his father's likely attempts to engage in intimate conversation. One subject in particular, their respective Protestant faiths, would seem to have been a likely topic for discussion—that is to say, for two men who were open minded to each other's feelings. The father was spiritually wedded to his Methodism, and the son would always energetically assert his devotion to Anglicanism, or the Church of England, affiliated with the Episcopal Church in the United States. If the father possessed an openness to fair exchange on the topic—and comments of those who knew him in later years suggest he would have—the son had no such openness, especially where the father was concerned.

As Bertram sailed each day with his father, esteemed in Brooklyn for bringing Wesleyan Methodist hymns and prayers to West Indian immigrants there, the teenager carried in his jacket a letter from his Uncle Willie de Grasse, introducing the nephew to any Anglican priest (or Episcopal priest, as they said in the United States) who might be inclined to help the young man in his first desire—to enter the Episcopal priesthood. The son of the Wesleyan Methodist minister wanted to be an Episcopal priest.[20]

Though Bertram would never again see his Uncle Willie, that de Grasse relative would remain planted in the young man's mind as a counterweight to his father, the Methodist minister. For Nevisian Anglicans, their faith was a way of projecting themselves onto a perceived and fitting rung of society. It also couched an elitism that had to do with breeding or ancestry, as well as with a level of education. (Bertram was baptized in the Anglican Church. It is not known whether Bertram's Methodist father, Rev. Baker, was on the preaching circuit at the time of the christening, a decade and a half earlier, or whether he had already left for Brooklyn, or had simply conceded to the English high church preferences of the de Grasses.)

Up in Brooklyn, where Rev. Baker's brothers were living, the brothers' spouses, the Huggins sisters, had both been raised as Episcopalians. But at that stage of their lives in America, the men were still making decisions having to do with big issues like the religions embraced by the households, and so the children attended Rev. Baker's Methodist services. There are some historical differences between the two forms of worship. Anglicanism was the Church of England and existed effectively as the official religion of the British empire. Methodism, on the other hand, circulated as a newcomer faith and made its way through the Caribbean in the early and mid-1800s. It was seen as more open and progressive when it came to the mixing of blacks and whites. It was also less rigid, more progressive, in its structure. While Anglican priests had to be educated at divinity schools, such as in England or at Codrington College on the island of Barbados (the colony that was called "Little England" throughout the Caribbean), a would-be Methodist minister could become a man of the cloth by apprenticing with an ordained reverend who would tutor and observe the newcomer.

As for the genealogical history of the Bakers, their records are mostly viewable in handwritten sheets kept by family members, as opposed to official records, many of which were destroyed in an 1882 fire. One of Rev. Baker's grandfathers is listed as William H. Baker, born April 3, 1829, on Nevis; a great-grandmother was Elizabeth Lowman, born in 1813. One wonders, especially because the father is not named, if Elizabeth Lowman was a free black or a mulatto who had children with a white Britisher.[21]

As the father and son sailed for a week up the Atlantic, it seems likely that they would have found time for a discussion of utmost importance to the boy—the race situation in the land they were entering. To Bertram, it must have seemed odd that someone like his dad, who could have passed for a white Englishman, given his features, complexion, and even, to the unaccustomed ears of some Americans, perhaps his accent, would be considered an African.

But there on the manifest of the *Parima*, the same *Parima* that ten years earlier had brought the reverend to New York, under the column marked "Ethnicity," was the notation: "Great Britain, African."[22]

The truth is that Rev. Baker and his relatives were all descendants of Africans, but being called African was likely a bit jolting to Bertram, not because he felt that his African-ness was something to be denied, but because he had lived in an environment that did not define him by it.[23]

And so now here was Bertram, on the evening of Saturday, March 20, 1915, arriving finally in that place of limitless possibilities. Brooklyn on its south and west was bordered by water, as Nevis was all around, but Brooklyn was heavily developed with brick and brownstone row houses, stretching for miles and miles, and the downtown neighborhood onto which they finally completed their journey boasted many commercial buildings, government offices, warehouses, and churches, so busy all, that any comparisons between Brooklyn and Nevis fell with a clunk.

Ellis Island itself must have been especially striking and perhaps a bit intimidating. Arrivals had to go through interrogations and medical examinations before placing their feet on American land. Bertram's situation was relatively free of the strain and anxiety that so many others experienced. That was because he was accompanied by his father, who had legal residency (though not citizenship) in the United States. Some immigrants arrived panic-stricken, knowing perhaps that they carried infections that might be discovered in the physical examinations. Others would have to stay at Ellis Island because their sponsors could not arrive in time to sign as their guardians and escort them off the island. Some black arrivals had memorable recollections of the entry, made especially poignant with the passing of time. There were West Indian arrivals who would pass along, from one to the other, the same fist-held wad of two U.S. dollars required as proof of self-sufficiency.

The Statue of Liberty loomed in New York harbor as a heartening site, welcoming Bertram as it had welcomed so many previous newcomers from eastern Europe and Italy over the past two decades. After riding a ferry from Ellis Island to Brooklyn, it would have taken Bertram and his father about an hour to walk to 235 Smith Street, but they likely took public transportation, either a trolley car or a horse-drawn carriage. Rev. Baker would have pointed out, there in the distance, the arching expanse of the Brooklyn Bridge, built three decades earlier, and within days Bertram would travel over it with his cousins to visit family friends in Manhattan and to attend recitals there.

Rev. Baker did exceptionally well as a clergyman in Brooklyn. Methodist churches had existed in the United States for a long time, but the racial segregation of the churches, with blacks consigned to certain pews, infuriated black Methodists, who formed their own breakaway denomination called the African Methodist Episcopal church, generally shortened to A.M.E. For newly arrived Nevisians, the A.M.E. services were too emotive for their conservative inclinations. And so the Baker brothers, Edwin and Ned, together with other recently arrived Nevisians, had organized the Ebenezer Wesleyan Methodist Church; and with their brother Rev. Baker, Bertram's father, as the pastor, they worshipped in the relatively subdued and British ways to which they had become accustomed, over generations, on the island of Nevis.[24]

It was precisely the respective postures on religiosity that would take Bertram from his father. To put it another way, the oppositional belief systems, however nominal they might seem to some others, gave Bertram his out. The seventeen-year-old young man adamantly insisted on the trueness of the Anglican faith of his maternal ancestors, the de Grasses. He still wanted to enter the Episcopal priesthood, he would confide to cousins who would politely listen. The split between father and son occurred soon after their arrival in Brooklyn in the spring of 1915.

It's not in Bertram's diary, but according to what he later told his wife, Irene, there came a Sunday morning when Bertram's father and stepmother were preparing to leave for church. Bertram, rather than readying himself, knelt at the side of his bed in prayer. When Rev. Baker walked in, he looked in puzzlement at his son and asked why he wasn't getting ready to leave for church. Bertram replied that he was raised as an Anglican and he would remain an Anglican for the rest of his days, and that he wasn't going to worship at a Methodist church, even if his father was the pastor there. In disgust, the father shouted, "You'll never again get a red cent from me!"[25]

And so on that Sunday Bertram left his father's home at 235 Smith Street and went to the Lawrence Street home of his cousins, the Bakers Dozen. There he rented from his Uncle Ned a single room that would be his residence over the next four years. He paid his rent out of his $6-a-week salary from a job at the Abraham & Straus department store on Fulton Street in Downtown Brooklyn, just four blocks from Ned Baker's home.[26]

While Bertram said he left his dad's home because his soul could not bear a renegade denomination like the Methodists, the fact of the matter was that the Lawrence Street household was also Methodist. Ned Baker was Rev. Baker's brother and had helped organize the Ebenezer Wesleyan Methodist Church, where Rev. Baker was the pastor. The family attended Methodist services on Sunday, and Bertram lived with them and put up with it. On Sundays, he would go to St. Augustine's Episcopal Church, which was largely black and at that time located in the downtown neighborhood.

But was this division over denomination much ado about little? Should it have led to family breakups?

"When I was in St. Vincent I was an Anglican," said Jessie Warner (now deceased), who was born on the then-British island of St. Vincent in 1894 and immigrated to the United States in 1923. "But my husband [Gerald Warner] was a Methodist, so we got married at the Anglican church, and on some Sundays I used to go with him and some Sundays he would go with me. . . . And then I came to [the United States] first and I went to St. Phillips, which at the time was on Dean Street. But after my husband came here I tried to get him to go but he wouldn't. So I went over with him to Ebenezer and that's how I became a Methodist.

"There's not much difference. For a long time, I used my Anglican hymn book at Ebenezer, because it's the same thing. It's the same service. The only thing is the communion service is a little longer than what the Methodist book has. . . . I felt that when myself [sic] and my husband get older we can hold hands in the same church." The Warners had two children, she said. "My first child was baptized Anglican, the next Methodist."

Interviewed at her Bedford Stuyvesant home on October 7, 1995, at the age of 101, she added, "John Wesley himself [the eighteenth-century founder of the Wesleyan form of worship] always said he would die an Anglican . . . so however we worship, it's the same thing."[27]

The four years following Bertram Baker's arrival in Brooklyn moved along swiftly. He had steady work and stayed safe from the overseas war that pulled a number of men, including some black immigrants, off the streets and onto battlefields. Bertram earned his first paychecks sweeping floors and delivering packages at Abraham & Straus, where persons of color could aspire to a job no higher than that of elevator operator. And during the 1917–18 involvement of the United States in World War I, he avoided the draft. Because of his overall physical fragility, Bertram did not pass the fitness exam and was exempted.

At the age of twenty-one, he was ready for marriage and life on his own. And the young lady with whom he pledged a lifelong bond was his eighteen-year-old first cousin Irene, whom he deemed a proper spouse for a man of his talent and ambition. It was perhaps all for the good that Bertram's father had decided to return to the West Indies before the wedding. He had left in 1917.[28] It would have been awkward, after all, for Rev. Baker, the respected Methodist pastor, to be standing off to the side while the wedding ceremony of his son and niece was performed by an Episcopal priest.

That priest was Father George Frazier Miller, a man of color, born in the American South. He grew up during the era of Reconstruction when the southern states were renouncing efforts to give Negroes rights thought to have been won in the Civil War. Miller came north, entered the priesthood, and began to make a mark on life in Brooklyn. He also became a father figure for young Bertram Baker.

Miller was the rector of St. Augustine's Episcopal Church, the main parish of those Negroes who adhered to the beliefs and practices of what in effect was the American Church of England. Rector Miller, as he was called, was about fifty at the time of the wedding of Bertram and Irene, and he was an established figure in the black community. Miller had a reputation for being a radical, someone willing to stand up to the white power structure.

Between 1917 and 1918, when America was involved in World War I, Rector Miller had refused to fly the American flag outside his church, as a protest against a war he considered immoral. Miller was, in fact, a committed socialist. This was the period when the U.S. government was forming a federal investigative agency, and it became well known throughout the black community in Brooklyn that agents were attending Miller's Sunday masses and taking notes. Although Bertram never publicly identified with socialism, it was clear he greatly admired Rector Miller for his strength of conviction as well as for his eloquence and charm, all of which meant more to Bertram than the man's politics.

Speaking many years later of Rector Miller, Bertram Baker said, "He called himself a socialist, and the federal government knew of his activity, and they posted in his church from time to time men, FBI men, to record his sermons and so forth. But he was fearless because he said that, because of the segregation in the United States . . . the American flag meant nothing to him. It was just a piece of bunting. And for that, of course, these men were stationed in his church. And he said: 'I'm not afraid. I'm not afraid of you. You can record what I say.' That's the type of man he was."[29]

The emergence of Rector Miller as a Brooklyn spokesman for blacks coincided with the rise within the federal bureaucracy of a man named J. Edgar Hoover, and it was around this period that the federal government began sending black spies who would attend black events and surreptitiously inform the government about the goings-on of note in the black community. This intrigue would surely have drawn Bertram Baker into its web. The point of convergence would have come through Marcus Garvey. Garvey, like Bertram, was a West Indian making his way in the land of the color line. But Garvey was overt in the venting of his anger and of his increasingly militant beliefs that blacks should return to Africa.

Rector Miller had connections to Garvey.[30] On February 26, 1920, Miller appeared at a massive gathering of Garveyites, attended also by Garvey himself, at the Brooklyn Academy of Music. In attendance that evening also was a federal agent who took notes and passed them on to higher-ups:

> Next was a thrilling address by the Rev. George Frazier Miller of the St. Augustine P.E. Church of Brooklyn. Rev. Miller opposed such men as Booker T. Washington and [others], claiming that they have no initiative and had to . . . report [to their] white associates whose sole interests are to keep the Negro in a subjective capacity. . . . During his address, he referred to the late war and stated that the Department of Justice had held him under observation as an unpatriotic American. He also stated that he remarked during the war, and does now remark, that "the war was not fought for the

purpose of making the world safe for Democracy, but for the purpose of making Wall Street safe for foreign loans." (This latter statement met with overwhelming applause.)[31]

It is not known whether Bertram attended that event.[32] But for the next two decades he remained on good terms with Rector Miller, and an ardent admirer. However, Bertram clearly came to feel that that sort of radicalism, and being followed around by federal agents, was not in his best interests. This would have been especially true at the time of the wedding—which was the time of that meeting at the Brooklyn Academy of Music—because Bertram was not yet a U.S. citizen. As for the Jamaican-born Marcus Garvey, who like Bertram was technically a citizen of the United Kingdom, Garvey was eventually tried for and convicted by the U.S. government of fraud for swindling his members in back-to-Africa ship purchasing deals, and he himself was shipped back to Jamaica in 1927. Such outcomes were not in Bertram Baker's plans.

Notable about Rev. Miller was his role in officiating at Bertram's marriage, on December 10, 1919. The marriage to Irene Baker took place at the small East New York, Brooklyn, apartment that Irene's father, Edwin Baker, was renting at the time. A son concerned about the reputation and feelings of his father, who happened to be a minister, would have tried to have the father at least be present as an officiator at the ceremony. But Rev. Baker was gone, having returned to the Caribbean, where he would live the rest of his long life, except for one short visit in the 1930s, detached emotionally and in every other way from his ambitious, up-and-coming son. There, instead, was Rector Miller, and Bertram was pleased with his presence.

There was one glitch, however, that exuded meaning even as it remained silent. Ideally, the wedding would have been held at the St. Augustine Episcopal Church, which was then located in the downtown section where the Lawrence Street Bakers and the black activists were centered. But, given that Bertram and Irene were first cousins, Rector Miller knew that his officiating at their marriage would not be formally accepted by his church.[33] And that was the reason the exchanging of the vows took place at the home of Edwin Baker—Bertram's new father-in-law—rather than at the church. The radicalism, even of one so militant as George Frazier Miller, went only so far, it seems.

Despite his affection for and even adoration of Rector Miller, Bertram Baker was starting to realize that becoming a priest in the American Episcopal Church would be too difficult a hurdle for a West Indian immigrant, especially one who, like him, had not come to the States with a divinity degree already in hand. So he satisfied himself by moving onto another path to power, politics.

Before signing on with the local Democratic Party in the Bedford neighborhood of Brooklyn in 1924, the year he took his oath of citizenship, Baker knew he had to find a way to earn a living. So he acquired an accounting certificate from the Chicago-based correspondence school LaSalle Extension University. To support himself, Irene, and their two girls (Lilian, born in November 1920, and Marian, born in June 1925) he did taxes and other bookkeeping work for local black residents and businesses in the community. To make connections he joined organizations and fraternal groups, notably the local chapter of the all-black American Tennis Association; a local group associated with the Garvey movement; and the Prince Hall Masons. As for the Democratic Party, he did the yeoman's work of walking through the neighborhood and trying to talk residents into signing petitions for the candidates supported by the Brooklyn Democratic organization.

When things got financially tight, as they did during the late years of the Great Depression, Baker looked to the island of Nevis for help. And it was not his father, back in the Caribbean, whom he asked for assistance, but his de Grasse uncle. William de Grasse (Uncle Willie) had continued with his business successes through the 1920s and '30s. Even while he and other Nevisians were strongly buffeted by the Depression, he had managed to hold on to a number of his properties. He owned and sold, for instance, Kades Bay, on the island. That, plus Uncle Willie's other holdings, could keep a family, even a business one, in financial shape.

Apart from money, Uncle Willie wielded clout on Nevis and in the wider British Caribbean, as a representative of commercial interests. On January 1, 1939, Uncle Willie spoke at what was described as a mass meeting of Nevisians. He was not a government official. He was, rather, a local man of respectability, of substance, of birth.

In 1938, King George VI decided to conduct a survey on the economy of the islands, and he sent his representative, Lord Moyne. The January 10, 1930, session with the king's representative was a huge deal. Large numbers of Nevisians gathered outside the meeting hall in Charlestown. And who made the welcoming speech? Bertram's Uncle Willie. The *St. Kitts–Nevis Daily Bulletin* covered the event and ran an article with this headline: "Nevis Makes Deep Impression on Members of Royal Commission."

Bertram, working at the local polls in Brooklyn and struggling to pay the rent in those tough years, must have known about his uncle's very prominent role at that moment. How proud he must have been! There is no record that Bertram's father, Rev. Baker, was involved in any way, although the reverend was in Nevis preaching at Methodist services and running a little bookstore where he sold pencils and notebooks for children. In the newspaper, Uncle Willie was referred to in the classic style of the British addressing men worthy of deference—as the Hon. W. B. de Grasse. (Uncle Willie, typically for such men, had three names before his surname, i.e., William Mortimer Bruce de Grasse.) His opening remarks to Lord Moyne were published in the paper:

> We are extremely grateful to his Majesty's Government for appointing such an able and distinguished commission to come amongst us, to investigate our social and economic conditions with the object of making recommendations for improvement. We are very poor people, very hard-working but we are [nevertheless] amongst the most loyal subjects of His Majesty the King. Memoranda have been forwarded to you which we trust will help you in your investigation and we sincerely hope that the result of this enquiry may be of such lasting benefit to the people of this Island that your names will go down in its history and be engraved in the hearts of its people with the loving remembrances and gratitude not only of this generation but of the generations to come.

At this point in his life, Uncle Willie was gravely ill. He had in fact told some Nevisians that he knew he would die soon. And he did pass away on January 15, 1939, at his home on the island. Bertram, upon learning of the death of his Uncle Willie, immediately began corresponding with Willie's brother, Bertram's Uncle Murray. Murray and Bertram filed the necessary papers making them beneficiaries of Willie's holdings, which likely totaled more than $10,000, a significant amount of money in those days. Bertram during the late 1930s of the Depression era was starting to feel a little desperate. A bank had foreclosed on his Throop Avenue house. Uncle Willie's estate, after the payment of debts, allowed Bertram and Uncle Murray to share what was left, at least several thousand dollars. And Bertram was able to acquire a lovely brownstone at 399 Jefferson Avenue, barely seventy-five yards from the Throop Avenue home that he had lost through foreclosure.[34] That became the home from which Bertram would rise up through Brooklyn politics. It was the home in which I was raised.

As for Uncle Murray, he had a little struggling business on the island of St. Kitts. In a series of letters, Bertram convinced his aging uncle to sell everything and immigrate to Brooklyn, staying with Bertram, Irene, and their two daughters at Jefferson Avenue, where Murray remained until his death in 1949, the year I was born.

Bertram shared few words with his father over the decades, seeing him only once in 1935 when Rev. Baker returned to New York to be honored by members of the two Wesleyan Methodist churches the Reverend had pastored in the earlier years of the century (Ebenezer in Brooklyn and Beulah in Manhattan). A flier for a special church dinner in Rev. Baker's honor said:

> Two hundred and more gather here this evening from many walks of life to honor you and to give public recognition to your years of service in the cause of religion in this city. You have brought to us encouragement and inspiration; you have made our adjustment easier and happier in a strange land; you have given us the highest ideals of Christian fellowship and today many "rise and call you blessed." . . . We gather with you this evening to rejoice in your foresight; to congratulate you as a loyal son of the King giving to humanity a life devoted to true Christianity. . . . [35]

Bertram and his family attended the event. For the rest of their lives, Bertram and Irene's daughters lovingly reflected on the time they spent with their grandfather during his brief stay in Brooklyn. (Oops, because Bertram and Irene were first cousins, Rev. Baker was their grandfather *and* their uncle. Oddly, they called him Uncle Fred. Perhaps it was because while Bertram never spoke of his father, Irene harbored a fondness for her distant uncle and wrote to him in Nevis.) He seemed always to have a smile on his face. His hair had begun to turn snow-white, and he had a drooping mustache that played teasingly with caring eyes. Marian was ten at the time of the reverend's visit to New York, and Lilian was fifteen. Foremost in their memories was a day at Coney Island beach, listening to Rev. Baker's stories of life back on Nevis and taking to heart his assertions of love for them. They were sad to see him leave, and ever after they noted the emotional distance between their father and their father's father. The warmth of their long-distance relationship with their granddad contrasted with the chilliness of their connection to their dad.

Correspondences between Bertram and Rev. Baker over the remaining years of the father's life were brief. On Bertram's part, the communications carried an if-I-only-had-time curtness that can hurt the recipient, especially a close relative. On Rev. Baker's part, there was humiliation regarding his son's absence, aggravated by the fact that it became known throughout Nevis and neighboring St. Kitts that Nevisian-born Bertram Baker had made a bit of history by becoming Brooklyn's first black person elected to office, in 1948.

One letter, dated September 4, 1951, and typed out (probably by his secretary Marie Smallwood) read:

> My dear Dad:
>
> I have been away and have just returned home so I thought I would drop you a line before I got too engrossed in the very many things which I now have to catch up with.
>
> I fully realize that you must feel very lonesome and I suppose this accounts for the many reports which I get here that you would like to come to America. This is something that you should decide for yourself after consulting with your physician. I simply want you to know that, if that is your desire, there is a comfortable home awaiting you here.
>
> You never mentioned whether you actually drew the $200.00 which I authorized the Bank to pay you sometime ago. If you decide that you want to make the trip and you need additional funds, I can authorize a further payment to you.
>
> I am glad that you are getting along so well that you are able to be out, however, do not permit yourself to worry so much or you may have a set-back.
>
> Drop me a line as soon as you can and let me know what you think best.
>
> Affectionately yours,
> Bertram[36]

In the late 1950s, Sharon Bourke (Ned Baker's granddaughter) traveled to visit Rev. Baker on Nevis. At that point Bertram Baker was a powerful Assemblyman representing the Bedford Stuyvesant section of Brooklyn. My dear cousin Sharon wrote:

> Uncle Fred, or Baker, as most people here call him, is bitter about the only child of his, who has lived in Brooklyn. This is Bertram, a member of the New York State Legislature, an educated, successful man who never writes his father, who seemingly doesn't care how the old man exists or what he feels. Bertram has become like a legend to Uncle Fred, the prodigal son who'll return some

day, so the old man believes. A letter from Bertram is expected any day now, Bertram is going to send a package, or money, etc., etc. When I declined a visit to Sunday service with Uncle Fred [author's note: Bourke is an averred non-churchgoer], he looked into space dramatically and said, "I wonder what church Bertram belongs to now."[37]

Rev. Baker, whose wife Eva died in 1950, operated a bookstore off Main Street in Nevis for the rest of his life. There is a picture of him counting change after a day's work, which was really not so much work as a day of neighbors and fellow Methodists coming to chat with him. The "books" were mostly postcards, school notebooks, and pencils. Relatives in New York City would send him the items that he sold and sometimes even a few dollars. The reverend had given up preaching two decades earlier, except for the occasional times during the 1950s when he would officiate at one of Nevis's Methodist churches on an as-needed basis. He openly spoke of the loneliness he felt in the decade-and-a-half since his wife's death.

Rev. Alfred Benjamin Blanchflower Baker died on July 26, 1962, at the age of ninety-one. His son, Bertram, did not attend the funeral.

2
Irene
Baker Forever, but Never a Boss

When not doing housework, Irene Baker was known throughout her adult life for jotting down random and sometimes literary thoughts on slips of paper, reading letters from friends and relatives and immediately replying to them, skimming through stacks of magazines and New York City newspapers (there were a dozen in the early twentieth century), chatting with friends on the telephone that she and others began using with regularity in the 1920s, and perhaps most impressively of all her activities, sketching and painting.[1]

By nearly all measures having to do with intellect, Irene Baker was at least the equal of Bertram, and had the workplace been fair when it came to gender, she would have had one notable advantage over her husband. She was a natural New Yorker, her parents, Edwin and Sarah, having arrived through Ellis Island from the Caribbean four years before Irene's birth in Brooklyn in March 1901.

As first cousins, Bertram and Irene were so closely connected by blood that the Catholic Church of Rome and the Catholic Church of England (and thus the Episcopal Church of America) barred them from being married, granting annulments to such unions, effectively asserting the marriage had never taken place.

The closeness of their ancestral ties showed strikingly in Bertram and Irene. Their hair was black and straight. At the time, they were both fairly thin and relatively short, Irene being five-foot-one and Bertram five-foot-seven. Their complexions could be described as *café-au-lait*, and their faces were smooth. Bertram spoke with a British inflection, and

Irene with a Brooklyn accent, both with suggestions of confidence in where they were respectively born and raised.

The differences between Bertram and Irene were also stark. He had about him the brusqueness and overbearing sense of superiority that turned off many, including the Baker girls at Lawrence Street, although it won over countless white professionals and those engaged in local politics with whom he would interact after he settled into his new land. Irene had about her a softness, a delicateness that in that time was the most admired of qualities for the wife of an up-and-comer.

Irene Baker had just turned fourteen when the seventeen-year-old Bertram arrived. She was an avid reader of novels and she loved to write, doing so frequently with a pencil at home while her two younger sisters argued and fought. From childhood, Irene harbored a desire to someday be a professional artist, a painter. But her father, Edwin, firm in the traditions of women staying at home, had made it clear that painting was not an acceptable ambition for a Negro immigrant's child, especially a daughter. It was a denial that would cause Irene pain throughout her life.

> My father once called my sisters and me together to discuss how things were going in school. I must have been fifteen. Of course, the others were younger. Anyway. He wanted to know what plans we had for our futures. Edna said she wanted to go into business. (Maybe that meant we were a little older. I don't know.) But he said, "Very good." And then he asked Vi. And Vi said she wanted to go into dressmaking. "Very good!" he said. And so he asked me and I said, "Really I would like to take art courses." Oh, he got so angry with me. He said, "You don't realize that people of your color can't get into classes of that kind. There's no future in that for you." And it killed me.[2]

Her style was not to openly rebel, especially against her father who, while not inclined to use physical force, was nonetheless the head of the household and one to be obeyed. Rather, Irene fought back in her own quiet way, reading books in the evening hours and sketching with pencils protected like precious little cakes.

Irene's 1914 graduation booklet from her elementary school, P.S. 93,[3] reflected her life in those days. The pages show the students to be literate and happy in a youthful way. It also revealed the presence of dedicated teachers in their lives. There were sorrows, of course, but also a reflective thoughtfulness. One can see incarnations of Little Francie Nolan of *A Tree Grows in Brooklyn*. Francie was born the same year as Irene,

1901, and Francie passed her childhood in Williamsburg, a quick walk north of Irene's downtown neighborhood. Irene's schoolmates, like Francie's, were largely second-generation Irish, with recent Italians and Jews sprinkled in. The graduation booklet reveals a togetherness that faded in the coming decades, as greater numbers of blacks made their way from the American South and the Caribbean, hardening the hearts of white ethnics toward fellow Brooklynites of color. The signees of Irene's graduation book were mostly girls, though the school was co-ed. In the excerpt that follows, a student connects with Irene on the topic of men seeking to control women. She exhorts Irene to be assertive with her future husband.

> To Irene,
> When you are married
> And your husband is cross
> Hand him the lemon
> And say, I am the boss
> —Your friend,
> Genevieve Williams

And then there was the girl who could not have known how funny her words would seem years later to Irene's friends and relatives.

> To Irene,
> Irene for now
> Irene forever
> Baker for now
> But not forever
> —Your classmate,
> E. M. Carson

One has to wonder if E. M. (her full name is not known, though I presume she is a girl like the others) ever learned that her buddy Irene Baker did indeed become Irene Baker Baker.

Of note also among those students was Adele McCooey, who wrote the following:

> Dear Irene
> I plant this seed in a lonely spot
> And it only means forget-me-not.

Researching newspaper clippings and U.S. Census data shows that Adele was the daughter of John H. McCooey, an Irish American who was then the Democratic leader of Brooklyn and who several years before had founded the Madison Democratic Club, which would shape Brooklyn politics over the course of the twentieth century and would become the borough's greatest dispenser of patronage, joining up in the mid-1920s with the corrupt Tammany Hall machine, which was based in Manhattan.[4] When he involved himself in Brooklyn politics in the 1920s and '30s, Baker initially accepted McCooey as the boss of the Brooklyn Democrats. But eventually, during the mid-'30s, Baker would lash out at him as an old-fashioned Irishman who would not give patronage jobs to blacks. Irene's background shows how connected she was and how powerful someone like her might have become, if girls had been allowed to have that kind of gumption and to cultivate within themselves a desire for power outside the home. Bertram never really conceded it, but Irene's experiences taught him much.

Bertram Baker would always assert that it was racism which kept him from pursuing his dream of becoming an Episcopal priest. The church presented too many obstacles to black men holding that ambition, he would say. It might be argued that if Bertram's hero, Rector George Frazier Miller, had become an Episcopal priest and succeeded, then Bertram should have been able to do so also. But Irene's first experiences in her parents' new homeland confirmed that the Episcopal Church there was, as Bertram would later assert, very unfriendly to black people.

At the time of Irene's birth in 1901, her parents, Sarah and Edwin Baker, were living in an apartment on Fulton Street near Kingston Avenue. That was in the heart of what today is called the Bedford Stuyvesant section of Brooklyn, but back then it was just the black part of what was referred to as the Bedford section. Elevated trains (demolished three decades later, in the 1930s) ran above Fulton Street as well as Atlantic Avenue, one block to the south, and those were the blocks on which blacks were allowed to rent at that time. It was the Bakers' introduction to racial demarcations in their new country, and they would find out that it divided just about all aspects of life in America: residential, economic, judicial, and spiritual.

Thinking of herself still as part of the Church of England (i.e., the Episcopal Church in America),[5] her mother, Sarah, took baby Irene to the nearest Episcopal Church, St. Matthew's, on Tompkins Avenue, to be baptized. She saw the priest there and requested that he baptize her child. Irene Baker would later relate that, to her mother's chagrin, the rector told her that, yes, he would baptize the baby, but that the baptism could not be entered into the church registry. The reason stunned Sarah.

"There is a church for coloreds," the pastor said, as Irene Baker related the tale in an interview in the mid-1990s. The colored Episcopal church to which the priest referred was St. Augustine's. The pastor there was Rector George Frazier Miller, the priest who, fifteen years later, would become a hero of Bertram Baker's. (At this time, Bertram was a three-year-old toddler still living on Nevis.)

The racism of St. Matthew's was crude and long lasting.[6] It was in fact harsher than what Irene's family would generally experience in their typical days ahead. But it would make them inclined to accept the snide remarks of some in later decades that the most segregated day in America was Sunday. The September 16, 1929, *Brooklyn Eagle* newspaper published an article about a St. Matthew's parish bulletin that said Negroes should stay away from their church. The rector of the church at the time was the southern-born Rev. William Blackshear, who was white and who declared, "The Episcopal Church provides churches for Negroes. Several of these churches are within easy reach of this locality. They are in need of the loyal support of all true Negro churchmen; therefore, the rector of this parish discourages the attendance or membership in this church of the members of that race."

Sarah Huggins Baker, for the rest of her life, stayed away from Sunday devotions. But the irony is this: Her resistance wasn't based on her anger at the white racist priest. She would willingly have gone to one of the black Episcopal churches, especially St. Augustine's. No, she stayed home because her husband insisted on taking the daughters to Sunday Methodist services. And she did not accept that form of worship. It would be all but impossible to confirm today, but it could be that when Sarah Baker took Irene to St. Matthew's, she was doing so against the wishes of her husband, who likely was at work at the time. (A similar scenario played out at the other Baker household in Brooklyn, where Sarah's sister, Frances, was married to Edwin's brother, Ned. But Frances seems to have accepted the Methodism of her husband more willingly than Irene's mother accepted her husband's Methodism.)

There is a chance that Bertram's later affection for Sarah Baker was based on their respective embracing of the Episcopalian faith, against the preferences of the other Bakers. Even after Irene's marriage to Bertram, he would write tender poems to Sarah, Irene's mother. In a recorded conversation in 1993, Irene's youngest sister, Edna, said she suspected that he and Sarah, two decades older than he, were in love. Irene, listening to the exchange, said nothing. (Out of politeness to my grandmother Irene, I never pursued the topic.)

The Baker world in Brooklyn was a girls' world. The three children in Irene's household were all girls (Irene, Violet, and Edna), and there were eleven in the Lawrence Street home, which was the Sunday gathering place for the extended Baker clan.[7] Teenage Bertram did not seem to have gotten along very well with the Baker girls other than Irene. They knew their place. None had ambitions to be a doctor or lawyer or politician. But they could be loud and overbearing in ways that Irene never was. And the fact that there were eleven of them meant the place could get noisy. Rose, one of the daughters, was born in 1892 in Nevis. She played the piano well. One Sunday afternoon at Lawrence Street she started banging out "It Takes a Long Tall Brown-Skin Gal to Make a Preacher Lay His Bible Down." Here is how the song went:

> For twenty years I'se pass'd Joy by, but now
> I'm goin' to get mine 'till I die
> I always thought the preachin' was my line
> But since I met this gal I chang'd my min',
> It takes a Long Tall Brown-Skin Gal
> To make a preacher lay his Bible down.

Irene's father, Edwin, didn't like it one bit when he heard the music and the lyrics. He went a little ballistic. "He went to their father and told their father to come into the living room and 'tell these daughters of yours to stop playing such music and singing such words.'" In his anger that evening, Edwin took his family (wife Sarah and the three children, Irene, Violet, and Edna) home, taking the trolley to Dean Street, about a fifteen-minute ride to the southeast, there to sleep it off.

As for Bertram, he would probably have enjoyed the jam session better if it had been a bunch of guys. But the loud women, in a way, intimidated the same teenager who, in two decades, would show little fear in his spirit, especially when it came to someone else's words. But his early years with Irene and the other Baker girls were a time of adjustment for young Bertram.

One of the worst occasions for Bertram, when it came to dealing with the Baker girls, was in 1917. He had returned home to Lawrence Street after his physical examination for the draft. The doctor checked him out to see if he was fit enough to serve in the military. This was as the country was entering World War I on the side of its Allies, England and France, against Germany and Austria-Hungary. It was to Bertram's great delight that his thinness and overall fragility led his examiners to conclude he was not material for a war uniform at that time. Surely he kept his joy to himself while at the government offices. Then he headed back home to Lawrence Street. "When he came to Lawrence Street and entered the room he said, 'I was excused! I'm exempted!' And he jumped up and down, he was so happy," his cousin Irene, then not yet his wife, recalled eighty years later.

His reaction was not well received in the patriotic household.[8] "They all booed him," recalled Irene, who was present but was not among the booers, given her demure, über-polite nature. "The whole Baker family booed him, all the girls. He didn't like being booed."[9]

For the rest of his life, especially in the 1940s, as he climbed the ladder of politics and gained power, Bertram would stay emotionally and physically distant from the girl cousins at Lawrence Street, even from his male cousin, Eddie. And throughout his career in politics, beginning with the founding of his political club, the United Action Democratic Association, in 1934, Bertram would always project himself as the active patriot. He served in official capacity on citizen groups charged with getting neighbors to safety in the event of an attack during World War II. He recruited returning black veterans, especially officers, into his political club on Hancock Street in Bedford Stuyvesant after he became a state Assemblyman and a district leader. And he would speak dismissively of the radicals who protested the draft during the Vietnam War in the late 1960s.

Though they never spoke of it, both Irene and Bertram benefited in significant ways from being fair-skinned and having straight hair. Whites accepted such people of African descent more readily. They would be quicker to make pleasant remarks about their looks and even their manner of speaking, as the eye affects the ear. Whites would see someone like themselves, and thus hear someone like themselves. But it did not serve Bertram Baker well to dwell on that aspect of his persona, as he sought to make his way in a world he increasingly saw riven by race. In ways political and mental, he would become blacker as the years went by. Still, that fact of acceptability to whites in those early days stayed in Irene's mind forever. For she and her sisters lived an up–North version of a reality that granted favors to those blacks who looked and sounded white, or close to it.

For instance, there was the Jewish fellow who made "kit bags" for soldiers, and who hired Irene and a young lady of Indian descent from the island of St. Kitts. He thought they were "good looking enough," Irene would say eighty years later, to sit in the window of his shop and do their stenciling of the kit bags, showing the passersby that he was doing good work for the country.

Many black families entertained suspicions, perhaps biases, that the fairest of the children in the family would have the greatest expectations of success. Such was the case with Irene's baby sister Edna, born in 1904. The girls' father, Edwin, loving though he was to all his children, did appear (upon my own thoughtful reflection) to have thought Edna had all that it took, in the visible respects, to go far in life—for a girl, of course.

Edna was the lightest in complexion. Her father encouraged her to speak like an English woman. And he told her to identify herself as British when she was asked in school about her ethnicity.

Edna would eventually pass for white, with her parents' blessing. But along the way it caused her considerable pain. It was Edna who, through the course of her early life, was able to get the kind of jobs so many young women yearned for. "She [Edna] was able to work in Manhattan at a very good job, as a bookkeeper," Irene Baker said. "But she worked as white and she was scared to death that she would be discovered. She said back then that she would never recommend to anybody that they do that."[10]

There was a time when Edna was on a bus with some of her co-workers and, from her seat, she spied a black man whom she knew about to enter. Her heart began racing as she jumped up and, barely without saying good-bye to her co-workers, ran to the exit door and hopped off the bus. She was embarrassed, even humiliated, by the experience.

Years later when it came time to marry, Edna wed a gentleman from the island of Barbados who was dark enough to pass for African. C. Holman Lovell had come to the United States with the goal of becoming a physician. When he took a trip to Jefferson Medical School in Pennsylvania, hoping to get an application form, the lady at the desk told him, "We don't accept niggers here." So he ended up studying medicine at the University of Edinburgh in Scotland. He married Edna and then set up a home practice in Bedford Stuyvesant, on Hancock Street, just a block from Bertram and Irene at 399 Jefferson.

It was eight months after Bertram and Irene were married[11] that the Nineteenth Amendment to the U.S. Constitution, giving women the right to vote, was ratified. There was no chance that Irene would ever run for office. That was what Bertram was aiming for, and he was to begin seriously working as a street canvasser in the increasingly black community of central Brooklyn (which would soon become Bedford Stuyvesant) after he became a citizen in 1924. Irene would soon become a canvasser also, gathering the signatures of blacks in the community, encouraging them to support the candidate of the Democratic Party and, after 1933, the candidates of Bertram's United Action Democratic Club. She was valuable because she was so likable. But she always did what Bertram told her to do. Her place was in the home and she knew and accepted it, with her ambitions held in check throughout her life, surfacing only in the evening writings, drawings, and paintings, and, for sure, the thoughtful, beyond-her-age, wisdom-filled conversations she would have with those who might be associates or wives of associates of Bertram. She was loving and dedicated to the two daughters she would bear with Bertram, born in 1921 and 1925, jotting down once, in later years, on a slip of paper, lines that were touching for their simplicity and their smoothness:

> The world is full of lovely
> Things
> Gardens where a robin sings
> Blossoms on the orchard
> Trees
> Wheat fields (swaying or waning?) in the
> Breeze
> Sunlight dancing on the waters
> —and my daughters—[12]

The passing of time, the decades, led to changes in attitudes, even in the Baker clan, as the girls contemplated heights previously thought to belong only to men. There was Bertram and Irene's daughter Lilian, who showed strong signs of intellectual ability from her earliest years. She and her sister, Marian, attended Girls High School in Bedford Stuyvesant, which just a decade before, in the early 1920s, adhered to rigid segregation policies. The black girls had not been allowed to attend the senior prom. But one of the students in the class of 1920 happened to be Yolande Du Bois. She was the daughter of the scholar and activist W. E. B. Du Bois, who raised a stir about the practice, causing school officials to change their policy and permit the interracial mingling. By the 1930s, Lilian was excelling there and was accepted into Hunter College.

Lilian, and to a lesser extent her little sister, showed signs of the rebelliousness and even ambition that increasingly came to be associated with being raised in America, even if you were a girl. Bertram Baker, for all his faults having to do with women, was not an abusive man, surely not by the standards of those days. He did believe in discipline when it came to his own children and did not tolerate dissent from those who were supposed to be seen more than heard. But it seems his enduring love for his late mother was settled in him. Later in life, Marian would relate the time, perhaps in the late 1930s, when her father became very upset with Lilian about something, which led her to answer her father back in a way he did not appreciate.

—"Don't you talk to me that way! I'm your father!" Which led Lilian to say:

—"That's not my fault!" At which point Bertram raised his hand as if to slap Lilian, prompting Marian to run up to him and grab his pants saying:

—"Don't you hit my sister!"[13]

And the tiger of the house bolted from the scene in frustration, mumbling words couched in anger. In all likelihood, Irene was standing nearby, partially in fear but partially also delighted at the boldness of her daughters.

Citing others, such as Ida B. Wells, the courageous black woman journalist who published articles against lynching for newspapers throughout the East and Midwest (black newspapers carrying her articles were banned in the South), observers have contrasted the experiences and achievement of middle-class native-born black women with those of their Caribbean immigrant counterparts. In a 1937 master's thesis for the City College of New York, Myrtle Pollard wrote, "The foreign born colored woman is satisfied—generally—to accept the role of home-maker. . . . Even when she is the bread-winner, this does not seem to rob her of her semi-submissive role. But her American sister has a different tradition. . . ."[14]

In her autobiography, the late federal judge Constance Baker Motley writes about the Nevisian background of her mother and father, and she comments on how sexist, how male-centered Nevisian society was, especially in the early and mid-1900s.[15] Even so, Judge Motley went from her home in New Haven, Connecticut, to successes and gender "firsts," such as becoming the first black woman to be a New York state Senator (in 1964), the first woman to be president of a borough in New York City (when she became the borough president of Manhattan in 1965) and the first black woman to be a U.S. District Court Judge (in 1966).

And perhaps no one represented the shift in West Indian chauvinism with the passing of the generations as did Shirley Chisholm. She was born in Brooklyn to immigrants from the island of Barbados and, though she returned to the family island for a stretch of years during her childhood, she was mostly raised in Brooklyn, where she attended Girls High School, like Lilian and Marian (and overlapping with both of them, in fact), and then Brooklyn College, where she obtained her bachelor's degree.

Shirley began ascending the political heights during the 1950s right there in central Brooklyn, which put her in Bertram Baker's yard, and they couldn't stand each other. The disputes were for the most part not personal, but it was clear that Bertram saw her as an uppity and bitter woman and that she saw him as a relic of a political past that was going the way of the old Tammany Hall. In Baker's retirement, he went through Chisholm's book *Unbought and Unbossed*, which was a kind of run-up to her historic bid for the presidency in 1972, and underlined all the statements, many of them, he thought, were factually incorrect or simply misleading. On a page on which Chisholm wrote that blacks, presumably including Bertram Baker, sat in segregated rooms at Democratic meetings in the 1940s, he wrote "untrue." Where she wrote that in 1965 the Democrats came to control the state legislature for the first time in eight years, he wrote that it was the first time in thirty years. And he also wrote "untrue," next to a line that must have stung very much, where Chisholm wrote, "Baker was not going to back me [for Congress] because in our assembly days we had crossed swords over a bill regulating pawnbrokers. I had implied that he was in league with the pawnbrokers . . . against a bill that could crack down on the loan sharks. There must've been enough truth in it . . . because Baker was my enemy for a while."

Back in 1968 when Chisholm made her historic bid for a congressional seat from Brooklyn—becoming the first black woman to win a congressional seat in U.S. history and the first black person in Brooklyn to do so—Baker supported another candidate, though to his credit it was another black woman, labor organizer Dolly Robinson.[16] One suspects Baker didn't mind so much being on the losing side, especially because he was slowly bowing out of politics at that point, but that he just could not have stomached supporting "Shirley."

But, especially after Bertram's death in 1985, Irene Baker would speak with a noticeable admiration for Shirley Chisholm. She said at one point that Chisholm had given Lilian valuable advice in the 1950s when Lilian, married to an electrician and deciding what to do with her Hunter College degree, pondered her options and desired wise counsel. Irene suggested that Lilian contact Shirley Chisholm. Chisholm was gracious and strong in her advocacy of teaching as the path Lilian should take, and Lilian went on to a satisfying career as a New York City school teacher and administrator. "I always appreciated her telling Lilian to go into teaching," Irene said.

As for Bertram, Irene acknowledged that while it was clear Bertram didn't like her, Irene herself felt a spiritual connection with Shirley Chisholm. That feeling was only strengthened when Irene made one of her few trips up to Albany in the 1960s and learned the challenges that Chisholm was facing, with Bertram and the other black males up there at the time disliking her, and the white legislators also adding the gender animus to their usual racial hostility. In a recorded conversation on December 18, 1995, Irene added:

> So I've always been friendly with her. And when I went to the Assembly room this particular day she came and she told me she was presenting a thought, that she wanted them to pass a bill against child labor and she told me of this place she'd been to—I don't know whether it was children—little children were pulling up weeds and working the gardens and she thought that it shouldn't be, that small children, as small as they were, should ... not be [doing that]. So I told her I thought to do it [Chisholm's bill] was a very good idea. And I think she told Bertram also. But he didn't have much use for her because I think he thought she may outdo him out of his Assembly seat. So he spoke to the other men and told them what Shirley intended to do ... and [that] he didn't approve of it. So they didn't approve ... it. And I was so sorry for her. I was so sorry I wouldn't speak to her after that. I just left.[17]

Irene Baker would survive her husband, Bertram, who died in 1985, by sixteen years. She passed away peacefully at a Bed-Stuy nursing home on January 11, two months shy of her hundredth birthday. The home was administered by the Episcopal Church and was named after the late black Episcopal bishop Henry B. Hucles.[18] The priest who officiated at Irene Baker's funeral service was a black woman, Rev. Bernice Colman. A woman in the Episcopal priesthood was unimaginable in the earlier decades of the twentieth century. Speaking to those gathered, Irene's grandson (the author) declared that had women been treated equally back then, Irene, rather than Bertram, might have been the one who gained notoriety for accomplishments. (Note: There are more details about the relationship between Bertram Baker and Shirley Chisholm in Chapter 9. Irene Baker appears throughout the book and is prominent in Chapter 10.)

3
Searching for a Band of Brothers

In 1920 Bertram Baker was not yet an American citizen. But he absorbed the happenings around him with the careful eye of a scientist looking through a microscope. He focused his vision on things that seemed to bode well for him, and those that didn't.

While Rector George Frazier Miller still commanded his admiration, Bertram, as mentioned, decided he would not easily be able to enter the ranks of the American Episcopal priesthood. It had become obvious the Episcopalian hierarchs wouldn't grant such a position to more black men than there were in black churches already. And in Brooklyn in those days, there were three black Episcopal churches: St. Augustine's, where Miller was the pastor; St. Phillip's; and St. Barnabas.[1]

The 1920s were a decade of hope and promise for so many Americans. Bertram had married the year before and had decided he was going to earn his livelihood for the time being as a bookkeeper. Ambitions swirled through his head, but where to begin? To whom should he turn?

One of the first brotherhoods Baker became part of was that of the African Orthodox Church, which had ties to the Universal Negro Improvement Association of the Jamaican immigrant and black nationalist Marcus Garvey. The African Orthodox Church was started by black Episcopal priests who had come to believe that they were not being treated with respect in the American Episcopal Church. The pioneer among them was considered to be George Alexander McGuire, a native of the then–British island of Antigua (near Nevis), who was raised as an Anglican and immigrated to the United States in 1893, becoming an

44

Episcopalian. But his experience serving at a black church in Arkansas heightened his sensitivity to the pains caused by American racism, and he became increasingly militant, eventually establishing the African Orthodox Church with its own black clergy in a number of cities throughout the United States.[2]

It is not known whether Bertram Baker was present at the Brooklyn Academy of Music in February 1920, when Rector George Frazier Miller, the outspoken black Episcopal priest who was a hero of Baker's, gave a speech at a Garvey rally, putting himself on record as embracing Garvey and rejecting American racism. But it's very likely Baker was there. He would have been careful about drawing attention to himself, knowing that federal agents were possibly in attendance (as it is now known that they were) and erring on the safe side, given his status as a foreign resident. In the months before his death, Baker would say that Miller showed himself to be a wonderful exemplar of manhood for Baker himself and for many others, including frustrated black Episcopalians. But Miller was one of those very few blacks who had salaried work, as a church pastor in the Episcopal Church in New York. Church officials would refer to such pastoral positions as "mission" jobs, because some of the money for the church's activities came from the wider diocese. A few priests from the West Indies had been ordained at Codrington College in Barbados, which began accepting blacks just after 1900. One black Codrington graduate was the Rev. Reginald Barrow, who in the 1920s and '30s operated in Brooklyn as a bishop in the African Orthodox Church.

Barrow would have continuing problems with U.S. immigration officials. There were allegations, perhaps encouraged by undercover federal agents who were beginning to insert themselves into the lives of outspoken immigrants, that he was in the country illegally.[3] Bertram Baker's connection with Barrow and Barrow's attempts to build an African Orthodox Church in Brooklyn lasted for several years, into the late 1920s. Baker served as the treasurer of the church in Brooklyn, which met on Carlton Avenue, in a building where many black organizations held their gatherings, but in his later years he did not speak much about his involvement in the African Orthodox Church. His wife, Irene, after his death did say on a few occasions that Baker had attended Marcus Garvey rallies (which were often organized with the African Orthodox Church officials, who considered themselves Garveyites, believing that black people could overcome white racism only by forming their own groups and businesses).[4]

One of the most revealing bits of information about Baker's connection to the African Orthodox Church came in 1995 from his sister-in-law Edna Baker Lovell (Irene's younger sister). Edna in the mid- to late 1920s was living in the home at 507 Throop Avenue of her father, Edwin Baker, who was an early black purchaser of a home in what would in twenty years become known as Bedford Stuyvesant. Edna lived in an apartment with her parents, Edwin and Sarah. Bertram, Irene, and their two daughters had their own apartment in the building. Edna said that Bertram had been insisting his father-in-law owed him money, money that Bertram wanted to channel to Bishop Barrow for construction of an African Orthodox Church building in central Brooklyn. Edna said Bertram showed up and began pounding on the door of his father-in-law's apartment, demanding the money he felt was due him. "I want my money now," he yelled, according to Edna. She also said that Bertram claimed to be holding a gun. (Other than the gun found in one of the drawers in his bedroom after his death, a .25 caliber automatic pistol, there are no other known anecdotes of Baker's using or being associated with a gun.) It is not known whether Bertram obtained the money.

There was infighting within the Brooklyn chapter of the African Orthodox Church in the late 1920s. It is notable that around this time, in 1927, the U.S. government deported Marcus Garvey. He had been accused of financial misdoings in his handling of the so-called Black Star Line that was supposed to generate income for blacks worldwide even as it helped frustrated blacks in the diaspora return to their continental roots in Africa.

In 1927, Bertram L. Baker published a classified notice saying he was severing ties with the African Orthodox Church.[5] Nothing more is known about this. It is perhaps understandable that a black person with serious local political ambitions in a borough like Brooklyn might have come to be extra cautious about a public association with Garvey or the African Orthodox Church.[6]

By 1930, Bertram came to believe he needed a group of like-minded brothers in spirit who would stand with him when under attack, a fraternity of high-thinking black men with eyes fixed on future successes. That was to be the Prince Hall Masons.

"Back in those days everybody who was anybody was a Prince Hall Mason," said Ludwick Hall, a Prince Hall Mason and member of Bertram Baker's Carthaginian Lodge, speaking in 2013. "These were the so-called strivers."[7]

The secret society known as the Masons, like much of the rest of

America, was segregated in those days. The black division, called the Prince Hall Masons, was started in the late 1700s by a Boston-based African American abolitionist named Prince Hall. It received a charter to start a lodge that eventually assumed his name. The Prince Hall Masons became national, with a group forming in New York state during the mid-1800s. In 1904, a number of black Masons living in Brooklyn requested the right to establish a lodge of their own, which they named the Carthaginian Lodge.

It was in 1931 that Bertram Baker first showed up in the notebooks kept by the Carthaginian Lodge of the Prince Hall Masons.[8] He went through the secret rituals and quickly became a Master Mason with the rights, privileges, and associations that in those days added cachet to a black man's name in New York. At that time, Bertram and Irene Baker were living with their two daughters in a brownstone house at 523 Throop Avenue in the Bedford section. They had recently purchased the building, which was on the very same block as the brownstone owned by Irene's parents. Immigration from the West Indies had eased considerably after the 1924 federal Immigration Act meant to curtail the influx of immigrants of all countries. But the Great Migration from the South continued. Plus, blacks of all backgrounds began moving from other parts of Brooklyn and from Harlem into the Bedford section, which would come to be called Bedford Stuyvesant in the 1940s. As an accountant, Bertram Baker was managing to pull in a modest income from tax preparations and other bookkeeping work, but a good part of his earnings came from renting out several units in the four-story Throop Avenue building.

Many of the blacks who had been moving into the neighborhood in the 1920s and first years of the 1930s were Prince Hall Masons, including one by the name of Arthur Schomburg. Schomburg's vast collection of books and documents led to the establishment of the Schomburg Center for Research in Black Culture, the renowned institution located in Harlem. Schomburg, a Puerto Rican of African descent, lived on Kosciusko Street, just several blocks north of Bertram's home. Like nearly all the other Prince Hall Masons in Brooklyn, Schomburg was a generation older than Bertram.

The Brooklyn Masons had their own building, located at 165 Clermont Avenue, in what became known as the Fort Greene neighborhood,[9] an elegant, mystery-invoking structure, with horizontal stars on its stone façade, which stands today, though ownership has changed over the decades. The black newspapers frequently carried articles about the happenings at the various lodges of the Prince Hall Masons, including

Christmas parties or social gatherings held jointly with their female counterparts, the Eastern Stars. The Masons often held charitable events, contributing money to such organizations as the Brooklyn Oldtimers home, a residence for elderly black residents. Bertram was sometimes referred to as the "baby" of his lodge, as many of them had been members since its beginning three decades before Bertram was accepted into the brotherhood. One early member was Harry Williamson, who was known nationally among Prince Hall Masons as the scholar of the fraternity, having written a number of articles about them. The Prince Hall Masons considered themselves to be the African American elite, in terms of literacy and commitment to success.

Bertram Baker was a man of his times. He embraced the go-along, get-along approach of the conservative black leader Booker T. Washington even as he showed inclinations to ruffle feathers the way Washington's polar opposite, the radical scholar W. E. B. Du Bois, did. Like Du Bois, Bertram believed in agitating to achieve political advantages for black people. Like Washington, Bertram liked to form cliques of associates who looked out for one another. Both Booker T. Washington and W. E. B. Du Bois were Prince Hall Masons. Bert Baker had a bit of both men in him.

Bertram could be engaging at social gatherings. He liked to toss one back, or even two or three. Even in his older years Bertram would refer to liquor as "hooch," the term in the 1920s and early '30s for prohibited alcoholic beverages that made light conversation even more smooth. It was widely known that, even in the middle of the Prohibition era, anyone with a little money could drink through the evening, especially in the increasingly black district of central Brooklyn. Bootleg liquor, hauled up in vehicles from the South, found its way into meeting halls of various social groups, including lodges of the Prince Hall Masons. The nominally illicit drinking would only further endear the young Baker to the older members, who also enjoyed taking a sip of the liquid stimulant from time to time.

But there was something else about Bertram that his brothers would have noted from his letters to them and from the letters he would write on their behalf to other Masonic lodges. He was not an elegant writer, but he clearly could express his ideas in what would have been called the King's English. For the most part, his writing was grammatically correct. He had the ability to be comical when appropriate and, most of all, to express righteous-sounding outrage when the occasion called for powerful and effective reaction.

Right after his acceptance into the Prince Hall Masons in 1931, Bertram came up with the idea of writing a weekly column in a black newspaper, the *New York Age*, which circulated through black Brooklyn and Harlem. Harlem was then the city's densest black community. Central Brooklyn's development as a "black ghetto" rivaling Harlem was still two decades in the future. The *Age* seemed an appropriate organ for Bertram. It had been secretly purchased in 1907 by the man who was considered the most politically powerful black man in America at the time, Booker T. Washington.[10]

Bertram's column was called "The Masonic Notes." At first the articles were simply announcements of goings-on among the members. He called the series "From the Record," and he told readers about gala events of the various lodges of Prince Hall Masonry in New York City. The column was also big on the history of the brotherhood. Bertram and the Prince Hall Masons were out to impress one another and the rest of the world. But Bertram also had a haughtiness, a self-righteousness that in the view of many who came to know him was impossible to ignore. He could sound as if he were speaking from on high, from the pulpit, as it were— which, of course, is what he'd wanted to do when he'd come to the United States fifteen years earlier. It was he who was on the side of the less fortunate. It was he who understood the difference between right and wrong. It was he who had the courage of his convictions and would refuse to budge when he sensed in his soul that he was on the side of justice.

In the fall of 1932, Bertram Baker wrote an article[11] in which he reported that a top Prince Hall official named W. J. Rawlins, whose title was Deputy of the Second Masonic District, had harshly criticized the Carthaginian Lodge at a Masonic meeting. According to Baker's article, Rawlins had complained that the Carthaginians had not paid their fair share of Masonic taxes. The issue of taxes caused bickering and infighting in the brotherhood, and the topic became more sensitive in the 1930s as the Depression took its toll even on members of the black "Talented Tenth" who, for the most part, were significantly better off in terms of income than the typical black migrant recently arrived from the South. But money was still money. Some of the taxes had to do with the need to pay rent or mortgages on various buildings used by the brotherhood. (Typically, local lodges—there were several throughout New York

City—would share a single building, as was the case with the one used by the Carthaginians and other Brooklyn-based lodges.) Some brothers in Brooklyn, notably members of the Carthaginian Lodge, felt that some of the taxes they were being asked to pay were ethically and legally improper. According to Bertram Baker in his *New York Age* article, the Prince Hall official Rawlins stated at the meeting that he (Rawlins) was going to take legal action against the Carthaginians for their hard-line questioning of some of the taxes. In his article, Baker, though a Mason for only a year, took great umbrage at Rawlins's remarks and said that Rawlins's charges against the Carthaginians were completely bogus. The tone of Bertram's article showed his irritation. He declared it was obvious that the funds being raised were for some purpose other than the feeding of the poor and the housing of the homeless. Surely, he must have known that, even beyond the fact that he was expressing disagreement with fraternal leaders, the airing of group differences in a widely circulated black publication would cause problems. But he wrote it anyway.

"The District Deputy Grand Master of the Second District recently called a meeting of Masters and Wardens of the district," Baker wrote in that column. "The purpose of the meeting, at first, seemed to be an endeavor to foster cooperation efforts among the Lodges." Plans to hold a charity ball were announced as well as intentions to distribute Christmas baskets to neighborhood residents during the upcoming holiday season, he reported. But soon, Baker wrote, the true motive became evident, and that was to take action, possibly even legal action, against the Carthaginian Lodge.

> Other matters of interest were discussed, and then the surprising, unbelievable, almost incredible thing happened. The self-same Deputy who pleaded for, and expected the cooperation of[,] all the Lodges not only in financing and successfully running the proposed charity ball, but also, in all matters pertaining to the district for which he is responsible, boldly announced that, he, as president of the Unity Holding Corporation, which holds title to the Temple, was leading a fight to bring suit against one of the very lodges whose cooperation he solicited.
>
> One wonders if that is a new way of fostering cooperation. If it is, we had not heard of it. We do not know what grounds the brother has for suit, and we doubt if the best lawyer in the land could figure it out for him.[12]

Almost immediately after that article appeared, Baker received a letter from Edward T. Sherwood Jr., who was the Grand Master of all Prince Hall Masons in New York state. The letter read:

My Dear Sir & [Brother]:
In the future all articles intended for the press written on any subject pertaining to Masonry must be submitted to our Grand Sec.... Arthur W. Handy, 235 W. 120 St. New York City and he in his turn, after same has been censored, will then give the submitted copy to the publishers.
Yours Fraternally.
[Signed] Edward T. Sherwood Jr., Grand Master.

And Baker right away wrote back:

M. W. Edward T. Sherwood Jr.
431 Quincy Street
Brooklyn, N.Y.
Sir and Brother:
This will acknowledge the receipt of your communication of October 27, which in effect is an order directing me to submit to the Grand Secretary "all articles intended for the press, written on any subject pertaining to Masonry."
I have no doubt that your letter was written without due thought and consideration, or surely you would not have so glaringly overstepped your authority.
Permit me to advise you that the "Masonic Notes" column appearing weekly in The New York Age is a "signed article," written under my personal signature, and as such, with the exception of the publishers, I am the sole judge of the subject matter of same.
Until such time as the Most Worshipful Grand Lodge of the State of New York (Prince Hall) controls the public press, the writings of no individual, on the subject of Masonry notwithstanding, can be subject to the censorship of the Grand Secretary.
I shall be glad to co-operate with the Grand Secretary at any time on any matter for the good of the fraternity at large, but regret that I cannot recognize his authority as Censor, or your authority to issue the order which is the subject of this letter.
Believe me to be,
Fraternally and respectfully yours,
(signed) B. L. Baker

Things only got worse. Sherwood and his then-deputy Francis Giles notified Bert Baker that he was being suspended because he had "revealed to the uninitiated proceedings of a meeting of Masters and Wardens of the Second Masonic District of this M.W. Grand Lodge" and had "unlawfully, publicly informed, advised and ranted . . . about an alleged difference between the author thereof and another lawful brother Mason." The Masonic leaders said Baker's article was "calculated . . . to bring Free Masonry in general into disrepute. . . ."

The revered Masonic historian Harry Williamson, who was in the Carthaginian Lodge with Baker, stated publicly that he was on Baker's side, and Sherwood immediately suspended Williamson along with Baker. The majority of Carthaginian Lodge members were so upset by these developments that they decided to take a stand. They elected Baker to the office of Junior Warden. And Baker did not try to offer any compromise. He took to the typewriter and began venting with a sarcasm clearly intended to anger, in a column headlined "Thoughts Worth Musing Over."

> Contrary to the opinions of some, Freemasonry is not a despotic institution. It is unfortunate, but nevertheless true[,] that some men, and I am speaking now of colored men, holding high positions in the fraternity would assume the attitude of despots, taking unto themselves the outworn and long since discredited doctrine of the "divine right of kings." Is it any wonder that our Caucasian brothers poke fun at us? In the "Brooklyn Times Union" of January 13, 1933, I came across the following, under the heading of "Jokes":
>
> "Boss: Rufus, did you go to your lodge meeting last night?
> "Rufus: No suh! We dun have to postpone it.
> "Boss: Why was that?
> "Rufus: De Grand, All Powerful, Invincible, Most Supreme, Unconquerable Potentate dun got beat up by his wife."
>
> To the other fellow it's funny. To those of us in fraternal life, and particularly to those of us in Prince Hall Masonry in the State of New York who have had the actual experience of having those in authority endeavor to impress upon us that they are, "De Grand, All-Powerful, Invincible, Most Supreme, Unconquerable Potentate." . . . Where is there room for the development of intellect? Where is there room for the quest (for) truth? TRUTH, the very foundation on which the institution is built, is dangerous if it affects the acts of one of these "All-Powerful Potentates." Dare to mention any such truth and immediately you will be subjected to Masonic

punishment, without benefit of trial, for the grave offense of violating your Masonic oath. . . . [13]

The Masonic leaders ordered Baker to be placed on trial and directed him and his chosen "counsel," the historian Harry Williamson, to show up at a special session. But Baker and Williamson thumbed their noses at the Grand Lodge leaders, and the leaders responded by suspending everyone in the Lodge. Baker was singled out for the strongest punishment, a ninety-nine-year suspension.

In 1975, a Queens College professor named William A. Muraskin noted that Bert Baker had become a thorny chapter in the twentieth-century history of that brotherhood of black male achievers.

> The Baker case, a *cause célèbre* which ultimately led not only to his exit from Masonry but also to the resignation of the noted black bibliophile Arthur Schomburg, to the suspension of the internationally known black Masonic writer Harry Williamson, and to the alienation of many others, is a flagrant example of the tendency toward despotism in the fraternity. The major difference between this incident and countless other suspensions without trials in other states was that columnist Baker and his allies were a highly articulate and forceful group and for years refused to allow the issue to die.[14]

The case wound up in court, although a judge decided that he had no authority to rule on it, because the organization was unincorporated; and the fighting on paper and in meeting halls continued through the rest of the decade. Baker continued to shoot arrows from the Brooklyn office of the *New York Age*. He gave the clear sense that he was fighting for truth and justice.

> It was extremely important that you should know the facts. Important—let us make it clear—not because of the individual or individuals involved, but because the very foundation on which our Ancient and Honorable Fraternity is built—Truth and Justice—has been threatened. . . . We DEMAND that every wrong be righted so that PRINCE HALL MASONS may hold their heads up as men, that they may not be ashamed to meet MASONS OF THE WORLD as brothers. . . ."[15]

Then Baker began to focus his ire on one of the most powerful brothers in the Grand Lodge. It was Francis Giles, a former Assistant United States Attorney, the first black one in Brooklyn, who was soon to become the leader of the Grand Lodge overseeing all of the black Masons in New York City. Baker began to write articles mocking the Grand Lodge proceedings that led to the installation of Giles as the New York City Grand Master.

"Mob Spirit Rules Masonic Conclave" was one headline. "Freemasonry in Burlesque" was another. Francis Giles became Grand Master of the New York State Prince Hall Masons in June 1933 and assumed leadership of the Grand Lodge in its battle against Bertram Baker and Baker's brethren in the Carthaginian Lodge in Brooklyn.

Giles had high upbringing. He was a 1923 graduate of Brooklyn Law School and had been a top federal prosecutor. He was also the son of the Rev. Francis Giles Sr., who was a minister of the African Methodist Episcopal Church and a 1901 graduate of New York Law School—quite an accomplishment for a black man in those days. Francis Giles the son and Mason was, furthermore, the brother of two physicians, Chauncey and Roscoe. Roscoe had created a stir in upstate New York in 1911 when he began attending Cornell Medical School. The hostility was so great that he began receiving numerous death threats that continued through his years there. Even so, in 1915 Roscoe Giles became the first black person to graduate from Cornell Med.[16]

Despite this family background, it seems Francis Giles did not possess the inner armor for the fight that was to come to him. And, thus, his downfall had elements of a Greek tragedy, with Bertram Baker playing a role that would lead to a striking collapse.

Bertram Baker and his brethren went after Giles at the very start of Giles's tenure as Grand Master. Baker had a bylined article whose headline was all but portentous, as it fingered Giles as the man now responsible for the asserted injustices done to Baker and his brothers in Brooklyn's Carthaginian Lodge. The piece carried the headline "Hail Grand Master!"

Attorney Francis F. Giles is the newly elected Grand Master of Prince Hall Masons of the State of New York. He served as Deputy Grand Master for the Masons in the years 1930, 1931 and 1932. His duties as Deputy Grand Master, if we are to accept as a fact the words of his predecessor[,] were, "Absolutely none!" In spite of this, however, during those three years he had the opportunity to "read, mark, learn and inwardly digest," and even though he then had no authority except such as was delegated to him at the pleasure of the Grand Master, he now has the opportunity to show what's in him.

The legacy which he has inherited is one which, to congratulate him on, would be deceitful. He is deserving of the sincere sympathy of every honest Craftsman. The office was not thrust upon him. He sought it, and having sought it with full knowledge of the gigantic task, we can only hope that he was prompted by a sincere motive to build upon the relics of the past.

He has realized his ambition to become Grand Master, but the price may be more than he bargained for.[17]

Although some of the succeeding *New York Age* stories about Giles did not carry Baker's byline, they bore his tone and style; it's reasonable to assume that he either wrote them or read them thoroughly before they were published. The first bit of reporting about Giles was actually newsworthy and objective. It informed readers that Giles "had retired from Assistant U.S. Attorney for the Eastern District," and it pointed out that the retirement had been expected, given the change in U.S. presidential administrations in 1932, from Republican (Herbert Hoover) to Democrat (Franklin D. Roosevelt). But then began the first of a long series of "disclosures" that were nothing less than personalized tabloid sensationalism—the very sort that Bertram would complain about decades later, when they were published by New York tabloids about Brooklyn elected officials.

The *Age* reported about "rumors of [Giles's] estrangement from his wife Mrs. Octavia Giles, and absence from their home at 564 Putnam Avenue."[18] Right after that, the newspaper published an interview with Mrs. Giles in which she said her husband was having an affair. She said that the affair—in addition to his new state of unemployment and "the worries he has had as a grand master"—may "have thrown him temporarily off his mental balance."[19]

Then came this screaming headline: "GILES' MOTHER ACCUSES SON'S WIFE OF MISCONDUCT WITH WHITE MAN," and then the following subheadline: "[She] Questions the Paternity of Youngest Child of Estranged Couple."[20]

Someone has to wonder: What was Mr. Giles doing while all this was going on? Was he somewhere deeply fretting, perhaps straining to suppress fits of anger—understandable given what his mom wrote in her letter to the *Age*, which it published:

I feel that since my son's wife has told her side ... I owe it to his father, the late Francis F. Giles, his two brothers, Drs. Roscoe C. and Chauncey D. Giles, and myself to defend the name as I know it.

My son, F. Giles, married Miss Octavia Gray, against the protest of his father ... and myself, when he was only 17 years old. His father wanted to have the marriage annulled. I persuaded him not to do it as his love for her seemed maddening.

He started out as fine a man and husband as any one would want to see and had his love been reciprocated I feel sure that they would have made a wonderful success.

My side of the case is this: Instead of the white waitress creeping into his heart, he says that a white man who could neither write nor read crept into her heart and life to the extent that a child came into the family—white as they get in color—with blue eyes and blonde hair.

Of course the colored folks said that it was not his. He did not seem to pay any attention to what they said.

When his wife was going around with this white boy friend everybody was talking about it. . . . He was always wanting to fight everybody that said anything about her. . . . [H]e loved his wife not wisely, but too well.

Well, one can certainly imagine a son's frantically yelling to his mom at this point, "Mom, what the hell are you doing?" Which is pretty much what happened.

There soon came an article with the headline "Attorney Francis F. Giles Wants Mother to Stop Writing Letters; Says He's Fully Nauseated Now."[21] The article, citing a letter it said was sent to the newspaper by Giles, quoted him as saying that the "whole proceedings are causing me no end of embarrassment, and I not only desire, but further direct, my mother to please cease." He said that, contrary to reports, he and his wife are enjoying a reasonably satisfactory relationship and that "[o]n this coming June 9, 1934, she and I expect to celebrate 25 years of married life." But there was to be no rest. Giles seemingly was falling apart.

Within the month, Giles was arrested with two others on assault charges, accused of "blacking the eye of Ellison Styles of 315 McDonough Street during a drunken brawl at 1485 Fulton Street Sunday morning while the church bells sounded their calls to repentant sinners."[22] It was beginning to seem as if the fall from the heights would have no end. But the end did come on September 20, 1934, when Giles was found dead on the train tracks of the elevated L line, which then ran along Fulton Street through Bedford Stuyvesant. The *Amsterdam News* reported that he had died after a fight with someone.

Francis F. Giles, of Brooklyn, died at Kings County Hospital Thursday afternoon, under circumstances described by the police as mysterious, a few hours after he was picked up in a coma from the elevated tracks on the Fulton Street line in Brooklyn . . . .

Police are working on the theory that he got into an altercation with an unknown person and after an argument was pushed from the platform onto the tracks, his head striking the rails, causing a deep gash on the scalp.

Baker's personal reactions, at his home and among his associates, to the death of Francis Giles are not known. The astounding tragedy is all but singular in the annals of the black Masonic brotherhood. Was Baker smirking with satisfaction that, as he had been suggesting, Giles was a man of weak character? Did he show any sadness at the drama-filled destruction of a man who once seemed on course to accomplish the very things Bert Baker believed were the epitome of achievement for a black man in urban America?

Five years after the death of Francis Giles, an article in *Age*, un-bylined, referred to the "Baker incident" and bashed Giles, saying that Giles "was, by virtue of his temperament, not qualified to have held such a high station in the Craft, therefore, nothing could have been expected." Giles must have been crouching in heaven or hell at the continuing assault on his character. Or perhaps he was by that time laughing at it all, having maybe in the final seconds of his life found some of the peace that all seek.

One by one, through the 1930s, the members of the Carthaginian Lodge were reinstated—all of them, that is, except Bert Baker, who remained under the ninety-nine-year suspension that would outlive him. Baker continued to write columns for the *Age*, profiling members of the Carthaginian Lodge as fine, upstanding men of color who displayed the finest qualities of character that one ever expects from another human.

At the Schomburg, in the archives, is a photograph of Bertram Baker and twelve other members of his lodge. They were dressed in formal attire, with black jackets and bow ties. Every face was serious. At the bottom, typed in with white numbers and letters, was the date, October 17, 1936, and the words "Men of Honor."[23]

That is the way Bertram Baker referred to his fellow Carthaginian Lodge members for the rest of his life. His brothers in spirit continued to embrace Baker as one of their own, but he was never again officially recognized by the Prince Hall Masons as a brother in the fraternity. In 1942 the lodge presented a petition before the annual gathering of the statewide Prince Hall Masons:

Brother Baker, during his early and active years in free masonry as a member of [our Carthaginian Lodge]... endeared himself to us all by his brilliance, his candor and especially his great zeal for the well-being of the Fraternity. Indeed, he is a very type of man in whom the Fraternity can very justly [depend]. . . .

The very long period since his expulsion in June, 1933, has been fraught with bitterness, sadness and regrets in and by the craft, particularly so in the Second District [author's note: the Second District was made up of all the Prince Hall lodges in Brooklyn]. . . .

We do hereby respectfully petition your august body and implore that you receive [this] with kind and fraternal consideration . . . that the world may see how masons love one another . . . by terminating at this grand session the period of expulsion meted to Bertram L. Baker, of June 1933[,] and thus restore to him all the rights and privileges of a Master Mason in good and regular standing. . . .[24]

But a later article reported that "No consideration was accorded the petition signed by the officers and a number of the members of Carthaginian lodge . . . ."

As for Arthur Schomburg, who in the minds of many came to symbolize African American history, not just in New York City but in the whole continent of the Americas, his biographer Elinor Des Verney Sinnette wrote toward the end of her 1989 biography of the effect that the Baker affair had on him. She said the episode had a deep impact on him because he had become "sick" of the way Baker and Williamson had been treated. She said Schomburg developed a "disenchantment with the black intelligentsia and with black organizations" that was related to the Baker chapter of the '30s. He had been a Mason for "more than 40 years."[25]

And so the Baker episode ended without ending. All I remember hearing from my grandfather over the years were his occasional references to his having been suspended from the Masons for ninety-nine years, something he would note with a kind of pride, as if to say, "This is the kind of man I am, one who speaks his mind regardless of the consequences." And he also noted that he eventually joined the Alpha Lodge in New Jersey, a racially integrated group. I don't believe that the relationships there were as strong and significant as the ones with his brothers at Carthaginian Lodge in Brooklyn.

In Chapter 4 we'll see how Baker began entering the field of local politics, which meant dealing on a regular basis with the Irish, Italians, and Jews who were then running the local Democratic Party. A number of other politically active blacks locally were also Prince Hall Masons, including Oliver D. Williams, who would one day with Baker's backing become a judge. Close at Baker's side was J. Daniel Diggs, another Prince Hall Mason, who would become Baker's right-hand man in the 1940s and would be his connection to the neighborhood real estate market, as one of the boss's closest and most trusted partners. Diggs was at the gathering in 1933 at Baker's 523 Throop Avenue home when a group of ambitious blacks formed the United Action Club and agreed that Baker would be their boss. Perhaps as Baker began writing his feisty columns bashing the big guys who ruled the Grand Lodge of the Prince Hall Masons, he was in a sense preparing himself for the fights to come. Other battles loomed with Irish political bosses. He was, effectively, brandishing his sword so that he could better sense when to attack and when to retreat, always with victory in mind.

There's no doubt that Baker's brother Carthaginian Lodge members were key to his development of a sense of brotherhood and common purpose, as well as a righteousness that would always protrude from his upper torso and neck, especially when standing before a crowd. The historian of the Prince Hall Masons, Harry Williamson, penned a touching reference to the Baker affair, undated but obviously written in the 1940s, when it became clear that the ruling Masons were not going to forgive Bert Baker and forget his arrogance.

Williamson wrote: "Perhaps some day this narrative will come to the attention of some brother who will examine the entire record impartially and in the light of the facts as here presented. To such brother do I leave final judgment concerning the conduct and the procedure of the 'Men Of Honor,' all of whom at that time will have laid aside the cares of life.... What will be the opinion of such future historian?"[26]

Author Commentary

I was stunned to learn in researching the Shakespeare-like tragedy of Francis Giles that I had a personal connection to him. That is to say, I actually was acquainted with one of the hustlers with whom he raised Cain on Fulton Street in the late 1930s. It was this very person, and his background as I knew it, that led me to postulate that Francis Giles's career as a black federal prosecutor is precisely what brought him down to the depths to which he sank in 1934. It's tempting to say that the white power brokers tossed Giles into the same basket as the Prohibition-era law-breaking blacks in Brooklyn of that era. But the truth is that white law enforcement men of that time also fell into the grip of the bad guys whom they were supposed to be watching and arresting.

It seems that Fulton Street of the '30s was as bad as the Fulton Street of the 1950s and '60s when I was growing up. My grandmother used to caution me, especially in my teens, about spending time on Fulton Street. Too many rough people, too many joints playing illegal numbers, too much music and dancing at night, beyond permitted hours.

I learned from a *New York Age* article of July 14, 1934, that Giles and a friend of his named Bill Doe had, according to police, gone "to visit the home of a Mrs. Elizabeth Helms, 59, of 289 Herkimer Street." The article reported: "Mrs. Helms said Giles had a relationship with her daughter, Isadora Helms, which she didn't regard favorably since he was married." It went on to report Mrs. Helms as telling authorities, "It was during this visit that she was struck in the face and about the body by the lawyer and his companion."

What struck me was the familiarity of the places, the streets. I could almost hear the sounds around the real-life characters and smell the aromas. And then there was even a name that jumped out at me.

Oh my God, that can't be the Bill Doe whom I knew as a kid, the guy from Jefferson Avenue, who owned the colonial, curving-staircase building three doors down from us, to the east, just short of Throop Avenue? The Prohibition era was three decades in the past, but Bill Doe was still making money off booze, selling it after legal hours from his house several doors over from ours, two houses west of Throop Avenue. Could this be the same Bill Doe?

It had to be! I thought. Whom could I ask? Several years ago as I pondered this, the only person I could think of who might remember was my Uncle John, the widower of my mother's sister Lilian, Bertram Baker's older daughter. Chatting by phone with me, Uncle John recalled how right after he and Aunt Lil got married in 1947 they went to Billy Doe and told him they were looking for a place to live temporarily and he got them a room in a building he owned on Hancock Street, right around the corner from our 399 Jefferson Avenue and close to my grandfather's political club at 409 Hancock Street.

At Billy Doe's Hancock Street house there were "women of the night living upstairs from us," Uncle John said.

"The women on the second floor would come down to use the bathrooms. They were whores," Uncle John recalled. "Two of them were up there. And late at night there were men knocking on the door. There was a lot going on, and I said this is no place to be, especially with Lil." And so they moved into the Marcy public housing projects, in Bed-Stuy.

Bertram Baker was unaware that his daughter and her new husband were living in Bill Doe's house. "He was surprised when he found out that Billy Doe had rented this basement apartment to me and Lil. And when he found out, he didn't want it to be known that his daughter and her husband were associated with somebody like him [Billy Doe]," Uncle John said.

As for Doe's house on Jefferson Avenue, Uncle John said, "I do remember that he used to come up from Carolina with several gallons of 'white lightning' [as many called illegal alcohol]. They made the liquor down there. He would bring it up in the trunk of his car."

I asked the question that I'd repressed for a while. Did Bertram Baker have any kind of relationship with Billy Doe? Uncle John said, "Billy Doe was never in, as far as I'm concerned, as far as I know, he was never in the company of Daddy B." John Bemus always knew Bert Baker was the boss of the extended Baker family, but he never held his father-in-law beyond reproach. And I truly believe he would have said Yes, had there been any connection.

I knew Billy Doe's grandson Stevie and used to play marbles and jump rope with him on the sidewalks of Jefferson Avenue in the mid-1950s. I would hardly ever see Billy Doe because he was always on the run, moving from one blurry deal to another. But Stevie would come up to Brooklyn every summer from down South. He was a cute kid, a year or so younger than I was. Then came a summer that I asked about Stevie and was told, by someone living in the house with Billy Doe, that Stevie had recently drowned. Presumably he had been swimming but I don't remember ever getting details. I remember once boasting about something to Stevie, and he said, "Yeah, but you can't do it better than 'Guard.'" For some reason his odd pronunciation of "God" stayed fixed in my head.

Anyway. I finally asked Uncle John the question I really wanted the answer to. Had he never in his nine-plus decades of living in the South, in the West (California), in the Northeast (New York), ever known anyone else named Bill or Billy Doe? "No," he said.

I did have to wonder whether Bill Doe knew who murdered Francis Giles, or whether somehow . . . . There's probably no way to find that out now. What seems clear is that Francis Giles had met Billy Doe in the Prohibition years before 1933, when Giles was an Assistant U.S. Attorney and handling the identification and prosecution of those operating speakeasies or profiting from them in other ways—guys like Billy Doe.

As for the family of Francis Giles, who had reached the highest points of achievement only to crash in such a tragic way, I've wondered about them. Francis Giles seems to have disappeared from the record of black historical figures in early-twentieth-century Brooklyn. Ludwick Hall, a twenty-first-century Prince Hall Mason, has joined me in an effort to find and embrace his descendants.

The "Men of Honor" who stayed with Bert Baker through the decade-long wranglings with Masonic higher-ups must have remained gently in his heart until his death, though he didn't speak much about the episode in later years. Through the late 1930s and into the '40s Baker had turned his energies to rising in the Democratic Party.

It wasn't until about fifteen years after my grandfather's death in 1985 that I began reading his articles in the *New York Age*. At first I read them on microfilm at the Schomburg Center for Research. I, his grandson the journalist, was impressed with his writing and passion. You'd think I would have had exchanges with him about what it was like writing for the *New York Age*. But I spent much of my time bouncing around the country and the world. Only in the four months before he passed away did I try to interview him on tape. I still have the tapes, but his body was weak and his memory foggy. Father, forgive me.

From his articles in the *Age*, I could feel the righteousness that had made Bertram Baker want to be an Episcopal priest in his mid-teens. I often use the word "vocation" to describe the motivations of young journalists. Like my grandfather, when I was in my teens I wanted to be a priest, in my case a Roman Catholic priest, as opposed to his Anglican ideal. I believe my discovery of journalism helped rescue me from confusion and dejection. For the best journalists, writing has been a liberating craft. Of course, one's ability to liberate depends greatly on the owner of the publication one is writing for. In my years of writing and reporting, I mostly was not able to spew venom. As a black journalist, I wondered, as I began reading my grandfather's columns in the *Age*: Who was the guy who let him write those searing, sarcastic, *ad hominem* articles directed at some of the most influential black men in New York?

The gentleman who had secretly purchased the *Age* from Booker T. Washington in 1907 was Fred R. Moore. Moore had been born in 1857 in Virginia to a black mother and a white father. He educated himself as best he could and moved to Washington, D.C., before coming to Brooklyn. In New York he entered into business relationships (nontransparent ones) with Booker T. Washington, the nation's most influential black leader at the time, and a man known for his conservatism when it came to challenging the white powers-that-be. In 1905, Moore started the *Colored World* magazine. In that publication and in the *Age*, Moore published articles that took positions much more militant than those of Booker T.

Washington. "The Negro should awake to the necessity of relying more on his own resources as an impetus to race progress," Moore wrote. "The race cannot expect the whites to do for it what it can do for itself. . . . We must learn to walk alone. If race prejudice shuts the door of hope in our face, we must turn our face in other directions. If opportunities do not come, let us make opportunities. How can this be done better than by patronizing race enterprises? . . . How can we expect to ever be anything but 'hewers of wood and drawers of water,' unless we . . . stand together in this matter of race patronage. Go out of your way to help the colored business and professional man. . . ."

In Brooklyn, Moore lived at 14 Douglas Street, in what's now called the Carroll Gardens neighborhood (contiguous with the downtown section of Brooklyn), according to the 1910 census. This is just several blocks to the west of where Bertram Baker initially lived with his father on Smith Street, and several blocks to the south of the Lawrence Street home where Bertram later went to live with his cousins. But whereas Bertram later moved with his family into the Bedford section where blacks increasingly were moving, Moore relocated to Harlem, which was turning black more rapidly. (Moore in fact was a principal in real estate transactions that brought some of the first black renters into Harlem.) In Harlem in 1927, Moore became one of the first blacks elected to office in the city, when he won a seat on the Board of Aldermen (the precursor to what's now called the New York City Council, which passes local laws).

The issue of skin color may have affected Moore's embrace of Bertram. It's not something blacks acknowledge openly, but many black people, in the early 1900s and later, preferred to have very light-complexioned blacks as their partners, in work or at home. That's why so many of the early Bakers in Brooklyn, who had been considered "coloureds" and not "blacks" back on Nevis, tried to slip into a white world. Fred Moore, the publisher of the *Age*, was identified as a mulatto, according to the 1910 census. What's more, a 1934 article in the *Amsterdam News* (a rival black newspaper of the *Age*) reported some blacks' saying Moore told Harlem merchants they would be better off hiring light-complexioned young ladies in their stores, rather than dark-complexioned ones. Moore denied this, but the controversy surfaced on more than one occasion. I do not know whether Moore was a brother in the Prince Hall Masons. He died in 1943, and his newspaper continued circulating through 1960.

As I tried to get information about the Prince Hall Masons in the decades following the 1930s and '40s, I learned they were still active in Brooklyn. Ludwick Hall, a retired New York City police lieutenant and a scholar by nature, was active in Bert Baker's Carthaginian Lodge of the Prince Hall Masons through the twenty-first century. Ludwick had heard about the long-ago Baker controversy and was disappointed that someone who turned out to be so important in black Brooklyn history had been treated so unfairly. He reached out to brothers in the Grand Lodge, and in 2015 they voted to posthumously reinstall Bertram L. Baker as a member in good standing of the Prince Hall Masons.[27]

4

A "Coloured" West Indian in the Realm of the Irish and the Jews

After his marriage to Irene in December 1919, the first thing Bertram Baker had to do was find a way to earn a steady income. In the following months he received his certification in accounting from the LaSalle Extension correspondence school based in Chicago. He then began working with companies whose owners were liberal enough to hire a well-spoken, good-looking black man. He was taken on as a bookkeeper by Cox and Nostrand, a lighting fixture outlet that later was to become known as Cox, Nostrand and Gunnison. Like so many of the others with whom he would work in those days, the owners whom Bertram dealt with at Cox, Nostrand were Irish.

Things were fine at first, but Bertram soon clashed with one of the owners, one of the Coxes, who had hired him. Sixty-five years later, Baker would recall, "He adopted this tactic of getting from me all that I knew and then he'd come back and tell me to do something and saying it as if it was his own idea."

The end of the line for Bertram was when the Coxes decided to give a job that he said was promised to him to another man. "He had been promised that once there was a vacancy . . . he would hold this position," his wife, Irene, would recall seventy years later. "Well, there was a vacancy but it was given to another who was working also in the company; so he stopped all the machines where the men were working . . . [and] Bertram got on a platform and told them that they had promised him this position and they had deceived him and they had placed someone else in that position and that he was quitting, and he left."

Baker himself recalled that a further insult came when, after leaving Cox, Nostrand and Gunnison, he learned that he had been effectively blackballed. "I went over to an Italian friend of mine in New York, by the name of Salvatore Iovin (who ran a successful tailoring business) and he agreed to employ me (handling his books)." But then Baker's former employers at Cox realized what was going on and "endeavored to induce Iovin not to take me on and they sort of threatened Sal, as we called him, threatening to make sure that their associates would drop their business with him." Bertram went back to his previous boss at Cox and "I told him he was a dirty dog," Bertram said. Baker afterward mostly made his money doing taxes and keeping books for various businesses and individuals in Brooklyn.

As for Bert Baker's behavior with the Coxes, calling one of his former bosses a dirty dog, Baker reflected his skills as a juggler of two sometimes competing tendencies: to be the gentle man in the room and to be the one you feared offending. Baker was often described as reserved and deliberate in speaking with colleagues. But he was also known for outbursts, calculated outbursts. "He was polite and all of that, but he knew when to yell and scream and when to use the kind of language that would get him what he wanted," said Josephine Bravo, who met Baker in the 1940s and during the 1960s became the female co-leader of his Democratic club in Bedford Stuyvesant.

Perhaps what Bertram Baker had going for him more than anything else, as a black man trying to make it in Brooklyn politics, was that he embraced the Democratic Party at a time when many native-born blacks were fearful and resentful of it. They still saw it as the party aligned with former slaveholders in the South, and of the whites there who in later decades repressed the freed blacks. But in New York City, the Democratic Party was becoming the party of power, and its rise in Brooklyn was especially striking. It was the party of the new white immigrants who were increasingly leaving their crowded, tenement-filled neighborhoods of lower Manhattan and crossing the Brooklyn Bridge into less congested areas of Brooklyn.

In 1924, the year Baker took his oath of American citizenship, he and his family were living with his wife Irene's parents on Throop Avenue, in what was the 17th Assembly District. The neighborhood was dominated by Irish politicians, some of whose families had previously lived in Irish wards of Manhattan and moved to Brooklyn because of the relative abundance of affordable single-family housing. The boss of the Democratic Party in Brooklyn was John McCooey, father of the same Adele McCooey who had written the tender "forget-me-not" note in Irene Baker's grammar school graduation booklet ten years previously, in 1914. McCooey had been chosen as the Brooklyn party leader by the various district leaders in the vast swath of the borough.

The McCooey family lived in one of the mansion-like homes on St. Mark's Avenue, a quick walk from the Baker household. In later decades, as whites moved out and more blacks came in, that home would be considered part of the black Bedford Stuyvesant ghetto. The name Bedford Stuyvesant wasn't used at all in the 1920s. McCooey and other Irish Democrats vigorously distanced themselves from hood-wearing white Klansmen of the southern states, although those southern whites were also militant Democrats. But those racist southern Democrats were not just anti-black, but anti-Catholic and anti-Jewish as well.

Even so, the Irish Democrats in New York had a fraught and peculiar history with local blacks. During the era of slavery, many of the New York Irish were strongly anti-abolitionist, fearing that blacks, if emancipated, would come north seeking their jobs at lower pay. During the 1863 Draft Riots in Manhattan, largely Irish crowds opposed to the Union war against slavery ran amok on the streets, even hanging blacks and attacking the Colored Orphanage in what today is midtown Manhattan. Many blacks fled to Brooklyn, where there were concentrations of blacks in downtown and other sections.[1]

Baker began visiting the Democratic clubhouse for his 17th Assembly District on nearby Gates Avenue. He let the Irish leaders there know he was interested in becoming politically active. He soon became an election district captain, with a responsibility for the black precincts of the assembly district. In that capacity he tried to get blacks to register as Democrats and then vote for the party's chosen candidates on election day. Blacks were increasingly moving into the community from elsewhere in Brooklyn, especially from the downtown area, and also in growing numbers from the American South, especially Virginia and the Carolinas, as part of the Great Migration that would radically transform Brooklyn.

Baker recalled the resistance of many local blacks. "They [the Republicans] were stronger [among blacks] because Negroes traditionally felt they owed their allegiance to [the Republican President] Abraham Lincoln who freed the slaves. I know of one instance where I went around here on Jefferson Avenue canvassing to get signatures on the Democratic petitions and a woman came to the door [and] looked at me astonished.

She said, 'Young man, I'm ashamed of you. I was a Republican born, I was Republican bred and I'll be a Republican when I'm dead.' Bam. And she slammed the door in my face."[2]

Baker was a devoted worker within the 17th Assembly District. The district leader was an Irishman named Ed Cadley. Cadley was very conscious of the increasing number of blacks moving into the district. He wanted the support of blacks but did not feel he needed them to win. Baker would later tell associates that he once spoke with Cadley at the district clubhouse, which was on Gates Avenue, about four blocks from where Baker lived. Cadley told him that blacks did not vote in large enough numbers to make an electoral difference anytime soon. Blacks could join the club, but he did not need them to stay in power. "He told Bert that, 'If you boys want to come in . . . you can. But we don't have to have you," said Everett Williams, a former shoe repairman at Abraham & Straus department store, who worked in Baker's political club from the '30s through the '60s.[3] What Baker and other blacks wanted more than anything else were political appointments, including nominations for elective office. Those were slow in coming.

Gates Avenue was a strip of strong resistance among whites in the community to the influx of blacks. In the 1920s white block associations began to form in the Bedford area, and the Gates Avenue Association was an early resister, holding its first meetings in 1922. Some of those at the meetings would express support for lobbying the Board of Aldermen (then the city body making local laws) to create racial zoning laws, in effect demanding a *de facto* segregation. The group supported the razing of the elevated train tracks running over Fulton Street. They concluded that the construction of a subway line—to become the A train that Duke Ellington made famous—would increase property values and thus discourage blacks. Among those buying properties in the early 1920s were Edwin and Sarah Baker, Irene Baker's parents. Bertram and Irene, with their two daughters, were to live with them at 507 Throop Avenue for five years, at which point they purchased their own four-story home right down the same side of the block, at 523 Throop Avenue. They would lose that home to foreclosure late in the Depression, in 1939. They would then rent a house nearby (on Madison Street) for a brief while before moving into the 399 Jefferson Avenue brownstone that became the Baker family enclave through the century and to the present time. Baker made the purchase using a loan acquired through political connections as well as some of the money inherited from his late uncle Willie de Grasse in Nevis. The Jefferson Avenue house was barely fifty yards away from Bertram and Irene's former Throop Avenue home.

Blacks like Bertram had stars in their eyes as they mulled the future, but the present presented challenges in the form of white dislike for them that compelled them to act. In late October 1930, a group of black men who were frustrated with their progress within the machine of Brooklyn Democratic politics gathered to come up with a plan to advance themselves. Perhaps the one with the highest stature, when it came to credentials and experience in the political arena, was one of Bertram's Masonic brothers, Oliver D. Williams. A practicing attorney and a 1924 graduate of Fordham Law School, O. D., as they called Williams, carried himself like the born and proud Brooklynite he was. He talked out of the side of his mouth, with an accent quickly and approvingly recognizable to the Irish men who ran the political show in town. He and Bertram wanted more than they were getting from their work in the Democratic party. Furthermore, they had developed strong resentments toward those older blacks who had been favored by the Democratic bosses. Williams and Baker considered those blacks selfish and undeserving, shufflers, ignorant and embarrassingly subservient. A 1930 article described how the two men felt. Baker was at the meeting but it was the older O. D. Williams who presided.

> As a result of their dissatisfaction with existing conditions in the Kings County [Brooklyn] Colored Democratic organization, a representative group of professional and business men met at the Community Center Building ... last Wednesday evening [Oct. 29] and discussed plans for the organization of a "strong, active, colored Democratic club, one that would function all year round and give all so desiring an opportunity to work for the success of the party."
>
> Although Attorney Oliver D. Williams, who presided, explained that the new organization will not fight any existing Democratic organization or individuals but will co-operate with them whenever possible, the meeting reached the point where nearly every speaker expressed his disapproval of the manner in which the Kings County Colored Democratic organization, "Chief" Wesley L. Young, leader, has operated.
>
> One of the speakers sarcastically referred to the opposition that he often met from "a lot of backward men" in the Kings County organization whenever he presented a constructive suggestion.
>
> Attorney Williams also pointed out that there are many departments in the city administration where no colored persons are employed and this condition obtains because no pressure has been brought to bear on those in charge of the city government. He said

that with a live and virile organization working in the interest of the Negro much could be accomplished. . . .

Among the things agreed upon by the organizers are that this new organization should outline a definite program beneficial to the colored people of Brooklyn and to the Democratic party . . . and make an effort to win the support of all progressive colored people in Brooklyn and perfect a plan through which there would be larger registrations and to develop an intelligent and efficient leadership, whose purpose should be service to the people and to the party.[4]

Three years later it was not Williams but Baker who convened a meeting of trusted associates at his Throop Avenue home. Bertram and Irene Baker lived there with their two daughters Lilian and Marian, who were attending nearby public schools (Girls High School and P.S. 44, respectively). The girls bonded with children of other West Indian immigrants and the children of black migrants from the American South, who would become their lifelong friends. Bertram and Irene lived on the basement floor of the four-story building, and they tried mightily to find tenants able to pay with some regularity during those Depression years. In that home at the northeast intersection of Throop and Jefferson Avenues, a new and soon-to-be powerful political organization was born. "We organized a political organization, the United Action Democratic Association, fully determined to concentrate our efforts toward breaking the barrier," Baker said in a 1976 speech at the Long Island Historical Society. The United Action Club members elected Baker their president and drew up a Constitution with the following preamble:

Whereas the Negro voters of the Seventeenth Assembly District are an integral part of the population, we do firmly believe that the accredited leaders, both Republicans and Democrats, have dealt and are dealing most unfairly with our people as far as political recognition is concerned. And whereas it is the belief that this condition will never be changed nor improved unless and until we ourselves have called for and demanded a change, we therefore now do constitute ourselves into an association in order to organize the Negro population of the district into a political unit having in mind the gaining of the political recognition which our voting strength might prove we are justly deserving of . . .

In what likely was a calculation, almost all of Bertram Baker's top associates in his United Action club were Brooklyn-born or had roots in the U.S. South. Perhaps Baker's most trusted colleague at the club meeting was J. Daniel Diggs, a North Carolina–born local realtor. Diggs kept track of who was moving in and out of their central Brooklyn Assembly district. Baker also always had trusted attorneys who would read the fine print of agreements. He was pretty good at reading the fine print himself. One of those early attorneys was Phillip Jones. Jones made notable gains and always showed allegiance to Baker and the United Action club. In 1939 Jones was named an Assistant New York State Attorney General. As for Baker, he continued through the Depression years of the '30s earning modest income through bookkeeping and tax preparation work, as well as the rent from his house. But his strongest interest was in a political position he thought worthy of him.

A number of independent blacks in those days felt uncomfortable pledging their allegiance to one party. One, notably, was Wesley McDonald Holder. Holder, known among friends and colleagues as MacD, was, like Baker, a West Indian immigrant. Born in British Guiana (the South American colony that later became the independent nation of Guyana), he came to the United States first and foremost to work with the black nationalist Marcus Garvey. Inspired by Garvey, Holder traveled the country trying to get blacks interested in Garvey's business ventures and to embrace Garvey's belief that black was beautiful and even superior. In the 1930s, Holder became the top black activist in Brooklyn working with white radical attorney Samuel Leibowitz, known for having defended the so-called Scottsboro Boys of Alabama, who had been sentenced in the rape of a white woman. Holder acquired considerable connections in 1935 when he helped lead Leibowitz's campaign as an independent against incumbent Democratic District Attorney William F. Geoghan. Leibowitz lost. (The attorney had mixed success in the Scottsboro case, winning the release of only some of the defendants.) Holder would later say that he did Baker a big favor in those days. Baker had asked him for the mailing list used in the Leibowitz campaign. Holder said he in fact gave Baker the list of names so they could be used by the United Action Democratic club.[5]

The members of the United Action club began calling Baker "Chief." But there had been a Chief before him. His name was Wesley Young, and, while he never achieved the glory of being elected to political office, he was for decades, beginning in 1900, the guy who could get things done for people of color, almost always men, seeking favors granted by the political power holders in the Democratic Party in Brooklyn. Blacks back then, in the very early 1900s, were scattered throughout Brooklyn. They owned homes in Downtown Brooklyn. They rented cheap apartments along Atlantic Avenue and Fulton Street, along the southern boundary of the Bedford neighborhood that it would later become. And they remained in wooden slave-era houses in the Weeksville community, just beyond old Bedford and old Stuyvesant. It was easy for the Irish bosses to ignore the overall black presence when it was so scattered. They paid tribute to blacks by giving cigars and a good job to their fair-haired black, Wesley Young.

Things began to change as more and more black people moved into the Bedford and Stuyvesant areas, which ran parallel to each other but a dozen blocks from each other. Blacks within that area coalesced and began giving expression to their desires for recognition.

In an interview with me in the 1990s, Justice James Shaw, who had been part of Bert Baker's UADA in the 1940s, spoke contemptuously of Wesley Young, even half a century later. Shaw referred to Young as a "turnkey." That was old slang for a guy who opens the door to let prisoners in and out. Young had been a chief guard in the borough's jail, located on Raymond Street in the downtown area. But, in fact, Young did more than that. He had also served as a Deputy State Superintendent of Election and had had small jobs with the Bureau of Highways, the Tax Department, and the Board of Elections. And he carried enough political weight with the Democratic bosses to secure prosecutorial positions for black attorneys, including a lawyer named Sumner Lark, who became an Assistant District Attorney in Brooklyn.

It was said that Wesley Young in 1900 had been the first black person to enroll as a Democrat in Brooklyn. Back then the borough was the province of the Irish and other whites who had either sympathized with the South during the Civil War or simply did not support blacks, whom they saw as potential competitors for jobs. Young had been born into slavery in Charleston, South Carolina, in about 1855. And in the early 1900s he served as the Democratic Party's bridge to the slowly growing black community. He would hold meetings at which the white elected officials would show up and hand out cigars. For him and those in his party organization, it was also about getting a bit of patronage from the Irish (and then Jewish and Italian) Brooklyn party bosses. Young's organization was called the Regular Colored Democratic Association of Kings County.

As suggested by the attitude of James Shaw, who dismissed Young as a black who did not demand enough and was largely uneducated, Baker and his black partners coming up in the 1930s all but ignored Young and the Regular Colored Democrats. They intended to overtake the slave-era Wesley Young, and they eventually did. By the late 1930s, Young was pretty much forgotten by Democratic leaders in Brooklyn, and the United Action Democratic Association led by Baker was the black force with which to be reckoned.

Baker's connections, especially with the Irish and perhaps to a lesser extent with the Italians, were likely helped by the naturalness of his inner feelings for the style of their Catholic worship, both the rituals and the beliefs, for example, in the Father, Son, and Holy Spirit. For being Anglican—or Episcopalian, in America—was also, by extension, being part of the Catholic Church, albeit the Catholic Church of England, as some Anglican Britishers in fact referred to their denomination.[6] But oddly enough, it was a Catholic woman who became one of Bertram Baker's most significant allies as he climbed the political ladder.

Early on, Irene, as well as Bertram, was aware of the bold steps being taken by a central Brooklyn woman of Irish descent named Minnie Abel, who was a Democratic co-leader (called "female leader" because the custom was to have two leadership positions at the district levels of the Democratic Party in Brooklyn, one for a man, the other for a woman), and Abel, though passionate and bold, was the second in charge, despite her significance that went beyond the co-leader title.

Though her birth records have not been found, Minnie Abel is believed to have been born around 1890. Her parents were Irish immigrants, surnamed Hagen. Minnie Hagen and her siblings grew up in central Brooklyn just northeast of Prospect Park. Catholic parishes began springing up around that wide expanse, to accommodate the borough's Irish and Italian newcomers. The Hagen family eventually settled on St. Gregory's Roman Catholic Church, there on Brooklyn Avenue, as its place of worship. Like other women of her generation, Minnie married young. She chose as her life's mate an ambitious young man named Robert Abel,[7] who saw in her strong chances of acquiring local power and steady income. Minnie would display an innate cunning that was the trait of successful Brooklyn bosses. She did not climb to the top of the ladder. But she put her feet on the high rungs, and as she moved upward she revealed calculating instincts of the kind that younger strivers, like Bertram Baker, would observe and make note of. Her ward was the 17th Assembly District, which covered the old Bedford neighborhood.

Things were opening up a bit, in small ways, for ambitious women such as Abel. It would be decades before they could get fair consideration for patronage jobs, but the door was opening slightly, and Minnie was the first to walk through.

By World War I Minnie Abel was making her voice heard by asserting herself through the population of women in the Bedford section. In the May 23, 1919, *Eagle*, for instance, we learn:

> Women Democrats of the 17th A.D., including a few mere male members of that organization, helped materially to swell the doughnut drive fund for the Salvation Army at the Orpheum Theater last night. It was the first big theater party of the regular women's organization of the 17th, of which Mrs. Minnie Abel is the leader, and nearly 900 turned out for the affair.
>
> Mrs. Abel's popularity, not only in her own district, but throughout the county, was attested by the fact that nearly every woman leader in the twenty-three Assembly Districts was also present.
>
> County Leader John H. McCooey and many of the district leaders of the men's organizations were also present. Sheriff's Counsel Peter Hanson, head of the 17th A.D. organization, shared the reception honors with Mrs. Abel.
>
> The Salvation Army collection at the Orpheum last night was one of the most successful yet recorded for the "doughnut drive" . . . .

Abel was the most vocal of the women who were active in Brooklyn politics. By 1925 the Cleaner Brooklyn Committee demanded that Brooklyn have female candidates for deputy street-cleaning commissioner. One of the first women mentioned was Mrs. Minnie J. Abel, Democratic co-leader of the 17th A.D.

Perhaps the most telling and enduring detail revealing Minnie Abel's importance to Bertram Baker is in Brooklyn's real estate records. By the mid-1940s Baker was beginning to gain serious power in Brooklyn, through patronage and serious campaigning for legislative posts. The United Action Democratic Association (UADA) club needed a home, and they bought a brownstone at 409 Hancock Street, one block south and half a block east of Bertram Baker's home then at Jefferson Avenue. The UADA purchased the Hancock Street building from Minnie Abel.

Though no letters or diary entries have been found to show much about their personal connection, Abel and her family were crucial in Baker's rise to power in the Depression years and beyond. It was an on-again, off-again relationship, with Baker often playing both ends against the middle, the respective "ends" being, one, Abel and her tight-knit powerbase, and two, the black community of the increasingly black Bedford section of Brooklyn, defined as the 17th Assembly District in the 1920s and '30s.

Bertram Baker had to prove himself to a series of white leaders in the Bedford district. He had to show that he could turn out the black vote. As much as anything else, he had to show that he would honor his word when he offered his hand for a dealmaker to shake, in a bargain having to do with the neighborhood.

Baker made his entrance into the power hall with the election in 1936 of Minnie Abel's nephew Stephen Carney as district leader of the 17th Assembly District, which included Bedford Stuyvesant, which in that day still had a substantial Irish population. The district also covered parts of other neighborhoods, such as Crown Heights to the south and East New York/Brownsville to the east, which had taken in growing numbers of Jews who had been moving into Brooklyn from the tenements of the Lower East Side. To the west was Fort Greene, with its nineteenth-century brownstones that were like Bed-Stuy's and which was also beginning to attract black residents, and to the north was Williamsburg, home to Poles, Italians, and eastern European Jews. With Carney came his female co-leader, his Aunt Minnie.

Carney and Minnie Abel, with the backing of Bert Baker's United Action club, beat the eight-year incumbent, Ed Cadley, who had worked closely with Manhattan's old Tammany Hall Democratic organization and had been considered undefeatable.

The election had Carney and Abel winning by relatively small margins, Carney with 4,441 votes in the primary compared with the 3,701 received by Cadley, and Abel getting 4,432 against the 3,805 garnered by her opponent, Rose Ray, who was the incumbent female co-leader. The leaders of the United Action club all but beat their chests in declaring that the club's work in getting black voters to turn out and vote for Carney and Abel made the difference between defeat and victory for the new leaders of the 17th Assembly District. The *Amsterdam News* declared that the "victory in the Democratic primaries in the Seventeenth was a victory for the United Action Democratic Association, in which was centered the opposition of Negroes to the regular candidate, Cadley."[8]

The blacks at Baker's United Action club were upset with Cadley and the regular bosses because, for one, they did not name a black Assistant U.S. Attorney to fill the position once held by Francis Giles, the

Republican black attorney who gave up the position after the Democrats came to national power with the 1932 election of Franklin Delano Roosevelt to the U.S. presidency. With Roosevelt's victory, Baker and other blacks expected there to be a flow of patronage that would have included the assistant federal prosecutor's spot that Giles once held. It did not come. A white was named. (Perhaps that was subconsciously or otherwise a factor as Baker fought brutally with Giles, his fellow Prince Hall Mason, in the mid-1930s, before Giles' tragic death, as Giles represented the Grand Lodge of the Prince Hall Masons, which had expelled Baker for Baker's outspoken columns in the *New York Age* newspaper.)

Be that as it may, Baker's battles within the Democratic party dominated by Irish New Yorkers became feverish also. The Brooklyn Democratic boss Cadley went after Carney, Abel, and Baker with a fury. It was a battle that strengthened (at least for a time) the relationship between Baker and Carney, and even more so between Baker and Abel. That latter point was true because, while Abel was the female co-leader, she was also the one with the "real balls," as the men might have said back then. Cadley fumed over Abel teaming up with Baker and Baker's renegades. Some would say that Cadley began "losing it." He declared that police should intervene to protect those blacks who felt threatened by the declarations of Carney and Abel's black allies. "The respectable element among the Negro voters have asked me to put a stop to it," Cadley said. "The respectable colored voters are in the majority and they will have no part in this movement."[9] If Cadley's statements were true, then the large number of blacks who voted in the election were irresponsible because they helped turn out the old guard and bring in the new leaders, Carney and Abel, who would hold on to power over the next fifteen years, giving Baker and other blacks pieces of the pie. Initially, for instance, Carney and Abel oversaw the election of dozens of black so-called committeemen, who were not elected government officials but rather party officials who were able to wield some influence in party policy.

The old-guard black Democratic leader, Wesley Young, had backed Cadley in the '36 race.

After the Carney–Abel victory, the United Action Democratic Association issued a statement saying, "We supported the Carney–Abel ticket in this last campaign because they have proven themselves to be friends of our group on many occasions, and we feel secure that the mantle that has been torn from the shoulders of Edward F. Cadley to be worn by Stephen A. Carney and Minnie J. Abel will bring to the Negroes of this

District some of the patronage which their voting strength warrants, for both Minnie J. Abel and Stephen A. Carney are very keen politicians and realize the growing strength of the Negro in this district."

As Judge Shaw said in speaking with me back in 1995, some of these politicians might perhaps have been considered progressives or liberals back then. But context is everything. Nineteen-thirty-six was a different time in Brooklyn history, before the real fight for civil rights had begun, a time when blacks had virtually nothing in the significant political sense, no elected officials at all. It's important to note also that Minnie Abel, though she was hailed as one who helped bring power to blacks in Brooklyn's black district, had at one time been, in the 1920s, a co-leader to the very same Cadley whom Baker and other blacks were calling racist in 1936. One thing is certain: Minnie Abel was one tough Irish Brooklynite. And the roots of her power could be seen right there in the Hancock Street brownstone that was to become Baker's base of power in later years.

Abel held the patronage position of secretary of the Board of Assessors for New York City. Her husband, Robert Abel, had his own political club on Sumner Avenue that allegedly, during Prohibition, doubled as a "hooch" joint, selling illegal alcohol. Robert Abel didn't speak publicly about his political club, or his businesses, or anything else. But his Sumner Avenue joint was around the corner from 409 Hancock Street, which Minnie Abel owned and used with her nephew, Stephen Carney, as their political club after their 1936 victory.

Politics back then, as now, was the art of careful shifting that is made to appear righteous. In a show of political *chutzpah*, Baker in 1937 turned against Carney and Abel. Baker was angry at Carney and Abel's continuing support of Assemblyman George W. Stewart, whom Baker accused of opposing progressive state pieces of legislation supported by liberal Governor Herbert Lehman and by the black assemblymen from Harlem, William T. Andrews and Robert W. Justice. Stewart was also said to have ties to the Midtown Civic League. That was the organization of white homeowners in the Bedford section opposed to the influx of blacks. The Midtown Civic League had issued aggressive denunciations whenever members learned that area whites were about to sell buildings to blacks.[10] Baker decided to support Stewart's challenger. That was Fred G. Moritt, who was Jewish. Baker was quoted in the *Amsterdam News* calling Carney and Abel "discredited leaders" and saying they would get "the surprise of their lives" in the upcoming primary. Baker and some other blacks issued a statement of protest against the Irish nephew-and-aunt team that, a couple of years previously, had been Baker's pals. Baker also spewed at Carney and Abel with seeming venom, something like the venom he had unleased at his black Masonic enemies. Baker declared that, after their 1936 victory, Carney and Abel had "turned out" blacks from the Carney–Abel political club.[11] He went on to complain that a Carney–Abel supporter named Reuben Smith had said it was "a relief" that the Negroes were no longer part of the club and that "We have purged ourselves." Baker called Carney and Abel "Jekyll and Hyde" for claiming to be supportive of the United Action club even as they took positions against blacks.

As Baker had predicted, Morritt won the election to the Assembly and would hold the seat for a decade, eventually moving on to the state Senate. Although they would battle from time to time, Baker and Moritt maintained fairly close ties over the years. What was different about Moritt, as compared with Carney and Abel, was that Moritt was one of the Jews who were beginning to step into the political arena in central and eastern Brooklyn. Slowly (over the course of four decades) Jews began replacing the Irish, who were at the top of the rung. Among the most influential was Irwin Steingut, who was a Democratic leader in the state Assembly from the early 1920s through the early 1950s. As for Baker and Moritt, it should be noted that Baker's closest personal ties over his career have been with Jewish politicians, including Moritt and Lloyd Herzka, who would become Baker's ally and friend in the 1940s, when they worked together in the office of the Brooklyn Borough President. Baker went on to win an Assembly seat and Herzka became a Supreme Court justice. Moritt, like many of the Jews going into politics in those days, came from the eastern end of the 17th Assembly District, the section that took in neighborhoods like Brownsville. His mother and father were immigrants from eastern Europe, the area now roughly considered to be Ukraine, and they set up a plumbing supply business. Their son Fred Moritt spoke only Yiddish until he was five years old. He later attended New York University and then Brooklyn Law School, receiving his law degree from the latter.[12]

But two notable things about the 1937 Moritt vs. Stewart race shed a light on Bertram Baker as manipulator and a compromiser—qualities he shared with the best of the Brooklyn Democrats of that era. One was that for all the posturing about the needs and rights of the black residents of the district, there was in fact a black man running for that office of Assemblyman and that man was Oliver D. Williams, with whom Baker had joined forces in the early 1930s, declaring it was time to take a more forceful approach against the white Democratic leaders. In fact, while the black press seems to have avoided attacking Baker directly on the issue, the *Age* took a dig by suggesting that significant numbers of blacks were joining forces with Williams and his ticketmate, Benjamin Butler, who was seeking a seat on the City Council. The two had the backing of the city's Fusion Party, which was the party that catapulted renegade Fiorello La Guardia to the mayoralty in 1934. La Guardia over the next decade would stand out as a city leader who went against both Republicans and Democrats on many issues. Williams and Butler also had the backing of the Negro Young Republican Organization.

The other telling aspect of the Moritt victory, and Baker's role in it, was that Moritt also had the support of none other than former Democratic boss Edward Cadley, the very same Cadley whom Baker and the United Action Democratic Association had denounced a year before for his anti-black policies and for not doing enough in the way of granting patronage to blacks. Baker's politics, like those of other politicians of that era, would have strange bedfellows.

A year after that 1937 victory, in which Moritt acknowledged that he owed his election to the black vote,[13] the Jewish Assemblyman was to irritate Bert Baker and other blacks by making alliances with the Midtown Civic League, the white community group that became increasingly frantic in its efforts to keep whites from selling homes to blacks. Baker accused Moritt of having "broken faith" and said Moritt had "proven himself unworthy of the confidence placed in him."[14] The *Age* called the Midtown Civic League a "race-baiting organization." In the next Assembly election, Baker's United Action club put up a black man, the Rev. Theophilus J. Alcantara, who had affiliations with the American Labor Party, against Moritt. In the end, Moritt was reelected to the Assembly. And, as happens over and again with politicians, the two erstwhile adversaries Baker and Moritt managed to again deal peacefully with each other in the coming years. Baker was showing that seemingly natural ability to apply what Okinawan martial arts call the *go-ju* system, which is the balancing of the hard and the soft, pushing and even punching for what's in your interest, and then backing off when there's no need for tension.

If there was a job that especially stood out in its appeal for Baker in the late 1930s, it was that of Deputy Collector of Internal Revenue, the position he was finally awarded as a patronage gift, well earned, in 1939. His salary was $1,800 a year, a pittance even in those days,[15] but the appointment made all the black papers, and Bert Baker's chest pushed out even more proudly.

Baker was not the first black in New York City to be named to that position. In fact, jobs in the federal tax office had for decades been given to politically connected blacks around the nation. Indeed, a 1936 article said that in the decades following the end of the Civil War, many non-southern areas of the country saw improvements in the distribution of government jobs to those with connections. "The political influence of the black voter has compelled recognition of the Negro in the distribution of both federal and state patronage," the author John G. Van Deusen wrote.[16] Among the positions listed in a footnote were those in the office of the "collector of internal revenue, New York City."

The employees of Internal Revenue, then, as today, were charged with helping taxpayers. By the end of World War I, the federal government was making energetic efforts to acquire the manpower to meet its needs. Baker must have had an appointment with the office of the Collector of Internal Revenue on his mind back then, in 1920, as well as in the coming years, as he saw whites with seeming ease acquire federal jobs that were the payback for their allegiance to the local Democratic Party. With the growing numbers and percentages of blacks in Brooklyn, Baker and his allies complained that blacks were not even close to having a fair share of patronage jobs.

Yes, obtaining the job of Deputy Collector of Internal Revenue was great for Baker's prestige. Although it was properly termed a "pittance," for Baker it was a boost. As mentioned, in 1939 he had lost his Throop Avenue home to foreclosure and had to live for a time in a rented apartment on nearby Madison Street.

But the job was far from perfect. Years later Baker recoiled at the memories of watchdogs in the Internal Revenue office, who tried to trick him into taking money left on the table, and who watched him through two-way mirrors.

"They had it set up so you couldn't see them on the other side but they could see you," Baker said, speaking with me in the months before he died. The irritation with the Internal Revenue office (no one seemed to be calling it Internal Revenue Service, or IRS, around that time) came at the very beginning, during his interview for the job. "The fellow who was interviewing me left papers there on the desk and walked out," he recalled. "I never touched the papers and didn't look at them. Later I learned about the mirrors, so obviously they could see what I was doing.

I didn't touch or look at the papers. So when he came back he just dismissed me and recommended me for the position in the office." Baker at first liked the idea of helping people confused by the tax directions or upset because they thought they were paying too much. "I applied there because the job is to give assistance to people who come in for help. I was trying to save the taxpayers some money," he said. But the distrust on the part of the higher-ups was irksome and insulting. Once they tried to come after him with a ruse. "I was called to the desk of the division chief who sat up front, and when I got up there, there was nobody there. So I went back to my desk where a taxpayer was waiting to see me, and the drawer was open and there was a roll of bills in the drawer. And I said to the taxpayer, I said, 'What's this for?' He said, 'That's for you.' So I told him then I could not take it. I never liked the [Internal Revenue]."

Baker said he was so disgusted that he put in an application for vacation time. He hoped to take the leave during the summer of 1941. "But they said I was not entitled to my vacation, because there were those who had seniority over me who wanted those dates." So he quit. Besides, he said, "I needed the time to complete my work with the American Tennis Association."

Baker might have felt personally targeted by those tactics. But the fact of the matter was that for decades, pretty much from the beginning of the federal revenue system, there had been concerns about patronage abuses and corruption carried out by employees of the federal agency. Some of the collectors made special arrangements with well-endowed taxpayers, helping them to reduce their payments or avoid audit or prosecution. In 1924 the federal government held hearings called by members of Congress who were outraged at what they saw as crass patronage in collectors' offices around the country. U.S. Senator William H. King issued a harsh condemnation of the federal tax agency and the practices that were being permitted at local levels around the nation. "Don't political appointments make for inefficiency?" said Senator King, a Democrat of Utah, who was at the time acting chair of the committee looking into the suspected abuses. "Isn't it true that the great majority of the 4,700 Deputy Collectors are political appointments without regard to merit?" As a result of the attention the issue received, the federal government made efforts to tighten its requirements for the positions and reduce opportunities for corruption.[17] This history explains what seemed to Bertram Baker to be the excessive effort to watch over and even entrap employees of the office of the Collector of Internal Revenue. A serious cleaning of the Internal Revenue office did not begin until 1952, after yet another federal investigation into corruption and administrative shortcomings. In 1951, a year before that major review was conducted, a black Collector of Internal Revenue for New York (Manhattan), James W. Johnson, was removed from his office as federal officials found that his operation was "administratively inefficient." He went into private practice, specializing in real estate law, and died in 1981.[18]

Regarding Baker's citing of the American Tennis Association as a reason for leaving the Internal Revenue office: He had been the Executive Secretary of the association for five years at that point, with national responsibilities that intensified during the summers as the national tournaments were held on campuses of black colleges around the country. And 1941 was to be a special summer. It was the twenty-fifth anniversary of the group, a very big deal for hundreds of socially prominent black New Yorkers and others around the country, coast to coast, east to west, all though the South, and even New England. The members were a collection of W. E. B. Du Bois's Talented Tenth,[19] wearing white shorts, white skirts, and (in the case of Bertram and some of the other male administrators) white summer suits and white ties. The ATA was growing year by year, and it was increasing Baker's renown in the black communities beyond New York City. It was one of his greatest ego boosters, and he wanted to give it all he could.

5

The American Tennis Association as a Brotherhood/Sisterhood

As the economy improved in the early 1940s prior to the American entry into World War II, Baker was able to use his skills as a bookkeeper and tax preparer with the growing number of blacks streaming into Bedford Stuyvesant, in the second big wave of the Great Migration from the South.[1]

The need for fraternity beyond the office was still strong. Baker spent increasing time with an association that was breaking down gender barriers in black communities around the country, as more and more middle-class blacks, men and women, took to the sport of tennis, not only as a physical activity but as a way of socializing with other middle-class blacks. Professors at black colleges, lawyers, doctors, would-be elected officials, and others, along with their families, made up the membership of the American Tennis Association, the ATA.

It wasn't that Bertram Baker was a great player of the sport. He seems never to have shown tendencies to athleticism. But he did see sports, especially tennis, as a character-building pursuit, and he especially saw tennis as a way of connecting with the very middle-class black Americans with whom he wanted to bond.[2] In the early years of the twentieth century, tennis was associated with Booker T. Washington's Tuskegee Institute (now Tuskegee University) in Alabama. But given that tennis had British roots, Baker knew of the sport back on Nevis, and he quickly gravitated toward it in his new country as a way to connect with up-and-coming black men and women.

By 1921, there was a very small group of black Brooklynites sprinkled through central Brooklyn, sort of on the periphery of what by the 1940s would be Bedford Stuyvesant, who met and formed a group called the Utopian Tennis Club. They would gather monthly, arranging competitions between their members and those in other nearby communities, such as throughout New Jersey. Many of them were, like Bertram Baker, West Indians. By 1928 he was the chairman of the board of the Utopian club, which was the largest of the local clubs in the nationwide network making up the American Tennis Association.

The motivations were as clear as they were sincere. As Baker searched for ways to gain footholds in the Brooklyn Democratic Party, then largely controlled by Irish politicians, he was also looking to gain social contacts and influence through his work with black Brooklyn tennis lovers. By the mid-1930s, a decade and a half before he would be elected Assemblyman, he had extended his reach so far among black tennis communities across the country—through the segregated South and into the West and all the way to California—that he became leader of the ATA. Every summer he would travel by car to the group's national tournaments, which were held on the campuses of various black colleges. In the summer of 1931 he was at Tuskegee Institute, which was celebrating the fiftieth anniversary of Booker T. Washington's college and the fifteenth anniversary of the ATA. By 1936 he was the national organization's chief operating officer, holding the title of Executive Secretary, a title he would retain for thirty years. He would go to the national tournaments held every year at a black college in the South, most often Tuskegee Institute and Hampton Institute in Virginia (now Hampton University) as well as Wilberforce University in Ohio. He often also traveled to the regional tournaments in Washington, or in towns in New Jersey or Massachusetts.

The very first Executive Secretary of the American Tennis Association was Gerald F. Norman, who, like Baker, was from New York. Like Baker, Norman had roots in the Caribbean. His family was from the island of Jamaica, also a British colony back then. Norman, a generation older than Baker, began in the early 1900s to dedicate himself to promoting athletic activities in Harlem. His first interest was basketball, then in its early existence, and he organized teams encouraging teenagers to not only develop their physical talents but also to see the interrelationship between the body and the mind.[3] He had the credentials to guide young blacks in the sphere of the mind, having gone to the City College of New York himself and become a public school teacher. He was identified in obituaries[4] as the first black person to teach in a New York City high school, Bryant High School in Queens. Norman was part of the group of blacks from around the country who in 1916 were found-

ers of the American Tennis Association. They vowed to make it an organization that would tie together black strivers throughout the country,
united in their ambitions for themselves, their communities, and especially their families.

Norman had a strong commitment to his own family. He had started
his basketball organization in Manhattan with his brothers Clifton and
Conrad. His son Gerald L. Norman was to become a well-known tennis
player and teacher in his own right. In 1929 when the son was attending
Flushing High School in Queens, something of an uproar arose when it
became known that the U.S Lawn Tennis Association would not let the
son participate in its national youth tournament. The white alumni of the
high school publicly backed him, attacking the action of the U.S. Lawn
Tennis Association. "It indicates that they are afraid of colored competition and must be shielded if they are to win, whereas in reality the majority of white tennis players are very good in sports and do not want the
sort of victory that is even in part decided before the tournament starts
by the elimination of good players," wrote Spear Knebel, a white alum-
nus who was a Board Secretary of the Christian Social Services agency
of the Protestant Episcopal Church. Knebel's letter had been sent to the
relatively new organization known as the National Association for the
Advancement of Colored People, which released it to the public.[5] But
it would be another two decades before white tennis officials around the
country took seriously the demands that black players be allowed to participate in the tournaments receiving national attention.

Norman, the father of Norman the high school player, saw something he liked in Bertram L. Baker. Perhaps their shared backgrounds in
the Caribbean had something to do with it. Though Baker was some
thirty years younger than Norman, the two men saw the world around
them with similar eyes. Tennis could be both a source of relaxation and
a physical uplift but also a way of asserting oneself in a world that often
appeared hostile to their desires and ambitions. Norman held the title of
Executive Secretary of the American Tennis Association for twenty years,
from its founding in 1916 to his retirement in 1936. Baker's thirty years as
successor to Norman gave him some of the greatest pleasures he would
find outside of work.

Both Norman and Baker are mentioned in the 2014 book *A Spectacular Leap: Black Women Athletes in Twentieth-Century America*, written
by Jennifer H. Lansbury and published by University of Arkansas Press.
The very title notes a relevant truth about the American Tennis Association, especially for black men like Norman and Baker, coming from their
chauvinistic West Indian culture. Unlike the Masons and other groups,

the ATA was welcoming to the spouses and children of its members. In fact, it was decades ahead of other black institutions with respect to women's performing administrative duties within the organization. Even more meaningful, women were front and center on the tennis courts that were the organization's *raison d'être*.

Bertram Baker's wife, Irene, and his daughters, Lilian and Marian, went with him to the summer national ATA tournaments, which were held at the black colleges. It was a chance for them all to become friends with other black girls like Eleanor Chippey, whose father taught from the 1940s through the '60s at various colleges through the South, and with Frances McAllister, whose family came from Springfield, Massachusetts, and who would marry a professor of history at Howard University.

The significant turn for the ATA and for American tennis began to take place in the late 1940s as a young black woman from Manhattan began to show her talents on the tennis courts of New York City as well as at the black colleges where the ATA held its yearly national contests. By 1950 Bertram was engaged in serious discussions with white tennis officials about allowing a black person to compete in the theretofore segregated tennis events held in New York and around the world. By arrangement, the person tapped to be the entrant onto the then—all-white tennis stage was the young black woman from Harlem, Althea Gibson. The June 1951 Executive Bulletin of the ATA shows, on its cover page, Bertram Baker proudly shaking Gibson's hand as she was about to board a Pan American flight for London and the Wimbledon competition there.[6] Gibson would win a number of major tournaments over the next several years, but it was in 1957 that she rose to stellar heights of popularity, forever erasing the image of tennis as a whites-only sport.

That was the year she won two prestigious championships, at Wimbledon in England and at Forest Hills in Queens, New York. The Associated Press voted Gibson the Female Athlete of the Year. She was on an ascent in popularity that would last until her death in 2003 at the age of seventy-six. The moment of the 1957 Wimbledon victory was special for Bertram Baker as well.

He held a celebratory bash at his home on Jefferson Avenue, inviting activists and black political officials for breakfast, where he gave a toast to the new queen of tennis and drank "high balls" of Old Granddad whiskey and ginger ale, as he slapped backs and made the most of the moment. Gibson sat next to him at the dining room table, with Baker's family (including the author, then eight years old), friends, and members of the community. Soon would come other spectacular moments for him, as for example when he rode in the limousine with Gibson in the ticker-tape parade thrown by Mayor Robert F. Wagner in her honor. Gibson and her proud surrogate dad Bertram Baker waved as the parade moved along Broadway and television cameras recorded it all for history.

Some who knew him over the years saw Bertram Baker as an overly constrained man when it came to his social interactions. Almost always in New York he was attired in dark suits, pinstripes on one occasion, dark blue on another, dark gray on yet another, with matching vests. He frequently went all out on the formal route, with tuxedos, at the annual dinners of political clubs and various organizations he had connections with. But at the social events of the American Tennis Association, the suits were white, a color that went well with the soft, warm evenings at the black colleges where the tournaments were held. The nights were free of the tensions that marked workdays in the hometowns of respective ATA members. It was the quintessence of the work-vacation. There was dancing on the grass at nights, with bands playing bluesy and calypso tunes. His daughters appreciated those excursions, as did his wife, because those were among the few occasions when he would socialize with them.

However, there came a time when he would find a way to go to the events alone, in large part because he was traveling with his female secretary who would stay in a room next to his.[7] Marie Smallwood, who worked as his secretary back in Brooklyn, was a buxom woman born and raised in a black middle-class home in Washington, D.C. Marie once had the hopes of making it in New York as a singer or actress. Instead, she embarked on a career as the right-hand lady of Assemblyman Bertram L. Baker. Many, if not most, of the men who were administrators in the ATA had wives who were active also. It was expected. But everyone in the ATA knew that Miss Smallwood was Bertram Baker's mistress.

The openness of this must have been painful to some. Marie Smallwood's hotel room was always right next to Baker's, and there was always a door between the two that could be easily opened. Nevertheless, this was an era in which such behavior by a man of power would have been easily excused.

And so, for all the good things he extracted from his ties with brotherhoods/sisterhoods like the African Orthodox Church, the Masons, and the ATA, Baker clearly retained unresolved conflicts in the recesses of his personality, his id, that made for a fundamentally unhappy home. It was only Irene Baker's extraordinary character, her interest in art, her love for her children and grandchildren, that kept her walking with head erect and the home intact.

Author Commentary

By the time I was living in the Baker household and was at the age where I could travel with him, in the late 1950s, my grandfather started taking me to the tournaments, sometimes to Central State University in Ohio, and other times to Hampton University in Virginia. I missed out on the Tuskegee tournaments, which hosted the events in earlier decades.

Even a stupidly shy kid like me was stimulated by being around so many super-smart, ambitious, and health-conscious people of color from all over the country. At Hampton I played around with a kid whose older cousin would hang out with us sometimes. That older cousin was Bobby Scott, who several decades later would become a Congressman from Virginia. I also got to see the young Althea Gibson play, as well as the young teen Arthur Ashe. Though I was a baseball lover, I started playing tennis myself and entered some of the regional tournaments, though I never played at the ATA nationals. I made friends with kids my age who were the sons, daughters, nieces, and nephews of racket freaks from middle-class black communities, from Washington, D.C., to Mississippi and to California. I would hit balls across nets with them, and we would make our own bats and play a little baseball, or go fishing, or swim, and tell stories about our hometowns, and—in the case of Newport News, Virginia—get my first exposure to racial segregation. Once in Virginia I went to the beach with a friend of my grandfather's and that friend's family. We stayed the whole time on the "colored" side of the beach. But heck, for me, being at a colored beach was really kind of like being with folks from Bedford Stuyvesant. I had a decent time.

Inevitably, given my natural bond with my grandmother, I developed a bundle of resentments about the ATA. The submerged bitterness had to do with my grandfather's relationship with Miss Smallwood, who came along with me and Bertram Baker on the trips to the national tennis tournaments.

"Puddin'," she always called me, and I reacted with stiff silence. I absolutely detested the idea of spending so much time with her. In Brooklyn, I had to go to her house on Midwood Street and wait for her to get ready for our car trip together to Virginia, or to wherever that year's tournament was taking place.

The trip always seemed long, hours of driving, as my grandfather sang songs in a voice that seemed incapable of being on key. We stayed once at a hotel in Pennsylvania on the way to Central State College in Ohio, to avoid being on the road at night. After arriving at the college campus, whether Central State or Hampton, I would have my own room and Miss Smallwood would have one next to my grandfather's.

I don't remember hearing my grandfather yell at the tennis tournaments, as he did back in Brooklyn, on the phone or wherever. It almost seemed as if Miss Smallwood was able to keep him in check. I especially remember one time when we were all at an evening party. It was outside in the warm summer air. A band was playing calypso music, and there was my grandfather, wearing white slacks and a white shirt without a jacket or tie. He was shaking his hips as he moved with the others in a circle, holding the waist of the person in front of him, as all danced rumba-like to the rhythms of the drums and the horns.

It was in 1941, before the author's birth, that Bertram Baker threw himself most intensely into the administration of American Tennis Association activities. He had just resigned from his job as Deputy Collector of Internal Revenue, citing the importance of the ATA work awaiting him. But what Baker wanted most of all was a taste of power. And he set himself about acquiring it, even as world events played a role.

Nineteen-forty-one was a singular year in American history, for reasons having to do with the economy and America's relations with the outside world. In December 1941 the Japanese bombed the U.S. naval base at Pearl Harbor in the Pacific Ocean, and Bertram Baker's adopted country entered the Second World War. Young men in Brooklyn and around the nation, blacks and whites, were drafted to serve as soldiers in that conflict, including many from the Bedford Stuyvesant neighborhood. During the war Bertram and middle-class blacks all over the country made public their allegiance to their country, even as they continued to demand the civil rights still withheld from them. The *Pittsburgh Courier* came up with the idea of a "Double V" campaign, promising support for America's actions against Japan and Germany, even though the U.S. military remained segregated and blacks were denied opportunities to purchase homes wherever they wanted in Brooklyn and the rest of the nation.

Generals and political bosses like Bertram Baker know that one must never lose sight of one's goals, even in the thick of battle, real or figurative. Baker stayed focused. It happened that soon after he left the federal tax office, and as the country was stepping onto battlefields afar, Bertram Baker was named by Democratic county leaders as the official choice of the party to run for a seat on the City Council. Baker was ecstatic. Steve Carney, still the 17th Assembly District leader, strongly backed Baker for the City Council candidacy, as did the Brooklyn Democratic leader, John Cashmore, another Irishman. Many hailed the candidacy as historic, given that it had been a long while since a black person had been taken seriously in a campaign for elective office in Brooklyn. The *Amsterdam News* declared: "Political history was made in Brooklyn last week when for the first time a major political party nominated a Negro for county-wide office."[8] Baker celebrated and went to work campaigning.

But there was a problem. In those days, City Council elections were conducted according to what was known as the proportional representation method. That meant candidates had to appeal to voters borough-wide, not just in their respective districts. While that system was good for candidates running on transcending themes, like socialism, it was deadly for blacks who could not draw votes from whites living outside Bedford Stuyvesant. (There were still relatively few blacks in Crown Heights, Brownsville, Canarsie, or anywhere else in Brooklyn. Downtown was being transformed and the once all-black Weeksville, the famous black neighborhood of the late 1800s and early 1900s, was just a southern extension of Bedford Stuyvesant by the 1940s.) Baker did not win that Council seat in 1941.

6
Climbing the Ladder to Elective Office

The New York City Council defeat in 1941 left Bertram Baker without a full-time job, and he relied, as he did in the 1930s, on consulting-type work keeping books and doing taxes, often for small businesses including candy stores in Bedford Stuyvesant. He wanted a steady, paying job. The Irish guys around him had jobs. Stephen Carney, for instance, was a Democratic district leader, a job that paid no salary, but he was also employed with the Water Commission and in 1948 was named Commissioner of Water, Supply, Gas and Electricity; Minnie Abel, Carney's aunt and his co-leader, had a longtime civil service job (which, as with her nephew, meant a pension) as a secretary with the city Board of Assessors. John Cashmore was the unsalaried Democratic County leader, but in 1941 he was elected Brooklyn Borough President, which paid him even as it let him wield more clout in making appointments and influencing decisions at City Hall. Back then the office of the Borough President carried much more power, as the respective presidents were part of a (now-defunct) Board of Estimate and voted with the mayor on major matters of public policy.

Cashmore, nudged by Carney, chose Bertram L. Baker to be his Confidential Inspector. This job would be the direct line to Baker's victory to the New York state Assembly in November 1948, and he would never again be unemployed, until his retirement in 1970, after twenty-two years in the Assembly.

In 1945, Baker began his new job as Confidential Inspector in the office of the Brooklyn Borough President, carrying in his pocket a shield that was similar to a city police detective's badge. Baker was above all a liaison to the black community in Brooklyn, especially those who participated in black politics, which in those days largely meant those in the United Action Democratic Association. An elective office was still the goal. That same year, 1945, Baker was nominated again by the party to be a City Council candidate. But some blacks maintained that Baker acted against the interests of black people in that contest, out of selfish loyalty to the Democratic Party. A black woman of ambition, a Republican named Maude B. Richardson, was planning to run for the City Council and, concerned about the black vote's being split, she reportedly asked Baker if he planned to run. She said Baker told her no, but after she began her campaign she said she was startled to learn that Baker was in fact entering the race as the Democrats' candidate.[1] According to Julie A. Gallagher in her book *Black Women and Politics in New York City*, in that election, still carried out under the old proportional representation method, Baker (who had the Democratic and American Labor Party nominations) received just over 10,000 votes and Richardson nearly 6,000. Neither had enough for a seat on the Council.

For all the fire that would sometimes erupt from his mouth, Bertram Baker could be a patient acolyte when it came to honoring the wishes of the party bosses. He wanted power, but he saw the order of things. When blacks from other parties faced off against one another, he let them offset one another. A most notable moment came in 1946, when there was an opening for a seat in the state Assembly. Republican Maude Richardson decided she would run. So did Ada Jackson, another black woman, who was with the progressive American Labor Party. In the contest also was a Democratic Irishman named John Walsh. The two black women ended up splitting the black vote, and Walsh crossed the victory line first, by inches. Walsh received 9,691 votes, Richardson got 9,614 votes, and Jackson of the ALP, 4,199 votes. Maude B. Richardson had lost by 77 ballots.

Both Jackson and Richardson had roots in the American South. Like Baker, they had reputations within Bedford Stuyvesant for involvement with black organizations, such as the local office of the NAACP. The political ambitions of Jackson and Richardson could not be attributed solely to ego and a desire for steady employment. Jackson in particular was known for devotion to her four children and a concern for young people, especially in the black community. She also had ties to labor organizations, and she was a consistent choice of the leftist/progressive American Labor Party. Richardson, on the other hand, while also steeped in social activities in the community, was a confirmed Republican and remained so even after the vast majority of the city's other black Republicans had made the leap from the Republican Party, which was once considered the party of the Union Army that fought to end slavery. Even Irish Democrats of New York went out of their way to distance themselves from the nigger-hating Democrats of the South. But, as late as the late 1940s, there were still some blacks, such as the Arkansas-born Richardson, who could not bring themselves to drop the association with the old party of Abraham Lincoln.

Speaking years later of the race in which Maude Richardson came so close to winning, Baker would say, "The handwriting was on the wall." The Irish leaders in Bed-Stuy knew the end was coming for whites who, for decades, had been fearing black power. They "realized that, shall I say, the jig was up," Baker would say. To put it simply, the Democratic bosses cut a deal to get Baker into office. They did so in a slick way, all the better to trick the racist whites in the district who hoped a black would never be elected.

The Democratic leaders used a ploy that Democratic leaders use even today, way into the twenty-first century, even as they maintain that the days of bossism are over.

The Democrats made a secret deal with John Walsh, the Irishman who had won the election to the Assembly, defeating the two black women. For the 1948 race, the leaders named Walsh as the candidate. But election law allowed the candidate to decline the nomination. And at that point the district leader, Stephen Carney, could appoint a replacement. That replacement was none other than Bertram L. Baker. In other words, Baker won the primary without even running for it.

"I then became the candidate in the general election and Maude Richardson was the Republican candidate. And the breakthrough was at hand because . . . I got the Democrat[ic] and the ALP [American Labor Party]. . . . One of us had to be elected and we knew then that . . . the final barrier would be broken down," Baker recalled in 1976.

On the voting day, November 2, 1948, "I received 21,189 votes and Maude B. [Richardson] got 11,567 votes. The final barrier had at last been broken down, for a Negro . . . to be elected to public office."[2]

And so a question would be, How did Carney get Walsh to decline? The word was that Carney had offered him a judgeship. But Carney ended up with a political enemy when Walsh didn't receive the judgeship. Carney had given it instead to Lloyd Herzka, who was Jewish and one of Bertram Baker's best friends.

On January 6, 1949, as Baker was up in Albany wetting his feet in the pond that would be his place of work for the next twenty-two years, the *Brooklyn Daily Eagle* published a finely written "Man of the Week" article that noted the historical significance of his election.

The article was headlined "Negroes Win Strong Voice in Election of Bert Baker," and it said:

> A young man came to Brooklyn from Nevis, the "Queen of the Caribbee islands," in 1915. He was 17 and he soon got into the swing of things—Brooklyn things—that led him to a unique and enviable position in the community.
>
> At 50 Bertram L Baker is the first Negro elected to public office in Brooklyn. He was voted Assemblyman from the 17th A.D., which takes in the Bedford-Stuyvesant–Eastern Parkway area, and began work last Wednesday.
>
> . . . "I came to Brooklyn with the idea that I'd study for the Episcopalian ministry," said Bert. "I wasn't a Methodist like my father because of the influence of my grandmother, who brought me up as an Episcopalian."
>
> He looks much younger than 50, stands about 5'10" tall, has a full pleasant face, quiet eyes and wavy black hair, parted neatly and showing scattered strands of gray.
>
> "However, I found it necessary to work to make a living," he explained. "You see, I married when I was 21. My first job was as a messenger boy at A. & S. Later I ran elevators at various places. I wanted very much to learn a profession so I soon began a correspondence course with La Salle extension University. I learned bookkeeping and accounting that way."
>
> . . . Mr. Baker's extracurricular interest is tennis. He is executive secretary of the American Tennis Association, the Negro counterpart of the United States Lawn Tennis Association, and president of the New York State Tennis Association.
>
> "In my travels I've seen a lot of segregation," he said. "In Brooklyn, we have segregation, too. It's not forced on us, of course. But we still have it. That's one reason my people need spokesmen in government. . . ."
>
> Mr. Baker's election was a milestone in Negro progress in the community. He knows that the eyes of thousands, Negroes and whites, will follow his progress at Albany.

And so a milestone had been reached in the history of black Brooklyn and in the history of Brooklyn itself. Baker was just beginning the phase of his life for which he would be known by family, friends, and hyper-local historians.

Although Baker was half a century old at the time of his historic victory, he still had life in him and would serve a total of twenty-two years in the New York state Assembly before retiring. And along the way he continued to make marks on the history of his adopted borough, city, and state, such as sponsoring one of the nation's first laws against housing discrimination, and such as when he became the Majority Whip of the state Assembly in 1965, the highest state position ever achieved at that time by a black person. Bertram Baker did not want to have a life of rest until such a life was forced upon him.

Please note the following, dear readers: There had actually been a time, almost thirty years previously, when a black came within one vote of doing what Bertram Baker did in 1948. Some say that that election had been stolen from the black candidate at the last minute by racist whites. It was a Brooklyn story made for the ages. Had that man won, he, and not Bertram Baker, would have been the first black person elected to office in the county of Kings.

It happened in 1920, four years before Baker took his oath as an American citizen. The man who ran for assembly back then was Franklin Wheeler Morton, and like most blacks in those days he was a Republican.

Morton was a true up-and-comer, a graduate of New York University Law School. He had a unique lineage. His father, Dr. Walter Alfred Morton, was a physician with degrees from Bates College and Dartmouth Medical School. His grandmother Verina Morton Jones[3] was also a physician. She had turned her house at 105 Fleet Street in Downtown Brooklyn into a social service center for less-fortunate blacks in the borough. Franklin Morton decided he would run for a seat in the New York state Assembly, representing the downtown district, known as the 1st Assembly District of the borough. According to the first reports of the primary contest, Morton did well. He won, in fact. But the race was so close that the loser, a white Republican named J. A. Warren, challenged the results. A judge (white like everyone else in political office back then) ruled that there should be a recount. When election officials tallied up the ballots again, they concluded that Warren had actually won by two votes. Morton challenged that recount and asked for another. The final result was conveyed in a headline in the *Brooklyn Eagle* of October 3, 1920: "Warren Wins Over Negro by One Vote." Every black person in Brooklyn of voting age believed the victory had been stolen from Franklin Morton.

Morton, whose two-year-old daughter had died of pneumonia that very same election year, fell into a depression and alcoholism. It perhaps gave him a slight feeling of achieved vengeance when, in the 1930s, he renounced the party of Lincoln and became a Democrat. Franklin W. Morton died in 1943. After World War II, Morton's son, Franklin W. Morton Jr., was honorably discharged after service on the battlefields of Europe, and he joined Bertram Baker's United Action Democratic club. He graduated from St. John's University Law School. With Baker's intervention with Democratic bosses in the 1950s, Franklin W. Morton Jr. became one of Brooklyn's first black judges. (Judge Morton is mentioned further in Chapters 8 and 11.)

Elected officials cannot dwell on the past. They are concerned about the present and the future. Yes, Bertram Baker had to be aware of racial indignities that had caused suffering and grief to blacks earlier in the century. But certain discriminatory patterns remained as fixed in Brooklyn as they did in the American South. High on that list was the embedded practice of refusing to rent or sell housing to blacks.

The Charlestown Methodist Chapel in 1802. Slave women are in the foreground. Five years previously, a pro-slavery mob set the chapel on fire, but the fire was extinguished and the chapel survived into the nineteenth century. The poster belonged to Irene Baker.

Reverend Alfred B.B. Baker, a Wesleyan Methodist minister and father of Bertram L. Baker. The picture was taken on Nevis, year unknown.

Pictured here are Bertram Baker *(standing at far right)* and his "brothers" in the Carthaginian Lodge of the Prince Hall Masons. They called themselves the "Men of
Honor." The designation came from their loyalty to Baker in his fight against Prince
Hall Mason superiors. The superiors had expelled Baker because he'd refused to
submit to them for prior approval the columns he was writing for the *New York Age*
newspaper.

```
Back Row.(left to right))
         William A.Sellers; Constantine Thomas
         Alexander Fenner; Bertram L. Baker
Middle Row.(left to right)
         Archibald Millard; Daniel Brathwaith;
         Harry A.Williamson;Louis A.Jeppe;
         Ferdinand Washington; John Helps
Bottom Row.(left to right)
         Cyril Robinson; James Yearwood;
         George Fleming
```

The names of the "Men of Honor." Perhaps the most notable was Harry A. Williamson, who during the early 1900s was considered the historian of the Prince Hall
Masons. Louis A. Jeppe was one of the original members of the Carthaginian Lodge,
started in 1904.

Lawyer Succumbs

Francis F. Giles.

LAWYER DIES
IN MYSTERY

From a front-page September 22, 1934, article in the *New York Amsterdam News*. Francis F. Giles was the first black from Brooklyn to be named a federal prosecutor. He was also a powerful member of the Prince Hall Masons. After leaving the U.S. Attorney's office in the early 1930s, he was found dead, beaten, on the tracks of the "L" line at Fulton Street and Reid Avenue.

Bertram Baker in an undated photo, probably when he was in his early twenties, in Brooklyn.

A 1940 New York City tax photo of 409 Hancock Street, the home of Bertram Baker's United Action Democratic club. (The numbers 1836 and 69 in the photo refer to, respectively, the block and lot numbers used to identify properties in the city.) Courtesy of the New York City Municipal Archives.

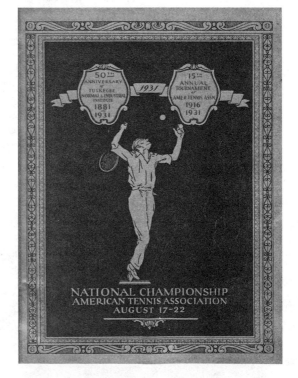

The front page of the 1931 annual journal of the American Tennis Association. Nineteen-thirty-one was the fifteenth anniversary of the ATA and the fiftieth anniversary of Booker T. Washington's Tuskegee Institute, considered the birthplace of black American tennis.

Young Franklin Morton Sr., who almost won an election for the state Assembly representing the Downtown area in 1920. Photo acquired from Rebecca Morton Johnson, granddaughter of Franklin Morton Sr.

Verina Morton-Jones, M.D., was one of the first black women to practice medicine in America. She was the mother of Franklin Morton Sr., who almost won election to a seat in the state Assembly representing Downtown Brooklyn. Photo acquired from Rebecca Morton Johnson, great-granddaughter of Dr. Verina Morton-Jones.

A 1940 tax photo of 399 Jefferson Avenue, the brownstone home that Bertram and Irene Baker purchased in 1942. It's where Baker lived until his death there in his bedroom in 1985. (The numbers in the photo, 1830 and 50, refer to the block and lot numbers used by the city.) Courtesy of the New York City Municipal Archives.

The swearing-in of Bertram Baker as a member of the New York state Assembly on December 21, 1948. Among those with him are his wife, Irene; his close friend Lloyd Herzka (*second from right*), smiling at Bertram; the Reverend John Coleman, wearing the minister's collar, who was the rector of St. Philip's Episcopal Church in Bedford Stuyvesant; and state Supreme Court Justice E. Ivan Rubenstein, who is on the far right wearing the judicial robe and administering the oath of office.

Bertram Baker's four grandchildren, who lived together in his house in the late 1950s, on Easter Sunday, exact year unknown. (*Left to right*) Lynn Bemus (now Prime); Ron Howell, the author; Diane Bemus (now Patrick); and John Bemus.

Bedford Stuyvesant children celebrating Christmas in the late 1950s at Bertram Baker's United Action Democratic club on Hancock Street.

Baker in 1963, at 120 Schermerhorn Street, the Brooklyn Criminal Court. Attorneys from Baker's United Action Democratic club were there. His lawyers were representing those arrested for protesting discriminatory hiring policies of contractors building Downstate Medical Center.

Bertram Baker is pictured here in 1963 with blacks who were growing in number in the New York state legislature during the mid-1960s. Sitting next to Baker (who is on the left) is Assemblyman James "Skiz" Watson of Harlem, who later became a federal judge. Standing, far left, is Bronx state Senator Ivan Warner. Second from left is Assemblyman Lloyd Dickens of Harlem. Next to him is Harlem Assemblyman Mark T. Southall, and standing on the far right is Brooklyn Assemblyman Thomas Russell Jones.

Wilfred DaCosta Howell, father of the author, who was a U.S. Marine Corps corporal during World War II. Wilfred Howell's two brothers also served in the military, upsetting their father, the Reverend Charles G. Howell, who was angry about racial segregation in the armed forces.

Reverend Charles Garfield Howell, the author's paternal grandfather. He was a writer and Episcopal priest and immigrated to America from Barbados in 1912.

Black Population of Brooklyn (Kings County): 1790 - 2015

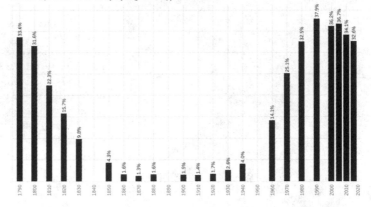

Note: Data not available for 1840, 1890, and 1950.

The population of Brooklyn was one-third black in the years after the Revolutionary War (see 1790). It went down to 1 percent black by the time the first Bakers came there (see 1900). By the end of the twentieth century, the black population had soared and, again, was one-third black (see 1990). The latest numbers show the effects of gentrification, which is taking down the percentage of the black population once again (see 2000–2015). Chart prepared by Jeff Bloem and Michelle Pratt at the Minnesota Population Center.

Election poster used in Bertram Baker's last campaign, in 1968.

Bertram Baker shakes hands with fellow Assemblyman Guy Brewer in 1970. Brewer was the first black person elected to political office in the borough of Queens, in 1968.

Althea Gibson, soon after her historic 1957 Wimbledon victory, visited City Hall, where she and Bertram Baker were greeted by Mayor Robert F. Wagner.

On July 16, 2011, scores gathered to celebrate the naming of Jefferson Avenue (between Tompkins and Throop avenues) as "Bertram L. Baker Way." The tall man in the rear is Robert Cornegy, who later became a City Councilman. Others (*left to right in the foreground*) are the late John Bemus, Baker's son-in-law; Ron Howell, the author; Diane Patrick, Baker's granddaughter; then–Massachusetts Governor Deval Patrick, Diane's husband; Letitia James, who later became New York City's Public Advocate; Altovise Fleary, president of the Jefferson Avenue TNT Block Association; Marty Markowitz, then the Brooklyn Borough President; and Hakeem Jeffries, who later became a U.S. congressman representing parts of Brooklyn and Queens. In the background, left side, are friends of the Baker family: Ed Rhodes (*left*); Joanne Edey-Rhodes (*right*); and Asha Rhodes, their daughter (*middle*).

U.S. President Lyndon Baines Johnson at Borough Hall in Downtown Brooklyn in 1964. Bertram Baker brought young Bedford Stuyvesant resident Karen Willis with him to meet the President.

Bertram Baker in 1965 with Assemblywoman Shirley Chisholm and state Senator Willie Thompson. They are meeting at the Bedford Stuyvesant office of the Brevoort Savings Bank.

Bertram Baker meeting with judges, including Oliver D. Williams, whose right hand is shaking the hand of another judge. Williams was appointed in the 1950s with Baker's backing.

In December 1957, J. Daniel Diggs (*second from left*), a loyal member of Bertram Baker's United Action Democratic club, was sworn in as Brooklyn's first black City Councilman. To the far right is Baker. To the left of Diggs is then–Brooklyn Borough President John Cashmore.

Through the early and mid-1900s, Harry Williamson was recognized as the historian of the Prince Hall Masons in the United States. He was suspended from the black fraternal group in the 1930s along with Bertram Baker. Williamson was later reinstated, but Baker remained suspended for the rest of his life.

Josephine Bravo, who served during the late 1950s and the 1960s as Bertram Baker's co-leader. She was also the Secretary of the New York state Labor Department. (Note: Not *a* secretary but *the* Secretary, i.e., the leader of the New York state Labor Department.)

Lawrence Pierce worked loyally with Bertram Baker in Baker's United Action Democratic club in the 1950s. He then became a federal judge and then a judge on the U.S. Court of Appeals.

Boys who played on the Cardinal Realty Bears baseball team, c. 1968. The team was sponsored by the Cardinal Realty Company, which was based in central Brooklyn. Various Bed-Stuy businesses contributed to the funding of the United Action Democratic club's baseball teams. Kneeling (second from right) is Ronnie Bish, from the Bish family that managed Bertram Baker's United Action Democratic club.

The author's mother, Marian Baker Howell, in her twenties.

Albert R. Murray, known to some as Bertram Baker's most trusted follower, being sworn in as a Criminal Court Judge in 1965. Photo acquired from Albert R. Murray Jr.

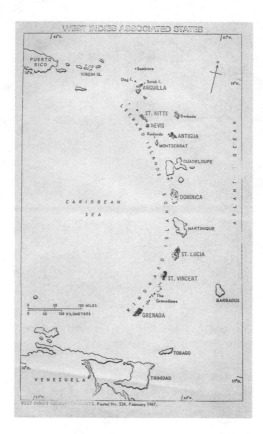

Nevis is among the so-called Leeward Islands, on the eastern side of the Caribbean Sea.

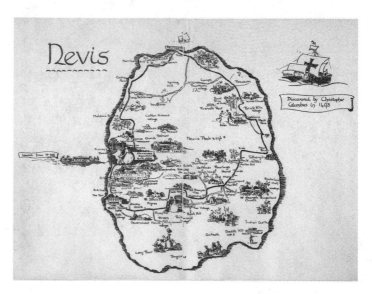

Nevis is one of the smallest populated islands in the world. Charlestown, the capital, is on the left (west) side, about midway up.

Bertram Baker in his early sixties.

As pallbearers place Bertram Baker's coffin in the hearse, State Supreme Court Justice Franklin Morton II raises his hat in a final farewell to the man he and other black judges called "Chief." Courtesy the *New York Times*, which published Chester Higgins's photo on March 12, 1985.

7

On a Mission in the 1950s
Desegregation of Housing

In 1949, when Bertram Baker took his seat in Albany, *de facto* segregation in housing was the rule in New York City and state. The massive Stuyvesant Town housing development in Manhattan, built by the Metropolitan Life Insurance Company, began accepting tenants in 1949. Several years earlier the insurance company's executives were ratcheting up interest in the development, which was receiving huge tax benefits, and they openly acknowledged that blacks would be barred as tenants. "Negroes and whites don't mix," said Frederick H. Ecker, the chairman of Metropolitan Life. "Perhaps they will in a hundred years, but not now."[1] Robert Moses, the man who all but dictated city housing policy, was on the record as agreeing with Ecker. Moses told the city's Board of Estimate that the city should grant Ecker's wish, because if it did not, "it will be the death knell of slum clearance by private enterprise."[2] The Power Broker had spoken. All the residents of the more than 10,000 apartments at Stuyvesant Town were white.

Through the 1950s, Bertram Baker would be celebrated for a number of his accomplishments, such as, in 1957, the history-making victory of Althea Gibson as the first black to win a major tennis tournament, the fruit of Baker's efforts to integrate the sport of tennis. But in the realm of politics, it was the Metcalf–Baker bill that would sit most prominently on the list of his legislative accomplishments.

Baker began embracing the challenge of battling housing discrimination through the 1950s. In 1955, the *New York Times* ran an article mentioning Baker's speaking at a conference called by the Urban League of Greater New York, which fought to open opportunities for blacks in business and housing.[3]

The article said Baker was drumming up "support for four bills to end discrimination in publicly assisted housing," and it noted that the sponsors were Baker on the Assembly side and George R. Metcalf, a white upstate Republican, on the Senate side. According to the article, the Brooklyn Assemblyman "contended that Queens had frozen out the non-white populations from areas of new construction." The year the article was published, 1955, was the year that Baker's anti-bias housing bill passed and was signed into law by then-Governor Averell Harriman.

Reflecting on his career years later, Baker would say his greatest pride was that he was the New York state assembly author of one of the nation's first laws barring racial discrimination in the sale or rental of properties.

"WASP" is the term that George Metcalf used to describe his background. His family in fact went back to the beginnings of the American republic, and he represented a very conservative region of the northern part of New York state, the city of Auburn.

But Metcalf was also, against all expectations, a social liberal. He had started out as a journalist, graduating in 1937 from the Columbia University Graduate School of Journalism.

Metcalf and Baker were initially approached by a group called the New York State Committee Against Discrimination in Housing (NYSCDH), which was committed to the elimination of discrimination in housing in New York state. Metcalf said the group thought it would be ideal to have an upstate WASP paired with a strong and well-spoken black New York City legislator as the joint public face of the bill.[4]

As Metcalf wrote many years later, in a never-published work about housing:

> [W]hen he entered the Assembly (in 1949), Baker commanded an Assembly district which made him a prominent figure in the Democratic hierarch[y]. He held strong convictions and possessed the kind of absolute persistence the struggle would demand. And, of course, as a black person he knew prejudice and discrimination firsthand. Where I could talk about justice and prejudice in the abstract, Baker knew from personal experience the insults and humiliations that whites knowingly or unknowingly heaped on blacks. He sought public office because by writing laws, he could best help his

race. In addition, he unquestionably enjoyed one of the state's most eloquent and convincing voices on racial issues.[5]

Baker began working with Metcalf to get an anti-discrimination bill passed in the legislature in the early 1950s. Metcalf said he knew that the road would be uphill for him and his black legislative colleague. Whites, even those who in conversation seemed to believe in the idea of racial equality, would not go along with the suggestion of putting their names on an anti-discrimination bill, especially one involving housing. White legislators generally believed that their constituents wanted no law that would restrict them in their choices of whom to sell to or that might bring large numbers of black residents into their communities. Baker and Metcalf kept their bill at the top of their respective agendas for several years. They saw their opportunity in 1954, when the Democrat Averell Harriman was elected Governor.

There were continuing obstacles, but the bill finally passed in both houses and was signed into law by Gov. Harriman on April 15, 1955. Newspapers slowly began noting its significance as perhaps a harbinger of things to come in dealing with *de facto* segregation in the North. But the law covered only 200,000 units throughout the state, those that had been built with government money or in some other way had used public funds. And so Bertram Baker and George Metcalf knew they had considerably more work to do.

In January 1956 they introduced another bill that, according to Metcalf, "covered multiple dwellings [three or more apartments] and clusters of 10 or more homes on one site." The bill, said Metcalf, "broke open new frontiers in social legislation."

The opposition this time was greater. Baker sent a letter to his colleagues saying that the bill was absolutely needed. "Probably 99 percent of the private developments rent or sell only on a segregated basis," he wrote, according to Metcalf. "For the minority family, our system of free competition has broken down in the field of housing. In looking for shelter, it enters a market restricted on the basis of race and religion."[6] But such appeals fell flat, and the two legislators deemed it necessary to approach the press and take the message to voters around the state.

Up against so many obstacles in getting support for their strengthened measure, Metcalf said, "Baker and I devised a new strategy," which was to "carry our message directly to the people, trusting that the pressure would ultimately move their representatives." They held hearings around the state, something pretty much unheard-of in those days.

Decades later, Metcalf spoke glowingly of Baker's rhetorical gifts and his ability to connect with other politicians. "He was a really profound speaker because he seemed to know how to get into the heart of something," Metcalf said.[7] "He could make the whites feel ashamed of themselves."

Metcalf described a confrontation between Baker and a well-known conservative Assemblyman from Brooklyn named Vito Battista:

> Baker and I decided that the publicity of a public hearing might prove enormously helpful. Indeed, it . . . gave Baker a chance to confront Vito P. Battista, a white ethnic from Brooklyn, representing the United Taxpayers Party and Property Owners of Greater New York.
>
> Battista loudly proclaimed his support of civil rights, but not legislation which, in the name of civil rights, endangered private property. "This is forced personal integration," he cried. "The issue is not whether any racial or religious group is superior or inferior to another, the issue is whether a person, regardless of his race or religion[,] is to be free to exercise fundamental rights guaranteed by the Constitution."
>
> While he was holding forth, Baker became rigid and as soon as Battista stopped to catch his breath, he broke in. "I don't think there is any common ground on which we can meet, based on your remarks, but just answer me this one question: Do you believe that a property owner has the right to say to you, all other things being equal—your financial responsibility, your character, your ability to pay—that he will not sell or rent to you solely on the basis that you are an Italian?"
>
> "Mr. Baker," he answered excitedly, "I have been denied that many times. It is his right, if that is what he wants to do, if that is his property. If he doesn't like me because . . . he might think I belong to some criminal element, then he has the right to tell me I don't want you. He might want you instead."
>
> "I said solely on the basis of your race or your national origin or your religion," Baker insisted.[8]
>
> "I don't know if he would discriminate on that basis," Battista answered, trying to avoid the question.
>
> "I say, do you believe he has the right to?" Baker asked in one final fruitless effort to get a "yes" or "no." Battista refused to reply directly.

Eventually, with the hearings and the interest they generated, Baker and Metcalf were able to get another, stronger bill passed in both houses of the legislature and signed into law in 1961 by Governor Nelson Rockefeller. Over the following years their efforts to strengthen that law continued, with varying degrees of success.

Years later, summing up the benefits of the Metcalf–Baker laws, Metcalf wrote that they "were enormously helpful in breaking down the support [that] society gave to prejudice. They stripped away legitimacy from discrimination. They helped to educate the public to do a self-evaluation of its own conscience. The bigots were by and large squelched but not eliminated. In the dark corners of our communities, they still operate, but furtively like bookies and numbers operators in the streets." Metcalf sadly concluded that "like the early optimism which greeted the Supreme Court's 1954 *Brown v. Board of Education* decision on schools, the ardent hopes of the [Metcalf–Baker] architects proved unattainable."[9]

Author Commentary: The '50s, the Boss, and Me

In the early 1950s, as Bertram Baker began his rise to power, my mom and dad and I were living in the Fort Greene Public Houses. Public housing projects would later earn horrible reputations as places of gang warfare and hard drugs. But back then Fort Greene was integrated, and its residents were among the up-and-comers in the borough. Our neighbors across the hall were like my godparents. Their daughter and son were like my cousins. The Colluccis had a mixed marriage. The father, my Uncle Bob, was Italian American and the mom, my Aunt Pearl, was Russian Jewish-American. Living on the floor with us was a family with the last name Baden. Their teenage son Michael would go on to become one of the most distinguished medical examiners in the country, gaining wide national attention in 1994 when he gave expert testimony at the murder trial of former football star O. J. Simpson. I sometimes think it probable that my grandfather used his clout as a new member of the New York state Assembly to get us into the Fort Greene Houses. The project was at the eastern edge of Downtown Brooklyn, right across from the lovely historic Fort Greene Park, which was named for Nathaniel Greene, a hero of the Revolutionary War. Bertram Baker's other daughter, my mom's sister, Lilian, was living at that same time with her family (husband John Bemus and their three children) in the Marcy Projects, about a dozen blocks to the east of us, closer to Bedford Stuyvesant. In those days, using political clout to get your family into a public housing project did not elicit the outrage and tabloid headlines that would be the case two decades later, in the coming era of political reforms.

My dad, Wilfred, was studying law at Brooklyn Law School at that time when we were in Fort Greene. He was also in the early moments of a horrible addiction to alcohol, which kept him away from home, as well as away from success at school. One day in Fort Greene remains in my memory like none other. It was 1952. I was in my bed and heard my mother in another room struggling in pain as she tried to move her-self. I remember shouting, in my three-year-old voice, "What's wrong, Mommy? What's wrong?" It turns out that was the day the polio epi-demic put its ugly arms around my mother. "I can't walk," she said with a simplicity that almost equaled her agony. I recall feeling a searing power-lessness, but nowhere near the pain my mom seemed to be feeling.

Whether an ambulance came to rescue her, or she called my grand-parents Bert and Irene Baker and they came over, I don't know. Polio was a home-wrecker and a killer in that era. The outbreak wreaked havoc on the United States in the years after World War II. In 1952 alone there were more than 57,000 cases, leaving more than 3,000 dead and more than 20,000 paralyzed. Mom began receiving therapy for her paralysis.

There was no way my maternal grandparents were going to let a suffering daughter and grandchild stay in circumstances such as those, the daughter unable to walk and dejected, the son-in-law drunk and absent most of the time. So Marian Baker Howell and her son Ronnie (me) went to live with the Bakers at their three-story brownstone in Bed-Stuy. It had been built in 1886 and stood firm. To me, it was like a magic ship on the high seas. The bedrooms were on the top floor and at night one could see the dark blue sky, stars, and moon pulling with a gentle tenacity that made dreams easy. Mom spent much of her first months there in bed. She had grown up in that abode as the younger of two children, two girls, playing girlish games and skipping to school with girlfriends. She spent her late teen years learning secretarial skills expected of young ladies of her background. This was true even as her older sister, Lilian, went to Hunter College in Manhattan and became a schoolteacher. My mom turned out to be tougher than anyone knew. Her vigor and battlefield grit had been below the surface in her growing years. But I saw her moving daily across those parallel bars, arms gripping them as she struggled to get from one side to the other, pain seething from the cells in her legs all the way up to her face.

After about a year, Mom was walking again. Then she was taking jobs—at the Department of Motor Vehicles, at the State Attorney General's office. It was only many years later that I reflected on and assumed that Mom's state legislator father had had a hand in her getting those state jobs. She came to love working and being out with friends for an hour or two on weekends, as my grandmother saw to my needs. We would hear word from my father's family of the battles that rivaled his time as a U.S. Marine in the Pacific during World War II. He was seen sleeping on the streets. He tried at least once to commit suicide. He would come by sometimes to read to me. He would "recover" in later years with the guidance of Alcoholics Anonymous.

Bertram Baker was therefore effectively my father. He gave me the shore-side haven that offered glances into distant places, the top-floor window of my bedroom that made the distant world seem touchable on clear nights. I slept by myself in a tiny rectangular bedroom next to the bedroom of my grandparents. My room and theirs, six times larger, were separated at the far, street-side end by a multi-paned glass door that stayed shut—except for when my grandmother came into my room to straighten it up, for a boy who, by expectation, could never do it with the same efficiency. My three cousins, Bertram Baker's only other grand-children from his only other daughter, my Aunt Lilian, had moved to Los Angeles in about 1954, there to start life anew. Aunt Lilian's husband, John Bemus, was a very fair-complexioned ex–Navy man from Mississippi who had been working at the Brooklyn Navy Yard after the war. The Navy had a reputation for being unfriendly to Negro workers of whatever skin tone. Besides that, John Bemus found the British-inflected world of his wife's West Indian parents to be at times pretentious and exclusionary for him. Gifted with a deep, melodious speaking voice and an ease with tools and numbers, he nevertheless showed no inclination for the efforts that would take him to law school and a likely future with the rising boss of black Brooklyn, his father-in-law. He thus contrasted with my father, who had been on the path to a career in law and perhaps in Bertram Baker's orbit, but whose weaknesses with the bottle yanked it all away.

At some point after she regained the ability to walk, Mom began dating a fellow named Gordon DelValle. Where they met, I don't know. Their relationship began in the mid-1950s, though Mom and Dad did not officially divorce until 1961. Gordon was Puerto Rican but looked like a fair-complexioned black person, with freckles, and spoke without a Spanish accent. Having "defeated" polio, Mom decided it was time for her and me to leave Bed-Stuy and make it on our own. So we packed up and headed west—like the pioneers of old—to begin life anew in Los Angeles, in the bungalow home of mom's sister, Aunt Lilian, and her family—her husband (my Uncle John) and their three kids (my loving cousins Jay, Lynn, and Diane). It was 1955. I was six years old and my grandfather's historic housing discrimination bill (Metcalf–Baker) was making its way through the state legislature and onto the desk of Gov. Averell Harriman. In Brooklyn I had been attending Our Lady of Victory grammar school and had been in the first grade.

California was, let's say, a very strange place for me. I remember my mom taking me to a nearby Catholic elementary school and, with me standing at her side, asking the nun on the first day of classes if she would be able to enroll me. The nun said no, that it was too late and there was no room. I have no idea what the tuition would have been, but likely not much more than the five dollars or so a month it had cost my mom for me to attend Our Lady of Victory in Bed-Stuy.

I'm guessing the nun was lying when she said there was no room for me. I say this without a lot of evidence. But the class was all-white, and in those days there wasn't much receptivity to having a black or brown kid mixing with the *blancos*.

I loved being with my cousins. We'd sit around the television at night and watch "The Mickey Mouse Club" on the tube. It was the early days of television. We were thrilled when Uncle John told us that while work-ing he had run into the leader of the Mouseketeers, Jimmie Dodd, and told him about us, and Jimmie responded that we must be "real Mouseke-teers." Can you get more cool than that? I attended the first and second grades there in South L.A., at a public school with my cousins.

Uncle John had a bunch of jobs, one of them as a Good Humor man driving an ice cream truck and selling cones. He was a great dad and uncle. He'd take us on trips to the beach, to Disneyland, to a cowboys' ranch where we saw re-creations of scenes from the 1800s when the pioneers first went out West. We sifted for gold on the shore and got to keep little bits of it in tiny bottles. At home we ate rabbit meat that Uncle John had bagged with his rifle. Mom's new boyfriend, Gordon, showed up in Los Angeles. How he supported himself, I don't know. But he went to the beach with us and everything else.

During our year and a half or so in Los Angeles, I assume, my mother was in regular communication with my grandmother Irene. My mother later would tell me she knew how much I missed my grandmother and how much I missed my grandparents' German Shepherd, Fella.

Next thing I knew, my mother announced we were moving back to Brooklyn and the Bakers' brownstone. I must have been overjoyed, as much as I loved being with my cousins.

Mom's boyfriend, Gordon, also returned from California to Brooklyn. The worst of it all was that, so I found out, Gordon was married with kids—and his two kids attended my school, Our Lady of Victory. One of the kids was in my third-grade class. In part because of Gordon, Christmas settled in my head as an unwelcome time of the year.

I didn't like Christmases much anyway. The one time in my childhood that my father came to the annual Baker Christmas dinner, he was flaming drunk and fell down the outside stairway, smashing his head. An ambulance came to take him to the hospital. Added to that was the fact that my grandfather was never at the Baker Christmas gatherings, which were held every December 25th at the home of my grandmother's sister Violent (Baker) Dash. We all assumed that my grandfather, the boss, was with his political buddies and his secretary, Miss Marie Smallwood. My grandmother had to put up with gauche references to her husband's absence. And I quietly felt her stoic embarrassment.

About 1957 or so my cousins and their parents came back to Brooklyn also. They stayed with me and Mom at Bertram and Irene Baker's Jefferson Avenue house for a couple of years.[10] They helped make Christmases fun. But sometimes Christmas was gloomy.

There was one Christmas when, before heading to Aunt Vi's, Mom and I went to the home of a relative of her boyfriend, Gordon. There was a Christmas tree there and all the supposed merry stuff. But there was also tension in the air. It had to do, I soon deducted, with resentment over Gordon's having left his wife and children. Gordon got into a fight with a man there, a fist-swinging, tumbling fight. Then, as Gordon was escorting us down the stairs, the other guy started yelling something in Spanish and Gordon ran back up after him, as everyone else screamed for them to stop. Mom and I left by ourselves and went to Aunt Vi's for the customary Baker family Christmas celebration. I remember once seeing a photo of us all around the table at Aunt Vi's that evening. I had a bewildered and sad look on my face, as did my mom. But we never spoke of the incident at Gordon's house to anyone, not even to one another.

An end to the relationship with Gordon was about to arrive. On a sunny afternoon my grandfather Bertram Baker came home and told me to go out and buy him the *New York Daily News*. He gave me a nickel. When I started walking down the block, I saw Gordon pulling my mother, trying to drag her up the steps of a brownstone apartment building across the street. I ran to them at full speed, not thinking about traffic, and I went crashing into Gordon and attempted to pull him away. I was crying and he started crying and the whole thing was an incredible

mess. (He had sensed, it seems, that my mom wanted to end the relationship with him, and he was distraught and wanted to meet with Mom in
the apartment of someone they knew in that building.) Emotions high
and public, we walked toward Fulton Street, the three of us. Gordon
was babbling, I was silent, Mom was thinking, "How do I get rid of this
idiot?" We eventually got Gordon to leave, and Mom and I headed home.
In the coming weeks, Mom would take different routes home from her
job, wanting to avoid Gordon. Finally the whole Gordon episode faded
into the past. I never saw him again and neither did Mom.

How much my grandfather the boss knew about Gordon, I wasn't sure.
He never asked me why I hadn't come back with the newspaper he'd
told me to buy. Did he know what had happened? I used to think it was
possible. But then again, Bertram Baker kept his mind so full of boss-type
obligations that there was often little room for anything else. He could
just shrug things off. For instance, there was the time my friend Joe Jones
came over to the house when I was there by myself. Joe was from North
Carolina. He was very fair-complexioned, maybe could have passed for
white. Even at the age of fifteen Joe smoked and drank. He was sitting
with me in the dining room, chatting, when he looked at the mahogany
cabinet in the dining room and saw a nice fat cigar. "Whose is that?"
he asked. "Can I have it?" I shrugged. He lit it up and smoked it. The
boss and my grandmother were out and Mom was at work. The smell
dissipated.

The next day I was in the dining room reading and my grandfather
walked in. He asked, "Where's the cigar President Johnson gave me?" Fear
gripped my stomach like a sickness unto death. It felt like minutes but it
was only two seconds. "Oh well," the boss said and went back upstairs.
Lyndon Johnson had given Bertram Baker that cigar when Baker had
been at the White House that week for the signing of the 1964 Civil
Rights Act. Johnson also gave my grandfather one of the pens used in the
signings. My grandfather kept the pen. I learned to be thankful for little
things.

I Owed Bert Baker My Track Medals and Much More

The early 1960s took me to high school. Looking back from the vantage
point of half a century—in other words, from now—I'd have to say that
my considerable successes were due to my high school. And I owe it all to
my grandfather. You see, I had heard of Brooklyn Preparatory Jesuit High
School and thought it would be a cool place to go; but I took the exam

and apparently did not do as well as I should have. I was rejected. Not to worry. It was an institution popular among middle- and upper-middle-class Irish families, with strong familial links to the Democratic Party in New York City and New York state. One of the graduates was Bert McCooey, grandson of the early 1900s Democratic boss of all bosses in Brooklyn, John H. McCooey. Bert Baker liked the idea of his grandson's going to Brooklyn Prep. So he made phone calls, and in short order I had an interview with the school headmaster and was accepted. That's what you call "pull." I did well. I was moved right away into the Advanced Placement class, and my grades were often in the top ten among the 250 slated to graduate in 1966. For all four years I was the only black kid in my class.

Even my athleticism I owed to my grandfather. I had played in his Little League baseball organization in my young years. And it was my grandfather who led the American Tennis Association, the all-black national tennis group, where I learned how to play that sport. Distant though he seemed in his manners at home, never hugging me or shouting congratulations, it was so quietly clear to me, from his smile that didn't come easily, that he was proud of every track medal I brought home while running sprint races for Brooklyn Prep. "You're bringing honor to your school," he said once, just after coming into the house, just before going upstairs to his office.

When Brooklyn Prep had a Father's Day event in about 1963, I kept it to myself, but the school apparently sent notices home and my grand-father decided he should go. Not only did he decide to go to the dinner, but he arranged to have his protégé Larry Pierce come with us and take us. Larry Pierce was chief of the State Division of Youth under Governor Nelson Rockefeller. He had a state car and driver who chauffeured us. Pierce was on his way up in the world. He had started as an ambitious lawyer in Bertram Baker's United Action club. Then he went on to be an assistant prosecutor. Later he was to be named a U.S. District Court Judge and then a U.S. Court of Appeals Judge. Larry, as everyone in our family called him, was also a devout Catholic, as I was at the time. He sat with me and my grandfather at the table, and Bertram Baker made a big impression with the Jesuits that night. Maybe that's why I never felt any overt discrimination during my years at Brooklyn Prep. Everybody knew Bertram Baker was a bigshot. And I was the bigshot's grandson.

8
Master of Black Compromise

Through much of the mid- and late twentieth century, many black leaders would shun an intellectual association with Booker T. Washington. Washington was known as the great black compromiser, the one who insisted that blacks tone down their militancy and instead seek gracious common ground with white folks who might share certain goals with them. He argued that blacks should focus on setting up their own businesses and other institutions, embracing a "separate but equal" view, a view that civil rights activists by the mid-1950s were roundly rejecting.

Bertram Baker did not publicly acknowledge a deep connection with the spirit of Booker T. Washington. But it was clear that Washington, who died in 1915, the very year Baker came to America, had a significant impact on him. Not only did Baker write for the newspaper, the *New York Age*, that Washington had purchased through intermediaries in the early twentieth century, but Washington's institution of higher learning, the Tuskegee Institute, was the birthplace of black American tennis. Baker came to have a deep bond with both the sport and with Tuskegee. For it was on the tennis courts of Washington's Tuskegee Institute that Bertram Baker and his American Tennis Association held their national tournaments.

A month before the November 1948 election that made him the first black person ever elected to political office in Brooklyn, Baker gave a telling speech at an event at the Carlton Avenue YMCA, located on the fringes of Bedford Stuyvesant and neighboring Fort Greene. The gathering was held to raise money for the Y. Baker was there, of course, to win votes. The brief and very favorable article by Edgar Lefevre reported:

> The Club Room was packed to the walls as over 800 people listened first to Bertram Baker, candidate for election. In a brief but well thought out address to those present Mr. Baker was most convincing in an adaption of Booker T. Washington's great theme— "cast down your bucket where you are."[1]

Among the books found in Baker's library after his death was a 1905 edition of Washington's autobiography, *Up from Slavery*. Baker had placed in the book an index card with "page 219" written on it. And on that page was a pencil mark around the words that Baker drew from when speaking to the Carlton Avenue Y. In that section of the book, Washington offers readers his 1895 Atlanta Exposition Address. That was the much-circulated speech in which he asked blacks to show humility and graciousness in dealings with white people. In the address, Washington used the analogy of a ship lost at sea, needing water and calling out to a "friendly" vessel in its sight. The friendly vessel then sends a message to the lost ship, telling it to cast down its bucket into the water. The lost ship then cast its bucket down and pulls up "fresh, sparkling water from the mouth of the Amazon." Washington concluded:

> To those of my race who depend on bettering their condition in a foreign land or who underestimate the importance of cultivating friendly relations with the Southern white man, who is their next-door neighbor, I would say: "Cast down your bucket where you are—cast it down in making friends in every manly way of the people of all races by whom we are surrounded."[2]

Washington was roundly denounced by black leaders, notably the scholar W. E. B. Du Bois. They wanted a more aggressive stand on race issues and advocated supporting politicians who took strong anti-segregation positions.

Even Bertram Baker's most loyal admirers saw him as a consummate compromiser. And the episode that stood out for the way he sacrificed principles for political gain occurred in 1953. Baker several years earlier had surmounted a significant hurdle when he won election to the New York state Assembly. But there was a goal that remained uppermost in the minds of blacks still working diligently in the political arena, especially black lawyers. That was finally to elect a black judge in Brooklyn. And the forum in which the black achievers felt they most strongly needed a jurist of their color was the Municipal Court. The Municipal Court, which no longer exists, was the legal battleground for disputes involving less than $3,000.

There was broad feeling among blacks who appeared in Municipal Court that the clerks and judges showed disrespect to blacks. Clerks and judges of the court, who were largely Irish, "did not have high regard for black people," said Lawrence Pierce, then an attorney. "Essentially it was incivility."

He was referring specifically to the Second Municipal Court, located on Schermerhorn Street in Downtown Brooklyn, which served the Bedford Stuyvesant area. Pierce, who was a member of Baker's United Action club, was upset about what he saw and bemoaned that there were no black Municipal Court judges in Brooklyn and especially none at Schermerhorn Street, given that many of those there for cases, as well as many of the attorneys, were black. Other blacks saw the same lack of respect Pierce saw and decided that immediate action was needed. One of those blacks was Wesley McDonald Holder, who in those days was working as a clerk in the office of the Brooklyn District Attorney. He would often have to go to courthouses and watch criminal proceedings. He did not like what he saw. "Some of the things I saw while I was there I couldn't stomach," he said years later. He mentioned judges' "turning to a black lawyer and asking him . . . 'How do you plead?'"[3] In other words, to some white judges, the black lawyers, despite their suits and ties, looked like the alleged criminals.

A black immigrant from Guyana, Holder had a background in progressive causes in the city, such as the effort in 1935 to get Samuel Leibowitz elected Brooklyn District Attorney. He had a reputation as a militant and a black nationalist.

In the late 1940s, Holder founded and led the Bedford Stuyvesant Political League, which led the effort to finally get a black judge sitting on the bench of the Municipal Court. The attorney who emerged as the League's favorite candidate was Lewis Flagg. Flagg had moved to Brooklyn in the 1920s from Baltimore, where he had gone to law school, and by 1930 he had become president of a distinguished organization of black attorneys known as the Brooklyn and Long Island Lawyers Association. Way back in 1932, as an independent, Flagg ran for the Assembly seat in the 17th Assembly District of Bedford Stuyvesant, opposing white Democratic candidate George Stewart. That was even before Baker had thrown his hat into the political ring. Flagg didn't do well in that effort to win political office. Stewart received 12,870 votes. Flagg received 254 votes.[4]

In 1953, Flagg again took on the Democratic machine, but his chances of victory were much greater than they had been two decades before. Flagg's position in the black community was helped greatly by the fact that the lawyer chosen by Democratic leaders to be the official Democratic candidate was a white person, a Jew, named Benjamin Schor, who had moved into Bedford Stuyvesant for the election. Schor actually lived in Brownsville, still home then to many Jews who had stayed in the neighborhood despite the influx of blacks. It was common knowledge that Schor had rented a room in Bed-Stuy in order to have what could pass for an official residence there.[5]

Despite the almost universal appeal of Flagg to black voters in Bed-Stuy, Bertram Baker stayed faithful to the choice of his Democratic Party, and he announced to his followers at the United Action Democratic club that they would officially be campaigning for Schor. "He said, whatever you do in the voting booth is your own conscience . . . but we have an agreement. I've given my word," remembered Albert R. Murray, a Baker loyalist at the United Action club from the late 1940s.[6] The vast majority of the club members wanted Flagg to win. But they were also intensely ambitious people, very much wanting the jobs that would give them prestige and income to assure a decent living for themselves and their families. They felt it was unlikely they would advance in Brooklyn without Bertram Baker behind them. "[H]e was the only black outside of Harlem who had any clout in getting jobs," said Josephine Bravo, who started out as a schoolteacher and later, in the 1960s, became a female co-leader of the United Action club and was appointed New York state Secretary of Labor.[7]

So the club members, chilled at the thought that they might contribute to a Schor victory, collectively held their metaphorical breath. They hit the streets, handing out Schor cards and saying little if nothing to support their nominal backing of the interloping white candidate. Bertram Baker told the members of United Action that he was their boss and they were his followers. "I have explained to you that there's a discipline that goes with being part of a regular organization, whether it's Republican or Democrat," Lawrence Pierce recalled decades later. "That was the message. We have our job to do. . . . We went out, did our thing. . . ."[8]

In the Democratic primary, Flagg beat Schor by a small margin (4,503 to Schor's 4,365), and he went on to defeat his Republican opponent in the general election. There was celebration in Bed-Stuy. "A lot of the black lawyers in the community and people in the community [had] rallied behind the effort to get Flagg elected as the Dem candidate," said Pierce, "and, by golly, they pulled it off. And those who had rung doorbells for Ben Schor were not at all displeased. We were glad that a candidate like Flagg won."[9]

Holder and others who remained active in the Bedford Stuyvesant Political League saw Baker's position in the Flagg campaign as tantamount to race treason, and tensions remained high. Holder ran against Baker or Baker's candidates a number of times, but Holder never won. He complained that Baker used his resources with the Democratic organization to have the petitions of opponents invalidated, a common complaint in New York City in those days among challengers to Democratic incumbents.

The Democratic organization swiftly compensated Baker for his ongoing faithful support. The job that Bertram Baker wanted more than any other in the whole political marketplace in Brooklyn was that of district leader. Since the 1930s, the district leader of the 17th Assembly District had wielded the real power in Bedford Stuyvesant. That power involved the selection of candidates for various offices and patronage jobs, little jobs like clerical positions in government offices, as well as promotions in the local post offices; and bigger jobs, like positions in the District Attorney's office and judgeships.

In a sign of Baker's clout in the higher rungs of the Democratic Party, the state legislature in 1953 redrew district lines in his favor. They created a new district, squeezing into it more blacks so that it would be likely to elect Baker as the district leader. Before the legislature acted, the leader of the 17th district was an Irishman, Vincent Carney. (He had taken it over from his deceased brother, Stephen Carney.) Vincent Carney wanted to keep the 17th Assembly District with a fairly strong number of whites, so that he could remain in power. But the power brokers went with Bertram Baker, and they created a new 6th Assembly District.

And so, in 1954 there was to be held an election that would likely result in a black district leader. The political *cognoscenti* knew such a victory would be as historic, in practical terms, as Baker's victory in 1948.

For Baker, there was one problem. Holder, still smoldering from Baker's failure to support Flagg in the race-tinged campaign of 1953, challenged Baker for the leadership. And Holder's Bedford Stuyvesant Political League put up a black attorney, George Fleary, to take on Baker for his assembly seat. Baker's United Action Democratic club won both races by a three-to-one margin.[10]

Around this time, Democratic party bosses agreed to support two of Baker's United Action club attorneys for municipal judgeships. There was thus developing a growing sense among black lawyers that the only place to go, if you wanted to eventually get a local job with clout, was Baker's club. Holder's Bedford Stuyvesant Political League had an ability to gather street support in a crisis situation, as when the renegade attorney Lewis Flagg sought to be the first black judge. But Holder's League lacked the intense, meticulous organization of Baker's United Action club, and of course it lacked United Action's continuing link to the Democratic machine.

So it came to pass that Baker got one attorney after another appointed to judgeships. One was Brooklyn-born Oliver D. Williams, an elder statesman of Brooklyn's black legal community. Williams had been an active Prince Hall Mason in the 1930s and in fact had taken a position against Baker in the so-called Baker controversy of that era. Williams had also backed Lewis Flagg when Baker stood on the side of the white machine-backed candidate Ben Schor. But politics was about letting bygones be bygones, and Baker saw there was value in supporting Williams at this stage. Urged on by Baker, Mayor Robert F. Wagner in 1955 named Oliver D. Williams to a vacancy on the Second District Municipal Court. A year later Williams was elected, with Democratic organization backing, to a full ten-year term. In 1963, he became the first black state Supreme Court judge in Brooklyn and a lifelong friend of Bertram Baker's.

Next in line for a judgeship, after Williams, was Franklin Morton Jr. Morton was the son of Franklin W. Morton Sr., who almost became Brooklyn's first black elected official in 1920 but lost by one vote, in what blacks back then felt was a rigged count. With Frank Morton Jr.'s appointment in 1958, blacks had all three of the judgeships in the Second District Municipal Court.[11] And black attorneys who had previously winced in fear when they walked into that courthouse now felt a bit of relief.

In some ways, the truly difficult task for Baker was to get his opponents to put aside their deep grievances and resentments. Baker took steps to do that. For one thing, he arranged to have Marie Flagg, the wife of Judge Lewis Flagg, named as his co-leader, officially called the female co-leader, of the 6th Assembly District. Not only did Marie Flagg become the United Action co-leader, but her erstwhile political boss, Wesley McD. Holder, decided to seek greener pastures and join up with Baker also. Holder became a member of the United Action club, continuing to work at his full-time job in an administrative post in the Brooklyn District Attorney's office. All appeared to be going well between Holder and Baker, the erstwhile enemies.

But Wesley McD. Holder was a tough one in letting bygones be bygones. In 1957, when a seat opened up for a new City Councilman covering Bertram Baker's area, Holder wanted it. The problem was that Baker had only one person in mind for that job. And that was J. Daniel Diggs.

Holder's loyalists maintained that Baker had promised Holder he would get the Council nomination, an assertion Baker denied. Among the angriest Holder loyalists was Marie Flagg, whom Baker had chosen as his female co-leader, in a peace offering to Holder. Flagg said Baker "was wrong in denying the designation to Mr. Holder after he promised it to him." She added, "[B]ecause of Holder's long outstanding services to the community and his outstanding ability, he is preferred." Flagg went on to attack Baker as a chauvinist. He "has no regard for the woman's point of view in the community," she said. "Let's put a stop to it now."[12] Holder was rigid: "I was promised the nomination two years ago, and I don't intend to let Bert Baker renege on a promise to me." He also called Baker's choice for the nomination, J. Daniel Diggs, "not qualified" for the job of City Councilman.[13]

But most of those at Baker's United Action club knew Holder had little chance of getting Baker to turn his back on Danny Diggs.

Danny Diggs was born in Sumter, North Carolina, in 1894, served in World World I as a private, and came to Brooklyn as blacks were starting to coalesce into the Bedford Stuyvesant area following the war. He was one of the dozen or so men who met in Bertram Baker's house on Throop Avenue in 1933 to form the United Action Democratic Association. By the consensus of club members, Diggs was Baker's most trusted worker. Diggs had attended City College for a time. He wore the same style of three-piece suits, dark in color, as Baker. As did Baker, he prided himself on his paunch, rubbing it frequently. Also like Baker, he had the habit, especially before embarking on a spiel among friends, of vigorously pushing his tightened lips out, like a child imitating a kiss, and then retracting them. Diggs was involved in central Brooklyn real estate. He was not wealthy, but he earned a decent living as a broker, finding apartments for hundreds of black renters coming into the neighborhood. That meant he was able to win lifelong friends, especially among those who had arrived as part of the Great Migration.

When it came to the prime work of clubhouse members—getting

votes—United Action old-timers said no one was better than Diggs. Those trusted with turning out the voters on election day were precinct captains. And Diggs was the general among the captains. Nobody could surpass him in getting Bed-Stuy registered voters to pull levers for Bertram Baker's candidates. "His relationships went back too many years. . . . He had done a lot of favors for people. He had gotten me my apartment, a very fine apartment, at [a] very reasonable rent," said United Action club member Larry Pierce.[14]

Holder, Flagg, and others, angry at the choice of Diggs over Holder, bolted from the United Action club. Holder directed his own rebellious campaign against Diggs. But Diggs won the election decisively. He thus became Brooklyn's very first black member of the New York City Council.

Baker survived the 1950s intact. He continued calling the shots with black patronage. He gained positive attention in the media for his involvement with the Metcalf–Baker desegregation law and became widely known for his work with the American Tennis Association. And among the families of Bedford Stuyvesant, he made strong connections through his youth baseball teams: the United Action Little League and the United Action P.O.N.Y. League, which he created in 1955 with the help of local banks, such as the Brevoort Savings Bank, the Lincoln Savings Bank, and the East Brooklyn Savings Bank. Hundreds of neighborhood boys found refuge and even stardom in those leagues, the Little League for nine- to twelve-year-olds and the P.O.N.Y. (Protect Our Nation's Youth) League for thirteen- and fourteen-year-olds.

Every year, to raise money for community activities and to promote his club, Baker would hold evening *soirées* at the St. George Hotel in Downtown Brooklyn. And every year the club would publish a journal featuring ad space purchased by local businesses, as well as others seeking the attention of The Chief. On the pages of the journal was a hymn to Baker. It was titled "The Battle Hymn of the Sixth [Assembly District]." It was meant to generate the feelings of "The Battle Hymn of the Republic," which to many blacks contained the emotions of the hostility to slavery a century earlier. It had once in history been sung with words praising John Brown, the white man who led a revolt of blacks in slave-era Virginia in 1859. The lyrics for the "Battle Hymn of the Sixth" were written by a former club member, attorney Phillip J. Jones. Jones had attended the first United Action Democratic club meeting at Baker's Throop Avenue home in 1933.

The Battle Hymn of the Sixth
For many years we've waited for this grand and glorious day,
To elect our own to office in the Democratic way.
He has been in many battles teaching us the civic stand,
As he goes marching on.

CHORUS:
Forward, forward with Bert Baker—
Forward, forward with Bert Baker—
Forward, forward with Bert Baker—
To the job that must be done.

We have seen battle forces, he has always won the fight.
We have seen him conquer evil, he has always fought for right.
We will see him now the winner, he has made a gallant fight,
As he goes marching on.[15]

Yes, Bert Baker was riding high, and he would go higher still. Through the early 1960s, Baker and Metcalf kept working to strengthen their Metcalf–Baker bill, and the two names together strode from Baker's pursed lips with pride. Sometimes when he referred to the bill, the "Baker" would precede the "Metcalf."

In 1965, Baker rose to the highest point he would get to on the ladder of New York state government. It was then that he became the Majority Whip of the state Assembly. That was the highest state position ever held until that time by a black person in New York state government. It was a big deal for Baker's family and his neighbors also. It meant that his license plate number was 5. It was jaw-breaking back then to see a classy-looking black Chrysler with a number 5 plate. He was outranked only by four others in the state: the Governor, the Lieutenant Governor, the Speaker of the Assembly, and the President of the Senate. Plus, as the Assembly Whip, his $10,000-a-year salary jumped to $15,000. And in addition to that, he got another $1,000 for "administrative expenses." Put into perspective, he was making twice what well-paid city cops were paid.

The younger blacks coming into the state legislature admired Baker's attractive personality, his skills as a speaker, and his civility with colleagues. Black legislators, including Percy Sutton—who went on to a long career as a Harlem political power broker, becoming Manhattan Borough President and owner of a black radio station—had formed a group called the Council of Democratic Elected Officials. They pressured the Democratic leadership to give more power to black officeholders. Baker, at that point, was at the top of the list in terms of seniority. In addition to being named Majority Whip, he was selected by his Democratic colleagues to be Chairman of the Education Committee.

Other young black legislators who were part of that effort to increase the power of blacks in the state legislature were David N. Dinkins of Manhattan (who two decades later became New York City's first black mayor); Basil Paterson, a state senator during the late 1960s, who went on to be (in 1979) the first black Secretary of State of New York; Charles Rangel, then in the assembly, who went on to be Harlem's congressman from 1970 to 2017; and a tough young Assemblywoman from Brooklyn by the name of Shirley Chisholm, who served on the Education Committee chaired by Bertram Baker and would one day trek along her own path to the mountaintop.

Bertram Baker's chest stood out as he strode through the halls of the Assembly chambers in Albany or the parquet floors of his United Action Democratic brownstone in Brooklyn. He did so even as he sometimes pridefully rubbed his protruding belly, all the better to feel the comfort of having arrived and done a bit of good for himself and his loyal followers. The *tempora* and *mores* had changed since the 1700s, but Baker began to note connection between himself and the other Nevisian who found success as a politician in America. That, of course, was Alexander Hamilton. In 1957 Baker sponsored a resolution in the Assembly honoring Hamilton as hero of successive American generations. High-blown stuff. But Baker knew black people were experiencing a shift that was unique at the time to their race. Whites were moving out of central Brooklyn, as more and more blacks from the South came to join those native-born blacks and West Indian immigrants who had planted their feet there after World War I. Bertram Baker's neighborhood had been called the Bedford in 1920s, when he and other blacks started moving in. He lived in the mid-area between Bedford and what was being called Stuyvesant Heights. By the 1940s, the outside world was starting to refer to the whole swath as Bedford Stuyvesant. And through the 1950s whites were increasingly calling it a ghetto.

Author Commentary

It was 1962 or thereabouts, lunchtime on a sunny day, and I was walking from my Our Lady of Victory grammar school to my home on Jefferson Avenue in Bedford Stuyvesant. Strolling several feet ahead of me were two police officers.

The officers noticed my grandfather's parked black Chrysler sedan, with its low-number license plate and state Assembly shield. One of the officers gestured toward the car, then looked at the beautiful single-family brownstone where I lived with my mother and grandparents. "Must be somebody's chauffeur," he said dryly.

That remark woke me to a harsh truth about the way whites, especially the police, perceived the neighborhood in which I grew up. Where I saw beautiful homes, and yards where children played marbles and slapball, they saw a ghetto. Where I saw people who worked as train conductors and salespersons and doctors and lawyers, they saw the residents of a ghetto.

Don't get me wrong. I don't mean to say that mine was the childhood of "Father Knows Best." The scourge of gang warfare that took hold of the city in the late 1950s struck fearsomely in Bedford Stuyvesant. When I was about eleven, I listened intently with a group of friends as a skinny little teenager who lived a block from me regaled us with tales of battles with rival gangs. I wondered how much was fiction and how much fact. Within a year came the news he had been shot to death in a street fight several blocks away.

The violence committed by a few seemed to become a convenient excuse for the city's police, who appeared to write off communities like Bedford Stuyvesant as morally intractable and unworthy of protection. When I was about nine years old, I saw a policeman from the 79th Precinct stand in a grocery store and observe coldly while an enraged black woman repeatedly swung a long kitchen knife at a black man. As a crowd gathered and tried to subdue the woman, the white grocer locked the glass door to his store. He and the officer stood and watched until the incident ended without bloodshed.

Whites in those days would say that Bedford Stuyvesant was not the nice place it was in the 1920s, when the Irish and other whites lived in the homes and ruled the streets. But I knew I preferred my Bed-Stuy to the old Bedford neighborhood of the 1920s, when my grandparents and other blacks were starting to move in. My grandmother used to speak of how groups of Irish boys would gather outside the family home at Throop and Jefferson avenues and yell cruel racial epithets, especially when she was there alone.

Mid-century Bed-Stuy was fine with me, call it a ghetto or whatever you wanted to call it. During my summer days, I played baseball with the Little League and P.O.N.Y.[16] League baseball teams that my grandfather had established in 1955. At first my family didn't want me to be part of the leagues. They had thought there might be gang members joining, like those in the Chaplains or the Bishops. But they came to see that baseball was good for me and the other neighborhood boys. I played first base, and some of the guys went on to play professional ball, like Rusty Torres, who was later with the Yankees and the Chicago White Sox. I had a photo of me with Rusty, when we were on Bertram Baker's All-Star team, Rusty from the Rockets and me from the Bears. But, damn it, I can't find the picture! When not playing baseball I and my partners from neighboring blocks would walk toward Bushwick, challenging other boys to games of stickball.

Between 1940 and 1950 the black population of Brooklyn doubled, to about 208,000, as 50,000 whites departed.[17] Bedford Stuyvesant thus, in the 1950s, was entering what outsiders considered to be a decline. One-family homes were being broken into apartments and rented out to families who had moved from elsewhere in New York City and from the South. And nearby public housing projects turned into lower-income areas, where gang fighting and later drugs became troublesome. The Chaplains of Bed-Stuy, one of the roughest street gangs in the neighborhood, feared the Chaplains of the Fort Greene projects, where I had spent the first three years of life, peacefully in a different era.

In 1947, Jackie Robinson came to Brooklyn as a Dodger, the first black professional baseball player in history. Bertram Baker, then a Confidential Inspector in the office of the Brooklyn Borough President, was part of a committee that raised money and held a welcoming party for Robinson at Ebbets Field. Robinson's first home for him; his wife, Rachel; and their baby boy Jack was in an apartment on MacDonough Street in Bed-Stuy. But while Jackie loved being a Dodger, he didn't seem to want to be a Bedford Stuyvesant resident for too long. Within about a year, he and family moved to East Flatbush, which then was mostly white; and then to St. Albans, Queens, and then to Connecticut. Poor Bed-Stuy.

By the time I was about ten years old and living with Bertram Baker, whites were leaving in a steady stream. Those who stayed behind were mostly Jews who owned grocery stores, candy stores, pharmacies, and hardware stores. But even they fled after the riots of 1964. Having lived through this era, I can understand why those disturbances were called rebellions. From the safety of my home, I heard gunshots ringing out through the night and the smashing of store windows. An older friend of mine was shot in the leg by police as he allegedly tried to help himself to a television at a shop on Fulton Street. Billy Bish was like an older brother of mine, and the incident hit me and the Bakers hard. Billy used

to take me to the Little League games when I was a batboy, aged seven
and eight. My grandfather and grandmother trusted him in large part
because his family lived there on Hancock Street and the Bish boys—
Billy and two of his brothers—used to take care of the United Action
club, cleaning it and looking after it when Baker and the others left to go
home. (I should update you and let you know that Billy, after being shot
by cops, was released from jail, served in the Air Force, and then went
back to using drugs. He lived as a homeless guy for years and then—by
the grace of a loving family—found sobriety and happiness after his
seventh decade. One of the Bish brothers went on to become a city police
officer, another worked as the district manager for a state Assemblyman,
another entered the ministry, and the fifth became a community activist.
The only sister, Jeannie, a nurse, was the loving force that held the siblings
together, leading to Billy's recovery.)

Besides the shooting of my "brother" Billy, other incidents hurt my
heart. One had to do with the family of Gilly Turner, who lived down the
block from us on Jefferson Avenue. One day Gilly's younger sister, in her
early teens, was in the street and was approached by another girl, who
was jealous of the sister's affection for some guy. The other girl pulled
out a knife and stabbed Gilly's sister, mortally. A dutiful neighbor rushed
down to Throop Avenue near Fulton Street, running the six blocks from
Jefferson, to tell Gilly's father, who owned a barber shop there. Gilly's
father had a heart attack, sank to the floor, and died. The raging insult,
perhaps more than the father's death, was that the killer spent not more
than several weeks in jail, and Gilly's family had to see the slayer strolling
around the neighborhood freely. I remember reading a book in my youth
in which the writer asserted that black killers of black people in central
Brooklyn in those days would rarely, if ever, do more than six months
in jail. During and after college I would show my empathy with Gilly,
buying marijuana from him and sitting with him in his dimmed room,
listening to Motown music and learning about his family's background in
the South and his partial Native American heritage.

For all my grandfather's absorption with his life in the political sphere,
people on the streets knew him pretty well. My closest friends feared
him in the filial way that I did. And while some were turned off by
Bertram Baker's abruptness or his perceived highfalutin way of talking,
many were more than impressed with the defiance Assemblyman Baker
sometimes showed around white people. I think this was especially true
of those recently up from the South. Among my closest southern friends
was Johnny Jones (no relation to the previously mentioned Joe Jones).

We bonded at Our Lady of Victory grammar school. He started attending there when his mom, who had been cleaning homes and doing other work, was able to afford to bring him up from Alabama, along with his grandmother, who had been caring for him there. Johnny was big for his age and muscular. He was a heavy hitter on our Little League team, the Tigers. It was Johnny who first told me about the Ku Klux Klan and about life in that part of the country that I knew only through television reports of the attacks on civil rights protesters.

One day, when I was about eleven years old, Johnny and I were in the back yard playing catch. My grandfather came by and told us to take a bunch of fliers from his office and go over and hand them out across from the polling place at P.S. 44, two blocks away. Of course, we did as we were told. Johnny seemed intrigued. I think his mom liked the idea of Johnny's hanging out with the grandson of Brooklyn's black boss. As we politely gave fliers out to adults passing by, we heard somebody screaming at the top of his voice inside the school, where the voting booths were. We crossed the street to get closer and look inside. It was my grandfather yelling like a maniac at a stony-faced white police officer whom Baker was accusing of rudely touching one of his female poll workers. Baker pulled out a slip of paper and a pen. "Give me your name!" he yelled. And the officer did so, gripping his nightstick tightly with both hands. There was otherwise nothing but silence. Baker shouted that he was going to see the commander of the precinct, who would sometimes show up at the opening of the baseball season when dignitaries came for the opening parade of Baker's Little League and P.O.N.Y. League. Things quickly started to return to normal, with poll workers returning to their tables and voters to the booths. Johnny was visibly stunned by the sight of a black man yelling at a white police officer, without getting arrested, beaten, or shot. As we walked back to give out more fliers, Johnny's face was frozen. Finally, he blurted out, "Boy, your grandfather told that white motherfucker off." I was just thinking, Yeah, but you wouldn't want to live all the time around all that yelling.

Being the Grandson of a Master of Compromise

I confess that I was a bit self-conscious about being the grandson of the boss. Once I was at the home of my friend Joe Jones, the guy from North Carolina (who was no relation to Johnny Jones from Alabama). Joe's aunt introduced me as the grandson of Assemblyman Baker, upon which a drunk guy started ranting about how he had once gone to the United

Action Democratic club and tried to give money to Bert Baker for a job, and Bert Baker told him to get out of his club and not come back. Joe's aunt was really embarrassed. She steered me and Joe out of the house.

But I didn't really have it hard. Some years later, fate would put me in my place and tell me to chill out regarding my hypersensitivity about being the grandson of Bertram Baker. One evening in the summer of 1981, when I was in my early thirties, I was roaming around Harlem, where I had an office as a reporter for the *New York Daily News*, and where I hung out quite a bit in bars, with eyes and ears open for good stories.

So I got to a familiar darkened nightspot, and I began sipping a beer as I sat and chatted with an old-timer from the neighborhood, who mentioned that he had recently met an interesting person at a community meeting. "Yeah, I walked over after it was over and said hi to Booker T. Washington," he said.

I choked and took a mental step back. "You said hi to who?" I asked.

He explained to me that the man he was referring to was Booker T. Washington III, grandson of the great Booker T. Washington, the original master of black compromise who was there in the background of so much of Bertram Baker's life. During his victorious campaign for the Assembly in 1948, the time he made history by becoming Brooklyn's first black elected official, Baker often quoted Booker T. Washington. In addition, Bertram Baker effectively took over Booker T. Washington's role as the boss of black American tennis. Despite these links, boss Bertram Baker had never met big boss Booker T. Washington. The older boss died in 1915, seven months after the younger one's arrival in America from Nevis.

I told my source that I really wanted to meet Mr. Washington's grandson—Booker T. Washington III—and I obtained his phone number. I called and was surprised at how easygoing and receptive he was, inviting me to his home on W. 137th Street, below the strip of Harlem brownstones known as Strivers' Row. It was a gorgeous place, and it reminded me of Bertram Baker's brownstone in Brooklyn. I remember being impressed by the classy wooden shutters protecting his rear windows.

Mr. Washington III was about forty years older than I was at the time, which was thirty-two. He lived with his charming wife, who worked as an administrator at a public school in the historic Weeksville section of Brooklyn. But he was a fundamentally lonely man, who loved books. And while proud of his profession as an architect, he clearly would have been pleased to pass all his days and evenings in the company of the texts that filled his library, which sat just off from the den where we talked—he smoking and talking, and I smoking, asking questions and taking notes.

On the surface, Mr. Washington was coping well. He defended his grandfather from the "Uncle Tom" label that the revolutionaries of my generation had pasted on him.

The grandson, as I reported it in the *Daily News*, said that his grandfather "took a 'ground floor' approach to gaining civil rights, encouraging blacks to learn a trade, even a humble one, to earn their keep and prove their social worth." He added that his grandfather's philosophy "helped build black businesses and other institutions, like Tuskegee."

"He was a revolutionist," the grandson declared, "in that he demonstrated at Tuskegee that blacks could move from poverty and helplessness to a reasonable degree of financial success."

But I quickly came to see a side of the grandson that revealed haunting legacies.

Mr. Washington the grandson told me how he used to love going through his grandfather's old manuscripts, wanting someday to put them into a book that he would publish. This lonesome scholarly activity appealed to the grandson much more than going out and speaking to community organizations and other groups that flooded him with invitations.

"Give me a break," he told me, chuckling as he looked over the pile of invites sitting nearby.

Then the grandson opened up to me about an incident that was as excruciating as it was telling, regarding the weight of his granddad's spirit upon him.

A heavy smoker, the grandson one day in the mid-1970s had finished going through some books left by his grandfather. Having decided he wanted to read that day's newspaper, he flicked his cigarette into the wicker basket near his desk and left. He purchased the newspaper at a stand nearby, and then, on his way back home, strolling toward his house, he saw fire engines outside the building. He approached in fear, his heart beating quickly, and he learned that his worst fears were true—the second floor, including the library on it, was ablaze.

As I wrote in the article, "Lost were 3,000 books, handwritten notes containing remembrances that his father, Booker T. Washington II, had passed down to him, and the unsalvageable manuscript he had been preparing on the life and times of his grandfather."

Mr. Washington had asked me not to write about the fire. "I'm not sure I could take it," he said. But I soothed him as best I could and told him that we and the wider world of black people would be better for the experience of learning what he went through. I only hoped that I wasn't bullshitting. There was no way I could have seen myself not publishing that part of the story. What I did do, though, was bury that part of the story far down into the piece, so it would not be as painful to him.

Funny how bonds like these are forged.

Exactly ten years later—in the summer of 1991—I was the cause of a fire at my own house on Midwood Street in Brooklyn. I had been cooking a duck in the oven and I irresponsibly left it in the oven cooking, as I went out in the car to buy some ingredients I needed. When I returned, and was around the corner, I could see billowing smoke coming from my block and several fire engines. Damn, I thought.

When I turned the corner I could see that all of the activity was in front of my own home. Fortunately, neither Marilyn nor Damani (then sixteen years old and out with friends) had been inside. The only one in there was the dog; and soon one of the firefighters came out holding our long-haired German Shepherd, Reina, by the collar. I was filled with joy at seeing her and grabbed and hugged her.

But I stood back and looked at the top floor where my den was and where I kept hundreds of books, some of them old and from the 399 Jefferson Avenue compound, having been left there by my grandfather. Up there also were audiotapes of interviews I had done with him, and pages and pages of scribbled-in notebooks about him and my beloved Bed-Stuy.

When the firefighters were finally done and exited the house, I darted in and then was pushed back by the lingering intensity of the heat. But I quickly recovered from that and ran up the two flights to my den, there to see that, though much smoke had entered, nothing had been destroyed.

Life was good to me that day. I refer to it as the day I got fucked by a duck.

Booker T. Washington III so clearly felt the weight of legacy. I could relate to it, for sure. I never wanted to be known as Ronnie Baker, as so many people called me as a child. How much heavier was that perceived load for my new buddy Booker T. the Third?

"People would expect me to be like my grandfather in every detail. And there's no way I could be like him," Mr. Washington told me.

And so in the early 1950s, when his wife from his previous marriage gave birth to his only child, a boy, he named him Lawrence.

At the time I wrote that article my grandfather was in his mid-eighties. I was not even aware of his deep, past connections to Booker T. Washington, the boss of black America. I may have mentioned my grandfather to Washington the architect. But I do not believe my grandfather was a significant part of the discussions with Mr. Washington, and I would visit him to chat a number of times before his death later in the decade. I do recall that when I went to visit my grandparents, soon after the article ran in the paper, my grandfather had a copy of it sitting on the dining room table. He had drawn a circle around the word "importantly" and proceeded to tell me it wasn't proper usage. I learned that the word had for sure seeped steadily into common usage by the late 1900s but was still resisted by many traditionalists. I stopped using the word for several years after that.

Even at that point, several years shy of his death in 1985, I knew only the salient details of my grandfather's public life. I was part of his private life. My cousin Diane Bemus Patrick, who would become the First Lady of Massachusetts in the early years of the twenty-first century, would note also that she was embarrassingly ignorant about what her grandad did in Albany as the boss of black Brooklyn. This was so despite the fact that all four of Bert Baker's grandchildren had traveled to Albany to be with him and meet Gov. Nelson Rockefeller in the 1960s. I remember saying to Rockefeller's guys that I didn't need to have my photograph taken with the Governor but that, yes, it would be great for him to sign his name in my notebook. My grandfather later found out and had a fit. There does still exist a great photo of a time when my three cousins—Jay, Lynn, and Diane—went to Albany and were not so stupid as to reject a chance for a picture with Rocky. They beamed in the photo. That was in 1962.

The 1960s was to be a long decade for Baker, with highs and also lows that are ever-present stuff in the lives of political bosses.

9
The 1960s, Political Reform, and Personal Tragedy

They were similar in many ways: Like Bertram L. Baker, Thomas Russell Jones possessed an ego that showed in his demeanor, his posture, the patrician manner in which he would pause while speaking, letting the listener know he was about to give important advice. Both men wore wire-framed glasses that suggested erudition and thoughtfulness. Baker and Jones were both sons of the Caribbean, Jones's family from the island of Barbados, considered by many the most British of the English-speaking isles, and Baker's family from Nevis.[1]

But there were also sharp differences between the two men that would ultimately affect the public positions they took and the ways they were perceived by others. Jones was fifteen years younger than Baker, and while he embraced his Caribbean roots, he had been born in Brooklyn, in 1913. Dark-complexioned and with a princely air that became more pronounced over the years, Tom Jones grew up in a tenement in South Brooklyn, not far from the East River shores that were the setting of the union gangster movie *On the Waterfront*. He had to fight continually as a boy, pushing back against the youths, blacks and whites, who poked fun at his proper English accent, which he said came from the stern demands of his dad, one of New York's first black podiatrists. Jones was able to take advantage of educational opportunities that had eluded Baker. He went to Hamilton High School (which was for commercial studies but nonetheless produced a proud group of successful blacks, including Oliver D. Williams, who in 1954 became, as previously mentioned, the second black judge elected in Brooklyn). He thereafter obtained a bachelor's degree from St. John's University and then a law degree from St. John's Law School. Further distinguishing himself from Baker, Jones fought for his country in uniform during one of the nation's major conflicts. Armed with his law degree, fit and trim, he was given the rank of first lieutenant in the segregated U.S. Army during World War II, and he served with forces that took part in the invasion of Normandy. Perhaps what made him stand out more than anything else from Baker was that Jones, in 1941, married a New Yorker named Bertha Kanter, who was Jewish.

When Jones came out of the army, he moved, like so many other blacks in those years, into the part of Brooklyn that by the late 1940s was becoming known as a black community, Bedford Stuyvesant. Jones decided that he had to find a way to make a decent living to support himself, Bertha, and their daughter (a son arrived later). Life was hard for a black attorney in those days. None of the firms were hiring blacks. Having political connections was the way to advance professionally, he decided. With that in mind, he walked over to the 17th Assembly District political club, on St. Marks Avenue near Kingston Avenue, with the hope of introducing himself and getting an appointment to meet the district leader, Steve Carney, or one of Carney's stand-ins. Even fifty years later, in 1995, as he recalled that visit, Jones showed evidence, in his voice and face, of the deep humiliation he experienced at Steve Carney's club.[2] "I lived up the street from there, about 40 yards or 50 yards away," he said. "And I walked into the club one night, and said, 'I want to join the club. I want to be a Democrat.' They looked at me like something the cat dragged in. 'Oh, you can't come here. You've got to go to the colored club on Jefferson Avenue.'"[3]

That colored club, said Jones, was Bertram Baker's United Action Democratic Association. (It was actually located on Hancock Street, one block over from Baker's Jefferson Avenue home.) Jones said many knew the United Action Democratic Association only as "Bert Baker's club." Jones stewed a bit over the experience at the St. Marks Avenue club. He soon began involving himself in an organization being formed by Wesley McDonald Holder, the Bedford Stuyvesant Political League. Jones said he came to detest what he saw in the Democratic Party: That blacks had to go to Bertram Baker for any favor or even to talk about local issues. Some of those in the Bedford Stuyvesant Political League maintained that blacks, when they attended district-wide meetings at Carney's St. Marks Avenue club, sat apart from the whites, in what they called a racial segregation. (Baker always denied that there had been segregation there.)

Jones's politics veered to the left. In 1955 he had represented Chinese workers whom the American government had accused of sending money to Communist China. The three workers were convicted, and Jones was unable to get the U.S. Supreme Court to hear an appeal.[4]

Jones eventually helped organize what he and his political allies would call the Unity Club, on the outer fringes of Bedford Stuyvesant, looping through an Assembly district that, while black and part of Bedford Stuyvesant, was outside Baker's new 6th Assembly district. In 1962, energized by the reformism of the 1960s, Jones decided to run for both Assemblyman and district leader. Those positions were held at the time by Sam Berman, who was Jewish. Berman, like other whites, could see that the growing number of blacks meant that sooner or later his time would be up. To try to corral at least some of the black vote, he decided to let a black man run for the Assembly seat against Jones, while Berman attempted to hold on to his district leader position. The leadership, after all, was where the patronage was.

And the black man Berman chose to go after the Assembly spot was none other than Wesley McD. Holder, the one who had long considered himself the anti-organization renegade. In the 1950s Holder had called out Baker as a white man's lackey. But the question in the minds of all politicians is, "Where's mine?" And now, after two decades of fighting in the political ring of Brooklyn and never winning a match, Holder saw his chance. But it once again escaped him. Tom Jones won both positions, the district leadership of the 17th Assembly District and the Assembly seat. And he thus became the second black Assemblyman and district leader in Brooklyn—the first one to hold those jobs having been Bertram Baker.

Jones stated that his priority was achieving not just jobs for well-connected lawyers but fair treatment of all blacks, especially the struggling poor, and trying to assure that blacks would be treated fairly by police.

Jones was setting the stage for the 1960s political players who would cause serious problems for Baker in the coming years. They were wrapped together under the umbrella of the reform movement, and they were out to upend the old-time boss roles of Baker and the regular Democrats over in Harlem as well. In Harlem there was J. Raymond Jones (not related to Brooklyn's Thomas Russell Jones), who in 1964 had become the first black chief of Tammany Hall (which the Democratic machine was called in Manhattan). J. Raymond Jones's struggles with reformers are detailed in his biography, *The Harlem Fox*.[5] There was also Hulan Jack, who in 1953 became the first black to be elected Borough President of Manhattan (actually, the first in any New York City borough, for that matter).

He also complained of his treatment at the hands of the reformers. He said they were behind accusations that led to his being convicted and sentenced in 1961 for dispensing political favors in return for expensive interior work on his home. That conviction led to his removal from the Borough presidency.[6]

Prominent among those giving support, financial and moral, to the so-called reformers were Eleanor Roosevelt and the rich Kennedy family. John F. Kennedy would win election to the U.S. presidency in 1960, and his brother Robert would begin setting his eyes on New York as a place where he, pursuing ideals espoused by the reformers, would become New York state's U.S. Senator. He won the election in 1964, and by virtue of money, personality, and contacts, he became one of the most powerful and influential figures in New York state and New York City. He would never be a friend of Bertram Baker's.

In Brooklyn, Baker maintained his allegiances with the regular Democrats, keeping his strong ties to the other bosses even as he attempted to work along with Tom Jones and the new black activists coming onto the scene. Hulan Jack's fall from on high, over in Harlem, was cataclysmic. But the dethroning process for Baker was slow.

When Robert F. Kennedy took office as a U.S. Senator in 1965, he began asserting his clout. Through his connections he set up the Bedford Stuyvesant Restoration Corporation, the goal of which was to promote businesses and boost the overall well-being of the neighborhood. And the black official who was the political liaison to the Bed-Stuy Restoration Corporation was Thomas Russell Jones.

Yes, Bertram Baker knew that times were changing. The most explosive transformations were occurring in the American South. The historic civil rights demonstrations were being led by the Rev. Martin Luther King Jr. and a young Alabama-born man named John Lewis. King would be assassinated like other prominent black activists of the era, and Lewis would go on to be elected to the U.S. Congress from Georgia, serving from 1988 to the writing of this book. The closest Brooklyn would come to seeing a steady stream of King/Lewis—type protests was through an organization known as Brooklyn CORE. Brooklyn CORE was the local chapter of the national civil rights group, the Congress of Racial Equality. During its first years in Brooklyn, CORE was composed largely of white activists of the kind who were identified with members of Thomas Russell Jones's Unity Democratic club. The group conducted interracial protests, such as the one against the racially discriminatory policies of building contractors. Outside the site where Downstate Medical Center was being built, Brooklyn CORE in 1963 conducted loud and angry marches that led to the arrests of many hundreds of protesters. The story of Brooklyn CORE's existence as an interracial protest group was told by the scholar Brian Purnell in his 2013 book *Fighting Jim Crow in the County of Kings: The Congress of Racial Equality in Brooklyn*. As Purnell points out, Brooklyn CORE by the mid-1960s would begin a transformation into a militant black nationalist unit whose members would veer off into various other organizations. Some of the personalities and organizations that sprang from that chapter of black Brooklyn history would strongly shape black Brooklyn in the years and decades after Bertram Baker's retirement and his death. Among them, notably, were Al Vann of the African-American Teachers Association and Sonny Carson, who would become the post–civil rights–era leader of Brooklyn CORE. Carson would also be convicted in connection with a murder and become one of the most controversial black activists in end-of-the-century black Brooklyn. Bertram Baker had to deal with these emerging personalities in the early and mid-1960s. He did not identify with them. He would not have called any of them his heroes. In fact, Bertram Baker is not even mentioned in Purnell's book. But he was in fact at those Downstate protests, and he did appear in court to give public relations–type support to the arrested demonstrators. He also designated some of his lawyers to represent some of those arrested. Baker operated in the slick way that pinstriped survivors do, the way he did in the 1950s as he showed his mastery of the art of compromise, using the get-along tactics of the man who sat always beneath his conscious political mind, Booker T. Washington.

Bertram Baker surely could see the end of the line in the visible distance.

But the end didn't come quickly, not for one as smooth and skilled in the game of local politics as Baker. The story of Baker's rise to the very top was a story of daring and deals. It was a game played by high-end slicksters, often with impressive words and often with silence. The most effective deals in old Brooklyn were not made on pieces of paper, nor with Yeses and Nos, but with winks and nods.

After being in the minority for thirty years, things were finally looking up for the Democrats in state government in 1964, but it was not the Democratic Party regulars who were the prime movers in the shift, but rather the reformers, led by New York Mayor Robert F. Wagner. Wagner had once been firmly entrenched in the Democrats' Manhattan Tammany Hall organization, but he began to turn against the old ways, for reasons of personal ethics as well as a sensing of the shifting political winds.[7]

In the last weeks of 1964, the time had come for the Democrats in the state Assembly to assert themselves. They had won a majority. They would rule. But a first order of business was to select the Speaker of the Assembly, the person who would be the prime mover when it came to deciding which bills would be submitted and passed, as well as who would get desired political appointments. The speakership of the Assembly was one of the most powerful positions in the state, putting the Speaker close to the governor in the wielding of clout.

On one side of the Democratic divide at this point were the Brooklyn old-time regular Democrats, whose leader was Stanley Steingut. Steingut's father was one of the first Jewish political powerhouses in Brooklyn, gaining increasing influence as he cut deals with the still-dominant Irish. Irwin Steingut, the dad, had come out of eastern central Brooklyn, and he was a harbinger of things to come, in the sense that Jews were beginning to assert themselves politically, to be followed soon by the Italians and then the blacks, and then (much later in the century) Puerto Ricans and other Latinos. In 1964 Irwin Steingut's son Stanley felt that this was his moment to shine. And so he put out the word, especially among the Assemblymen from Brooklyn, that if they wanted to be assured of decent treatment with respect to their choices for judgeships and other appointments, they should go along with the regular organization and assure the victory of Stanley Steingut as the next Speaker of the Assembly.[8]

But Steingut's ambitions were checked by the fact that another Brooklyn politician also wanted that job. That was a well-spoken Italian-American lawyer named Anthony J. Travia. His supporters made the case that it was only right and fair that the leadership of the Assembly should go to him, by virtue of his steadfast work in the party. In the background, though not as openly shared, was a sense that Travia was the more presentable leader for the party. He was admired for his informed eloquence, and several years later he would go on to become a federal judge. He could stand, without notes, and speak to a roomful of colleagues, entertainingly and informatively, for forty minutes.[9] Appreciating that kind of person, Wagner and others, such as the Kennedys and other reformers, threw their support behind Travia.

Both Baker and Tom Jones had lined up with the regulars. Jones later in life admitted that he was a bit divided about his choice. He felt somewhat skittish about the compromising of his values in lining up with Steingut—but he had come (painfully) to learn values of compromise, and he knew also that in Brooklyn's Democratic Party, being with the regulars was the way to get things done for yourself and your people.

Baker and Jones were crucial in the sense that the votes of the total number of Assemblymen were evenly split. If anyone at all bolted, that person
would be the key to victory for the would-be leader in question, Steingut
or Travia.

Jones recounted that he had received calls from the reformers Wagner
and Travia, who had asked him what it would take to get him to come
over to their side. Jones told them that he honestly liked Travia but that
he had already given a commitment to Steingut and couldn't go back on
his word.

"I didn't know how to be a politician in that circumstance," Jones declared somberly, saying of his ultimate vote for the regular organization
and Steingut. "I agreed that I would vote with him against Tony Travia, so
Stanley could become Speaker." Of his meetings with Wagner and Travia,
he said that perhaps he should have negotiated with them to try to get
some favors for switching his vote. "I didn't get commitments because I
wasn't smart enough to do that," he said.[10]

Baker, a tried-and-true regular organization man, had been expected
to go with Steingut, and he had been prepared to do so. But he didn't.
"Bert and I [had been staying] with Stanley and held the boat in balance. Bert's vote or my vote would have tilted it," Jones recalled many
years later. But "Bert broke. . . . Bert moved first against his old friend
[Steingut]." Jones added, "That's politics." Baker went on to give an ardent, almost preacher-like speech on the floor of the state Assembly, explaining why he was voting for Travia. The *New York Times* quoted Baker
as speaking passionately and "with a West Indian accent" as he made "an
emotional appeal" on Travia's behalf, declaring that the rejection of Travia would take the legislative body to a "day of infamy."[11] Shown on local
television stations, his voice rising as he came to the declaration that he
was casting his vote for Travia as the next Speaker, Baker was in the lime-
light for a few days.

"There should be little question as to the man who is justly entitled
to fill this position by virtue of his service and experience as the party's
spokesman in his present position as Minority Leader," Baker said. "Inter-
party differences and sectionalism should play no part in this selection. We
are called upon as elected representatives of the people to furnish responsible leadership, and this type of leadership can best be given by one who,
with devotion and sincerity, has carried the banner of the minority in
the Assembly through these many difficult years—that man is Minority
Leader Anthony J. Travia. I shall cast my vote for him as Speaker of the
Assembly."[12] Baker was pictured in newspapers afterward shaking hands

with Travia, the two men in glory. When the final vote came and Travia was elected, "Assemblyman Bertram L. Baker led Mr. Travia, who seemed shaken, to the big leather Speaker's chair on the rostrum."[13]

Reasons suggested for Baker's shifting from Steingut to Travia varied. Baker said he had learned that Steingut held secret meetings with someone Baker distrusted. Therefore, he could no longer trust Steingut, and he decided to back Travia. But more cynical suggestions about Bertram Baker's motives emerged.

Steingut allies and journalists came up with other eye-grabbing reasons for the switch: They said that Baker took the old-fashioned route of basing his action on "boodle," crass patronage that came from promises never written down, and certainly never notarized, but generally honored. Some would define the old term "boodle" as a bribe payment. The reward in this case was said to be a judgeship offered to Albert R. Murray, one of Baker's young and very much trusted toilers in the United Action club. The charge was reported in the *New York Times*,[14] and the *Amsterdam News* followed up with a headline based on a quote from Baker, who said, "I Took No Bribe."[15]

Al Murray was one of the southern-born World War II veterans who had come to Brooklyn after the war. He had walked into Bertram Baker's club, hoping for help in building a career of service and influence (as well as income). There were some in the club, notably the fair-complexioned and proper-speaking James Shaw, who were said to look down their noses at Murray, whose grammar was not always of the proper variety or with noun–verb agreement. Besides, Murray had a pronounced black twang that never receded with the passing of his years in Brooklyn. But he was a devoted worker in the club, and he was smart. Baker helped get Murray into Long Island University and then into Brooklyn Law School with letters of reference. His mind on money, in addition to patronage, Murray went into local real estate, eventually becoming a partner with a Jewish broker, Abraham Kaufman. Through Baker's United Action club, Murray became an Assistant Prosecutor in the office of the Brooklyn District Attorney. He did not get his name in the papers handling murder cases, but he did steady daytime work, and he was able, like others, to leave after sufficient hours of work and go to his other job, which in Murray's case was real estate. Because of his contacts and secure income, Murray was part of the United Action club's backbone. It was Murray who helped get local banks to support the hundreds of boys in the Little League and P.O.N.Y. League, the baseball organizations for local youth sponsored by Baker's club. Murray was comfortable. But a black robe was appealing and a sign of ultimate success for a lawyer like himself; and he had made it clear to Baker over the recent years that he wanted that or something like it.

In an interview a quarter-century after the Travia victory, Murray said that he did not believe Bertram Baker was capable of accepting anything that could be described as a bribe for Baker's vote. But Murray did acknowledge that, unknown to him at the time, Baker had in fact arranged with then-Mayor Wagner (who was aggressively backing Travia for the speakership) to have Murray's name submitted to fill the term of a Criminal Court judge who had died. "The first thing I knew about it was the 6th of January [about two weeks before Baker actually cast his vote on the floor of the Assembly for Travia]," Murray said. Murray was leaving his home on Jefferson Avenue. "I went out to get in my car to go to the office and a white man was across the street talking to a neighbor; as I came out he spoke to me, and I said, 'Yeah, can I help you?' And then he identified himself and said 'Your name's been submitted to the mayor's office for a position on the bench and I'm supposed to be doing the investigation.' And then I called Mr. Baker. And that's the first time I knew that he had made a deal with Wagner."

As for Wagner's reaction to the boodle reports, he told the *New York Times* reporter: "I did talk one time to Mr. Baker after he came out for Travia on his own about the possibility of having a Negro judge from Brooklyn." He also defended himself by saying that any candidate would have to go through the standard screening process.

Murray refused to call the agreement a bribe but conceded that there had been a *quid pro quo*. He also said that Baker had been nervous about whether Wagner would keep his word, because the arrangement was done in the old Irish way, the signature being a handshake, wink, or nod. In fact, he suggested that Wagner may have actually hoodwinked Baker, in a sense, because when it came time, in the spring of 1965, for Murray's appointment to the bench to be formalized, the appointment turned out to be for three years rather than the expected ten. (Mayors had the authority to replace judges who died or were moving on to other positions, and the time frames could vary, from one to ten years.) Murray said that a ten-year Criminal Court appointment went to another attorney, who was Jewish, apparently referring to Daniel Weiss, who was active among Democratic reformers.

Baker received more than just the appointment of an ally to a judgeship. He was also named chairman of the Assembly's Education Committee, an important assignment in those civil rights years, one that would come with a little controversy, as Baker was soon to learn.

At the end of that Travia episode, Baker was happy that Murray was equipped with a gavel and that he would be approachable for favors; but, according to Murray, Baker was angry that he had been betrayed by Wagner, giving Murray an appointment for only three years. "Mr. Baker was never friendly with Wagner after that," Murray said. "Wagner double-crossed Bookle," he said, using the nickname he had created for Bertram L. Baker.

Despite that disappointment, several years later, as Baker was in his retirement, Republican Mayor John V. Lindsay would name Murray to an opening on the state Supreme Court bench, and Murray remained on that court for a decade, until 1983. He retired to spend his remaining years managing a residential community and resort, called the Hillside Inn, which he had established in the Poconos with his wife, Odetta. He remained devoted to Baker, attending the gatherings of the "Faithful Few" at Baker's brownstone home every year and never allowing Baker's grandson (yours truly) and wife Marilyn and son Damani to pay even a penny when they stayed at his tree-strewn, spacious Hillside Inn resort in the Poconos.

In becoming chairman of the Assembly's Education Committee, Baker took up the cause of school desegregation and withstood public pressures from whites. He angered suburban whites in the state, and many white community leaders lashed out at him publicly. He seemed to be at peace with the balance he was maintaining. Bertram Baker was far from militant in his stances. In fact, he opposed efforts on the part of some Harlem politicians and black militant activists in Brooklyn to allow community control of schools in black neighborhoods, and he stood against militant Brooklyn demands to oust white school administrators and replace them with black ones. His overall conservatism would alienate him from black education activists such as Al Vann and Jitu Weusi in central Brooklyn. Vann would go on to a career in politics and become, after the mid-1970s, Bedford Stuyvesant's best-known and most powerful politician.

Baker's commitment to integration greatly upset whites on Long Island and in upstate New York. A case in point: Conservative whites wanted to pass a law that effectively would have overturned the practice of busing students to various public schools in order to achieve racial integration. As chair of the Assembly's Education Committee, Baker had the authority to lock up the bill so that it would not reach the floor of the Assembly to be voted on by the entire body. And that is just what he did. He locked up the bill.

All hell broke loose on Long Island, where the local newspaper, *Newsday*, published a March 16, 1966, article that quoted Baker as saying, "If this bill had been enacted, it would have tied the hands of [the state Education Commissioner] in his efforts to bring about quality education by the integration of the school system."

Then *Newsday* quoted Edward Nasierowski, a militant anti-busing activist from Malverne, Long Island, who was president of Neighbors United to Save Our Schools, who said, "We expected this because Baker is a Negro and said in the beginning that he would never allow the bill to be discussed. Baker is a nice fine southern Negro gentleman who says his grandfather was a slave and who would do anything to prove that the white people are wrong."[16]

Baker would later say he was stunned by the remarks. He said he had never made such statements. He had no family roots in the American South, though he did acknowledge being a gentleman.

Newsday furthermore quoted Charles Reardon, president of the Malverne Taxpayers and Parents, as saying, "I think it's a shame that a bigoted committee chairman refuses to allow the elected representatives . . . to vote on this important education matter." Reardon said his group would take further actions to express their anger at Bertram Baker. The article further said, "Baker could not be reached later for comment."

Baker denied that anyone tried to reach him.[17]

Baker knew well the art of political compromising, but he also knew the lives of the everyday black folks struggling to make it in Bed-Stuy, which many outsiders were starting to call a ghetto. And he tried to leave lasting impressions in his encounters that were open to the public.

Once, in the early '60s, Baker took more than a hundred of his Little League and P.O.N.Y. League ballplayers to Alley Pond Park in Queens, for a picnic of hot dogs and frolicking. Barely an hour into the afternoon, Baker was approached by a nervous United Action worker telling him that police officers on horseback had escorted several of the P.O.N.Y. League youngsters out of the park, saying they had molested a young lady. Baker responded with a verbal explosion that stunned everyone, including the white officers, into silence. He castigated the officers for violating the rights of boys who had been brought to a public park for an afternoon of relaxation by a member of the New York state Assembly. He demanded their shield numbers, which the officers gave him by pointing to their badges. He told the officers that he would be in touch with their supervising officers. The cops let the youngsters go, then trotted off from the area, and the picnic continued. Baker must have derived tremendous political benefit from the encounter with the white officers. While the incident did not make the newspapers, it was spread speedily by word of mouth and only increased the awe in which Bertram Baker was held by many in the Bedford Stuyvesant community.

Given the many radical changes taking place in American society during the 1960s, it was perhaps fitting that the black person who came to out-shine Bertram Baker in significance to black Brooklyn and, indeed, the country, was a woman. Shirley Anita St. Hill Chisholm (Chisholm was her married name) had been one of the younger aspirants in Thomas Russell Jones's Unity Club in the early 1960s, and she took his place after he changed careers in 1964, giving up his position as district leader and Assemblyman and becoming a judge. Not only did Chisholm then go on to serve in the Assembly with Baker, but in 1968 she became the first black person in Brooklyn elected to Congress. On a roll, she then sought the Democratic nomination for the U.S. presidency in 1972, be-coming the first woman of any race to make a serious attempt at the highest political office in the land. Ask many Brooklynites who the first black person elected to office in Brooklyn was and likely many would reply Shirley Chisholm.

There had always seemed to be bad blood between Chisholm and Baker. Perhaps it was in good part because of his lingering chauvin-ism. Bertram Baker's wife, Irene, had met Chisholm on one occasion in the Assembly and she expressed sympathy with Chisholm and her social causes, knowing that her husband harbored old Caribbean biases against women in power. In her autobiography, *Unbought and Unbossed*, Chisholm accused Bertram Baker of being in cahoots with ghetto pawnbrokers and their lobbyists. She supplied no evidence and Baker seethed at the accu-sation.

There's no escaping the fact that Baker disliked Chisholm. His passing references to her were always dismissive, that she was insincere and self-promotional. But he never called his feelings a dislike, and he never said that they had anything to do with his being offended by something she had said about him on the floor of the Assembly. It's also possible that Baker was much more concerned about the role of Wesley McD. Holder, whom Chisholm had chosen as her campaign manager. Through the 1950s and 1960s Holder tried a number of times to wrest Baker's lead-ership position and Assembly seat from him. If he didn't run himself, he supported others who opposed Baker.

Because Baker didn't speak much about Chisholm, he left an opening for speculation on the part of others. In 1972, Baker's former colleague George Metcalf (with whom he had sponsored the historic Metcalf–Baker law against housing discrimination) wrote a book about black American leaders in the early '70s. Titled *Up from Within*, it included a section in which he said why Baker had decided to back Dolly Robinson over Shirley Chisholm in the 1968 congressional race. The part about Baker began well enough, with Metcalf writing, "A twenty-year Albany veteran, Baker was, like Mrs. Chisholm, a West Indian native. Born on the island of Nevis, he had obtained an education with British overtones at the Cambridge University Preparatory School on St. Kitts. Now seventy, he was nearing the end of a distinguished career, with accolades for his part in promoting open housing."

But then came the part that caused Baker some irritation. Metcalf wrote that Baker did not want to support Chisholm for Congress because "... Mrs. Chisholm, with a burst of staccato mirth, had humiliated him on the floor of the Assembly, crushing his pride and leaving him frustrated." Baker had underlined that section in pencil and put a question mark in the column of the page.

In a 1995 interview (a decade after Baker's death), I asked Metcalf for details on what Chisholm had actually said. He answered that he did not know. State archivists say they did not keep transcripts of floor speeches in those days. Metcalf acknowledged that he had not reached out to Baker to see if the general assertion made by Shirley Chisholm was true.

"I did not question your grandfather to get his side of that whole thing and he was quite irritated about that," Metcalf said in the interview.

"He wrote me a letter. He was quite shocked that I would say something like that. But we made up after that."

I asked Metcalf if he perchance had kept a copy of the letter Baker had sent him, and he answered no. "It wasn't the kind of letter that I wanted to save."

Some of the tensions between Baker and Chisholm had to do with Chisholm's nominal embrace of the reformers of the late '50s and '60s, like the young Thomas Russell Jones. They associated Baker with the old Irish Democratic Party of Brooklyn, which they said was segregated and reactionary.

"The blacks sat on one side, the whites on the other," Chisholm wrote in *Unbought and Unbossed*. "There was no sign that said 'colored side.' It was an unwritten law. In many of the clubs even in the 1940s blacks were not welcome, unless they were brought in by a white member." In

Chisholm's vision, Baker's United Action Democratic Association was a kind of self-segregated political club that had been started by Baker right there in the 17th Assembly District, in what would become the black ghetto of Bedford Stuyvesant. In his copy of Chisholm's book, next to those lines quoted above, Baker penciled in, "not true."

Bertram Baker would assert, on those few occasions when he spoke of Shirley Chisholm, that she was not the reform idealist that many progressives believed her to be.

For one thing, her political boss, Thomas Fortune, who was one of her prime backers in the '68 congressional campaign, was the same one accused by Judge Thomas Russell Jones of demanding $50,000 for the judgeship that Jones received in 1964. Also, regarding Chisholm and the Bed-Stuy "reform" club that spawned her, there were the complaints that Chisholm, early on, acted as the Brooklyn version of U.S. Senator Joe McCarthy, weeding out the political radicals who might embarrass the club and its leaders. In his 1990 City University of New York doctoral thesis, titled "Building the Brooklyn Machine: Irish, Jewish and black political succession in central Brooklyn, 1919–1964," Jeffrey Gerson quoted Brooklyn activist Ruth Goring as saying:

> It was still the Cold War. People were afraid to even be seen talking to someone that they had known for years because that person had registered Communist because they were for the workers, and nobody was doing anything for the workers. And Shirley built on this, on this fear. And even when she was still in the club and she would stand up and make her speeches, she would always warn us against associating with people that were known Communists. . . .[18]

But it was Baker who, at the end of the 1960s, was tagged as the reactionary of black Brooklyn politics. Gerson wrote, "Baker became a symbol of the old, stodgy, failed black leaders. All black political party leaders of the day feared the same reference."

By some accounts, the beginning of the end for Bertram Baker came in 1964. There opened up a Senate seat in the Senate district that overlapped Baker's and Tom Jones's Assembly districts. This meant that blacks now had a chance they had been waiting for, to have someone representing them in the State Senate, although the choice as to who the candidate would be was no longer Baker's alone. Rather, it meant that Baker had to work along with Jones's Unity club. When that Senate seat opened up, Jones and Baker came to an agreement, a compromise, on who the black candidate for that position should be. It was a very fair-complexioned and socially connected attorney by the name of Risley Dent. Through political connections, Dent, a native of Peoria, Illinois, had served for two previous years as director of the Brooklyn office of the New York Rent and Rehabilitation Administration.

Dent was confident of victory. It was to be a great step up in the world—the world of black Brooklyn. For he would be the very first black person in Brooklyn to hold that office, New York state Senator. Manhattan had done it a decade before, in 1953, with the election of Julius A. Archibald, a Trinidadian-born lawyer from Harlem.[19] Dent, lively and a partyer, won the primary election as expected. He and friends then went to upstate New York, to the Concord Hotel in Monticello, to celebrate. It was the evening of June 7, 1964. The paunchy Dent collapsed amid his co-celebrators and died of a heart attack.[20]

This threw black Brooklyn into a tizzy, as the leaders would have to quickly decide who would be the replacement candidate to run in the general election. In the rush of negotiations and phone calls, Jones and Baker agreed to substitute a young, steadfast, very aggressive lawyer in Bertram Baker's club by the name of William Thompson.

Thompson had managed Dent's campaign. Apart from that, he was a quick-talking and well-trained lawyer, who could be counted on to offer advice, whether about election law or to advise a poor, black Bed-Stuy voter who came to the United Action club with a need for assistance. At that point Thompson was a close ally of Baker's. Unknown to most, Willie Thompson, like Bertram Baker, had roots in the St. Kitts and Nevis region of the Caribbean. Virtually no one at the time spoke about this connection. Indeed, it would not have been in the interest of either man to do so, given that such relationships could have raised accusations of prejudicial Caribbean bonding, at a time when native-born blacks with roots in the South were increasing even more in numbers, relative to Caribbean immigrants, because of the continuing Great Migration.

Willie Thompson was widely viewed as super-aggressive, a tendency seemingly held in check by a graciousness that also came bundled with the seeking of power. Some in the club suspected that Willie Thompson was a prime candidate among those who might one day use what they had learned from Bertram Baker and turn against him. Willie Thompson won the election, and it was, on the surface, a happy moment for Baker.

But Thompson was to be the major player in the endgame that took away Bertram L. Baker's championship title. Baker's loyal followers soon would begin turning against him one by one, joining the organizations of other leaders or starting their own clubs as rival leaders. It began in 1967 with a desertion by an attorney, James Shaw, who saw that his chances of winning a Supreme Court judgeship would be greater if he bolted to the Unity Democratic Club. Baker sponsored as his opponent a close club worker named Ben Headley. Shaw won the primary race.

In the old way of doing things, Baker might have made peace and supported the Democratic victor or remained impartial. To cross a Democrat and support a Republican was like treason. The Republican going for the judgeship against Shaw was Henry Bramwell, a black Brooklynite of West Indian descent. Baker decided to back Bramwell. He made the announcement at a United Action club meeting notable for the tension in the air. When Baker asked for reaction to his decision, one longtime worker, Henry Randolph Sr., one of the first black detective investigators in the Brooklyn District Attorney's office, raised his hand and told Baker that he (Randolph) thought the club should back the Democratic candidate, as it had always done. Baker said, without hesitation, "There's the door." And so Randolph, loved and respected by many in the club, walked out that door, never to return.

Others soon left the club also, including, most notably, Willie Thompson, who had earned his seat as a state Senator with Baker's backing. (Thompson, a future state appellate judge, was also the father of Bill Thompson, who four decades later would make credible, though unsuccessful, attempts to become Mayor of New York City.) Thompson and Baker would then become political enemies, and Baker's closest associates maintained that he suffered greatly, emotionally and even physically because of it. One of the painful contests came after the death of J. Daniel Diggs, the City Councilman, in 1968. Diggs had been with Baker since the 1933 founding of the United Action Democratic club. Diggs had acted as godfather to Baker's grandchildren, giving them gifts on special occasions and even sometimes transporting them to events.[21] The death hit Baker hard. He wanted Lyn Bell, who had the backing also of the National Organization for Women and the National Council of Negro Women, to succeed Diggs.

Willie Thompson decided to go after Diggs's seat himself, and he attacked Baker for breaking with the Democrats and backing the Republican candidate, Bramwell, for the judgeship. Baker's still-loyal followers considered Thompson a traitor who hurt Baker more than Baker would ever acknowledge. "He attacked Baker personally," Baker's loyal friend Albert Murray said of Thompson. "And that killed Mr. Baker, really. That's the one thing that just drove him in, and he didn't want to go out and fight. So I knew he wouldn't stay in the Assembly." Thompson won Diggs's seat on the City Council.

Baker's old buddy Everett Williams would say more than a decade after Baker's death, "The guy that really hurt him more—now listen to this, you don't have to print this if you don't want to—was Willie Thompson. That's the guy that really hurt him more than anyone else. He had faith in William Thompson. You see, he gave Willie the break."

As state Supreme Court Justice James Shaw explained when interviewed in 1995, Willie Thompson not only opposed Bertram Baker's candidate but also ran against Baker for the position that had once been the *pièce de résistance* in old Democratic politics—that of district leader, the one who sat with other leaders from around the county and effectively decided which local boss got his way. Willie Thompson won the races for Diggs's Council seat, and he won the leadership position. "Willie took vengeance from your grandfather," Shaw said. "And then what had been a trickle became a deluge."

Responding to those above assertions, Willie Thompson said that Baker had kicked him out of Baker's United Action political club because he—Thompson—had refused to go along with Baker's decision to back a Republican candidate over a Democrat in a race for a local judgeship. In his interview with the scholar Jeffrey Gerson in the 1980s, Thompson spoke of Baker in a way that seemed to show visceral dislike. "We had gone in Baker's club at one time and . . . it became a one-man gang. Bert Baker did everything," Thompson was quoted as saying in Gerson's 1990 doctoral thesis. "He was the leader, he was the Assemblyman, he ran the dinner dance. Nobody knew how much money was taken in. . . . [H]e was autocratic. He wasn't heavily involved in civil rights or anything else like that. Diggs did what he was told. I told Baker he could have done a lot more for the community, and Baker said, 'That's just the way it is. If you don't like it, get out.'"

Others have confirmed that Baker effectively told Thompson to "get out" of the United Action club. In a conversation with the author, Thompson attributed the true reason for Baker's decision to leave politics to something personal. Thompson said Baker's professional decline had more than anything else to do with his (Baker's) "girlfriend." Given the passing of time, almost fifty years, Thompson did not immediately recall the name, but then acknowledged he was speaking about Marie Smallwood, Baker's mistress.

Author Commentary:
The Tragedy of the Boss's "Gal Friday"

Marie Smallwood, forty-six years old at the time of her death in December 1965, was raised in a black middle-class family in Washington, D.C. She was buxom and always elegantly attired. Back in Washington, she had been trained as a seamstress, and she could type; she also had a beautiful singing voice and hoped that her talent would propel her to fame, or at least an income, once she settled into a new life in New York City.

Like others before her, her highest aspirations, to sing for audiences, were not realized, and she learned that Brooklyn was the place to which striving, middle-class blacks were flocking, for a nice home and a pleasant life, maybe the chance to do good for others.

Smallwood met and lived for a time with Albert R. Murray and his wife, Odetta, on Pacific Street. There at the United Action club, Murray was beginning a relationship with Bertram Baker that would take him to heights he had dreamed of as a youngster growing up in Georgia: a law degree, dealings (on the side) in real estate, a job as an assistant prosecutor, and finally a judgeship. Smallwood was introduced to Baker, and, like others, the young and impressionable Smallwood saw stars. Whether Murray encouraged the relationship is not known, but he certainly accepted it and facilitated it. It is believed that Murray helped find and acquire the home where Smallwood would eventually live, on Midwood Street near Prospect Park. In the 1950s, Smallwood was always there for Baker, using her skills as a typist, her gifts as a conversationalist, to be the Assemblyman's alter ego when answering the telephone or exchanging niceties with someone who rang the bell at his political club on Hancock Street, just one block south and half a block over, eastward, from his home at 399 Jefferson Avenue. Marie was sweet, even as she was tough, especially when arguing some point for Bert Baker. There were other pretty women high up on the administrative ladder at United Action, yes, but Marie was number one and served as Baker's personal secretary both at the political club and even at Baker's home on Jefferson Avenue, where he did accounting and bookkeeping work in his second-floor office. Sometimes Bert and Marie would walk from Hancock over to Jefferson, though generally they would step hurriedly into Bert's car and drive the three blocks, she up front on the passenger side, pushing back her hair or singing gospel songs.

Everyone knew that Smallwood was Baker's mistress. But at the United Action club, they all seemed to like her, even as they felt sympathy and even sorrow for Baker's wife, Irene, who bore the treachery in humble silence. The two women exchanged polite greetings and farewells but never words of anger. Smallwood was a sweet woman at heart, her friends at the club said. There was something forlorn about her. She loved children and obviously wanted to have a child of her own. And she obviously began to feel some guilt, and even inner torture, at her relationship with Baker. "It was like *Wuthering Heights*. You want to let go but you can't let go," said Smallwood's older sister, Loretta Smallwood Dehaney.[22]

It was the American Tennis Association that really pulled me personally into Bertram Baker's affair with Marie Smallwood. Bert Baker seemed to have his most fun when he was at the summer tennis tournaments. He would wear a happy white straw chapeau, as opposed to his customary fedora. The weeklong national tournaments held at black colleges, mostly in the South, made Baker feel like the boss of black America, not just of black Brooklyn. And there, on those campuses, Miss Smallwood was even more influential than she was in Brooklyn.

When I was about nine or ten years old, I began traveling to the tennis tournaments with my grandfather and Miss Smallwood. Before hitting the road, we would stop over in Flatbush to pick up Miss Smallwood, which meant I would have to sit and wait while she finished packing and prettying herself up. Then we had to take her stupid dog, Princess Margaret, to the kennel where she would stay until our return a week later.

The ride, once we finally began, was made all the longer by my grandfather's overly careful driving. He sometimes would sing, though he had a horrible, off-key singing voice. Miss Smallwood would sometimes pick up the slack and sing in a voice that would have seemed beautiful, I suppose, if I could ever have been objective in judging it.

Then there was the full week at the college residence, in Wilberforce or at Hampton, where I would have my own little room and Miss Smallwood would stay in a room near my grandfather's.

Back in Brooklyn at the Jefferson Avenue compound, Miss Smallwood would spend hours during the day typing away in Baker's office, sometimes calling down the stairs, "Yoo-hoo!" when she wanted to reach someone, like me or my grandmother.

As much as I disliked Miss Smallwood, I had to admit that she was a sweet woman at heart. There was something about her, evident beneath the surface, that was bluesy and painful. It likely had to do with unfulfilled wishes to be a singer or theater star or even perhaps to be a mother.

In any event, there came a night in December 1965, in other words while I was in the middle of my senior year in high school, that we received a call saying that Miss Smallwood was dead, that she had been found hanging in the basement of her brick single-family home on Midwood Street in Flatbush (a section now called Lefferts Manor). She was dangling from a pipe around which she had wrapped a clothesline that she had also tied to her neck. She had been alone in the house at the time, except for her blond cocker spaniel pooch that she called Princess Margaret. The real Princess Margaret, you'll recall, was the younger daughter of the Queen of England, and the real Princess Margaret's life was full of misery and illness, having been linked with suitors who proved an embarrassment to the Royal family, and who engaged in activities, such as heavy smoking, that harmed her body as well as her spirit.

I was aware the night of that tragedy that other lives, too, were being upset. A hush fell over us. I cannot say there was, within my grandmother, or within my mother, or even within myself, a desire to shout in triumph. It was beyond the reach of our experiences in life so far, and so there was silence. But then late in the night my grandfather came home, having passed the evening at Miss Smallwood's house with his close buddy Judge Murray, and with police. He entered the solemn quietude of the 399 Jefferson compound, not alone, but with Miss Smallwood's cocker spaniel, Princess Margaret.

But we already had a dog we loved, and her name was Ginger. And no one, except for the grieving Bertram Baker, loved Princess Margaret. Making matters worse was that Princess Margaret found that she could bully our Ginger, who was part Welsh Corgi and part God-knows-what-else. (We had adopted her from the Humane Society.) Princess Margaret would stare menacingly at Ginger, growling at her and chasing her around the house. One day, perhaps a week after Miss Smallwood's death, I lost control and started yelling at the dog and went and slapped her hard on the backside, at which point she cowered. My grandfather, hearing it all from his upstairs office, came down and said, "What's wrong with Ronald?" To my surprise he did not yell at me or give a lecture. Something tells me he understood.

I did not go to Miss Smallwood's funeral and for the life of me I do not have the faintest recollection of the preparations for it or even discussions about it. There was a concerted attempt, on the part of everyone else, to keep it all away from me.

It was much later in life that I came across the *Amsterdam News*'s coverage of Miss Smallwood's funeral. On the front page was a photo of Bertram Baker, looking stricken, and there with him, dutifully at his side, was Irene. Walking along beside them were Judge Murray and State Young Division Director Lawrence Pierce, one of Bert Baker's protégés, who would within a decade be named a Justice on the U.S. Court of Appeals. The headline blared across the page: "Bert Baker's 'Gal Friday' Is Suicide: Aide Hangs Self in Brooklyn Home."[23]

This would have been seen in black communities all around the city, because the *Amsterdam News* was for so many decades, and still is, the weekly organ of the black community in New York. This all occurred in my senior year of high school, though it's strange how successfully I repressed it. The story read: "Miss Smallwood's body, fully clothed except for shoes, was discovered, police said, hanging by the neck with clothes-line from a pipe in the ceiling of the basement of the well-appointed home at 80 Midwood St. in Brooklyn's fashionable Crown Heights–Flatbush section where she lived alone with only a cocker spaniel named Princess Margaret."

The newspaper reported that the house was owned by Bertram Baker and at least one other person whose name was not in the city documents. I am now pretty sure that was the late Supreme Court Justice Murray, Baker's close confidant. In recent years, through conversations with associates of my grandfather who were still living, I learned that Miss Smallwood had left a note and that she had been severely depressed, even to the point of contemplating becoming a nun. As I thought back, this made sense, because years before, when I was an altar boy at Our Lady of Victory Roman Catholic Church, a four-block walk from 399 Jefferson, I would sometimes see Miss Smallwood there at Mass, sitting in the pews, standing and kneeling at the appointed times. And I was there at the altar with the priest, holding the golden plate under the chalice that contained the body of Jesus Christ, in the form of wafers, seeing Miss Smallwood among the worshippers, but never coming to receive Communion. I do not believe I ever mentioned it to my mother or grandmother. And I certainly would not have said anything to my grandfather.

One day I came home from school to learn that poor Princess had died, that she had been in the back yard and somehow stuck her head between the wooden splats of the fence between our home and the brownstone next door, home of my buddies the Villanuevas, who were from Puerto Rico and always had dogs of their own. Everyone accepted the death with the proper solemnity.

It was only years later that I came to understand—to know, in a way that loved ones know—what had happened. My grandmother knew as no one else did how much I hated that dog Princess, how I wanted to strangle it that day when Princess attacked our meek little mutt Ginger.

It was a suffused bitterness that my grandmother saw every day and that she, long suffering as she always had been, identified with. Deep in my heart I came to believe that Princess had not died because she stuck her head between the wooden posts of our backyard fence. She died because Mommy I had held that dog's head between the posts, there to choke and die, and that my grandmother did that, not so much out of anger over the way she herself had been mistreated by my grandfather, but because of concern for me.

The exit from the long drama of the 1960s crushed the spirit of Bertram Baker. But it also damaged the ego of the man who had set out, at the beginning of the decade, to reform the political traditions of Baker and the other bosses of the Democratic Party. That was Thomas Russell Jones.

If Baker was a victim of the 1960s, then, in a sense, so too was his reformist counterpart, Thomas Russell Jones. Jones told me several years before his death in 2006 that he began to feel crushed in spirit in the mid- and late 1960s. The fighting and deal-making damaged his psyche and shamed his sense of right and wrong. Many had thought Jones would continue seeking power as Bertram Baker's opposite in black Brooklyn. But when an opening came up for a Civil Court judgeship in the mid-1960s, he went after it. He wanted out of the battles for legislative offices.

In 2003, Jones spoke to me for an article in *Newsday* and disclosed that he had secretly paid $35,000 for that judgeship four decades before. He said he had paid it to Thomas Fortune, the Democratic leader for that area, all in cash. Fortune had actually demanded $50,000, but Jones gave him only $35,000, the judge had told me. Both Jones and Fortune are deceased.

Though Jones had often criticized Bertram Baker for his old-line ways and devotion to the Irish and Jewish Democratic party bosses, he told the author in 2003 that he never knew, or heard, that Baker had demanded payoffs for jobs. But it came with the job of being a black political boss that there would be accusations of financial misdoings. Some said Baker effectively took a bribe from former Mayor Robert Wagner when Baker did Wagner's wishes and voted for Anthony Travia to be Speaker of the State Assembly. The payback was a judgeship for Albert Murray. And then there was a 1969 *New York Times* article that raised questions about the ethical propriety of another vote, on a horse-racing bill. The article said Baker and several other assemblymen had changed their votes and supported a proposal authorizing pari-mutuel betting on quarter-horse racing.[24] The suggestion was that there might have been payoffs for the vote changes. Baker himself never gave attention to the charge. In 1970, an *Amsterdam News* story quoted a source from the State Commission of Investigations, saying the group "has no evidence that Baker and the others who had switched their votes had been offered bribes to do so."[25]

Baker's former female co-leader, Jo Bravo, maintained that Baker stood out among politicians for not having an interest in making money. "I can say he was altruistic because he was never concerned about getting anything big for himself. He got things for people because it made him feel good to know that Bert Baker was responsible for it. I mean, that was his conceit, in a way. It made him feel good. . . . It made him feel important. It gave him a good reputation. He was respected. United Action was his baby. He felt he accomplished something and he did."

10

Irene, in the End, Became His Connection to Home and Mother

Irene was a Brooklynite, born and raised, and she lived there her whole life, until her death in January 2001. But her love for writing (simple, honest, and literate) always kept her in contact with lifelong friends and family members back in the place she always called "home," which was the island of Nevis. Furthermore, it was the women of the Baker clan (Irene and her two sisters, Violet and Edna) in Brooklyn who maintained possession of the two-acre tract of land in the Gingerland section of Nevis known as Bucks Hill, which had the old English blackstone remains of what in the 1800s had been the mansion of a sugar plantation. Some of Irene's cousins in Brooklyn had vivid memories of living on Bucks Hill, including her first cousin Rose, who was born in Nevis in 1892 and immigrated to Brooklyn eleven years later with her parents, Ned Baker and Frances Huggins Baker. Irene and her sisters eventually acquired possession of Bucks Hill, paying taxes on it and renting it out all through the Depression years that hit Nevis especially hard and all the years after. In 1969, when Bertram was hinting to Irene that he would soon retire from politics, she made her first trip to Nevis, flying by herself, finally visiting the ancestral property and getting to know in person the many Nevisians she had developed long-distance relationships with over the decades.

In a mostly faded note she made during that trip, Irene wrote that one of her cousins (unnamed) had invited her to have lunch by the beach. "It was the happiest day. . . . She [the cousin] had packed a picnic basket and ... we drove to a secluded spot near palm trees and a bay of water. I was elated with the beautiful sand and sea around us, of what was called Jones Bay, as I felt too that I was ... home. I played in the water as I don't swim, and I walked along the sand ...." When the week of fun was over, Irene returned to Brooklyn, where Bertram, who was showing Irene more attention than he had in his earlier years (for one thing, having just reached the age of seventy the year before, he no longer had girlfriends), showed up at the airport with a driver. (The driver was Bertram's hand-picked candidate for a judgeship, Ben Headley. In a sign of Bertram's diminishing power at that point, Headley lost the election.) In the coming years Irene would paint beach scenes of little girls in bonnets walking happily along the shores of Nevis.

It was to be six years later that Irene would finally convince Bertram to make his first trip back to Nevis since leaving there in 1915. It was the first half of Bertram's fifteen-year retirement stretch, a time when he would spend long stretches sitting by the front window, either of the ground floor or the parlor floor (in front of the office with his precious books), or making calls to former associates, telling them about the book he was contemplating, about blacks who "broke down barriers" in "various fields of endeavor," a book that never saw the black of print. Planning for the trip to Nevis perked Baker up. His daughter Marian, still living at 399 with her parents and working as a manager in the office of the New York state Attorney General, typed up introductory letters that her father then sent to friends and government officials on Nevis.

Setting foot on the island after half a century away from it must have numbed him to the point of fainting. But he was one to recover from such episodes in fractions of a second, especially if he knew he would soon be speaking to an audience. The main events at which Bertram Baker was a featured guest and speaker was at the Hamilton House, a museum in the capital city of Charlestown, named after Alexander Hamilton, the first Nevisian (although a white Nevisian) to achieve political notoriety in New York. The top officials of Nevis and neighboring St. Kitts attended. Irene evinced a pride and affection that some might have said only an angel could muster after the decades of inattention and outward eye-roaming on the part of her husband.

She wrote in a booklet that she gave afterward to her grandchildren: "The tears came to my eyes as 'B' started to talk, for I realized this was his most important event, and he wanted to leave an impression. He did. Especially the Americans formed a line to shake his hand. I watched them, and found they were intensely attentive as he spoke."[1]

That visit to Nevis was like a return to the womb for Bertram. He was back in his childhood, and he told Irene of sitting alone under a fig tree in 1900, mourning with his eyes and chest as toddlers do, while others attended the funeral of his mother. There was looking-back tenderness in his exchanges with Irene. He had become in life everything that his mom would have wanted him to become, and the development was continuing with Mom's spirt close by.

Unusually reflective at this time of his life, Bertram gave expression to a likeness he increasingly began to see between himself and the other Nevisian who had left his island at a young age, traveled to New York, and entered the political realm, affecting it in historic ways. The name of that Nevisian was to be remembered long after his tragic death by gunfire in 1804, but even more so three decades after the death of Bertram. That was *grâce à* the young, gifted writer of color (born to parents from the Caribbean, the Latin part) named Lin-Manuel Miranda. Miranda made Hamilton's voice heard around America and the world, from a stage on Broadway and way beyond. Had Baker lived into the second decade of the twenty-first century he would have ignored those family members and others who would have told him not to spend $1,400 for him and Irene to see a play about Alexander Hamilton, not when you have every single book ever written about him. Bertram would have gone, and he would have glowed for his remaining days. Hip-hop would have baptized its most recalcitrant convert.

In my collection of materials from my grandfather's home I found a nine-page publication, with a black-and-white cover carrying the title "The Voice of Nevis." An image of its northern shore and a midcentury vessel sailing its Caribbean waters rested at the bottom of the page. The publication contained a copy of the speech Baker gave during his visit at the Hamilton House (an old building used to store historic documents). On those grounds exist, still, the stone house in which it's said Alexander Hamilton was born on January 11, 1757.

In his speech, Baker noted how he had first become fascinated with Hamilton in 1957, on the second centennial of the Founding Father's birth. That was when he had pushed through the state Assembly a resolution honoring Hamilton, and he became lifelong friends with Hamilton's great-great-grandson Laurens Hamilton. Baker was aware of the debate over whether Alexander Hamilton's father was part black. Baker said he had read much about his Nevisian predecessor and did not believe there was evidence to assert that Hamilton was a Negro by virtue of the African blood of the father, as contemporary detractors of Hamilton had been saying. Because of the questions about Hamilton's paternity, his detractors (and their name was legion) loved calling him the bastard. A pertinent truth here is that, had Bertram Baker been convinced that Alexander Hamilton was in fact a black man, mulatto, or whatever, he would have seen his earlier countryman as even more of a hero, if it was possible for Hamilton to have existed on a higher plane in Baker's mind. At the time of Bertram Baker's talk, Nevis was still part of the British empire. It would not be until 1983 that independence would be granted to the new independent nation of St. Kitts and Nevis, which would be the smallest of all nations in the Western Hemisphere. Here are his words (as printed in a journal for Nevisian Americans started in the late 1970s by Eustace Huggins, a physician practicing in Queens, New York):

Today [January 11, 1976] we celebrate the anniversary of the birth of a great man, Alexander Hamilton. A man who was born, not only on the Island of Nevis, but history tells us, on these very grounds. There has been speculation as to the circumstances surrounding his birth. But be that as it may, Hamilton proved himself to be a great man. He left the island at an early age, journeyed with his mother to the Island of St. Croix, where he served, we are told, in the store of a merchant there by the name of Mr. Cruger. In 1772, at the age of 15, he journeyed to . . . America in quest of an education.

At the time that Hamilton came to [what would become] the United States, after some preliminary studies, he entered Kings College, which is now Columbia University. While [he was] a student there the conflict between Great Britain and the colonies was coming to a climax, and Hamilton had to choose. He had to make a choice whether to align himself with the American revolutionary forces or to throw his lot with the British Loyalists. And Hamilton, true to tradition, thought not what was the expedient thing to do. Possibly the expedient thing to have done then would have been to throw his lot with the Loyalists because the President of Kings College, Dr. Cooper, was a staunch loyalist. But, no, not Hamilton, not what was expedient, but what was the right thing to do. And so he threw his heart and soul with the American revolutionary forces. He distinguished himself as a soldier. He became the aide-de-camp to General George Washington, Commander-in-Chief of the revolutionary forces, and served in that capacity until the end of the war. It was Hamilton who wrote the draft of George Washington's farewell address to his troops. It was the master pen of Alexander Hamilton that wrote that draft.

. . . In his native State of New York, he was a delegate to the Constitutional Convention. He was elected to the Assembly of the State of New York in 1786 and took his seat on January 12, 1787 as a member of the Assembly of the State of New York.

In 1949, when I took my seat as a member of the honorable body I became the second, *and only other*, Nevisian to serve in the Assembly of the State of New York.

Alexander Hamilton became the architect of the political structure of the United States of America. . . . And from then on until today the likeness and image of Alexander Hamilton—the Nevisian—appears on every ten dollar United States bill that has ever been issued. Many of you have never thought of it.

. . . Historians may differ as to the circumstances of his birth, but history affirms two things, (1) he was a Nevisian and (2) he was one of the world's greatest statesmen.

Bertram Baker had wanted to travel yet another time to Nevis. His intense desire was to pay a posthumous tribute to his de Grasse ancestors, especially his mother, Lilian. Saving several thousand dollars over the mid-1970s, he arranged to have a new inscription placed on the tombstones of his mother, grandmother, and uncles in the graveyard of the St. George Anglican Church. He said that he was the most senior in that line of living de Grasses and that if he did not take such actions, no one else would.

In 1979, Baker dispatched his daughter Lilian and her husband, John Bemus, to Nevis to speak at a ceremony dedicating the plot to his mother, Lilian de Grasse. Baker was not able to make the 1979 trip because he was recovering from one of his recurring stomach ailments. In 1983, Irene accompanied Bertram to Nevis again on his last trip to his motherland. The occasion was to celebrate the independence of St. Kitts and Nevis from England. Once again, as ten years previously, Baker spoke outside the Hamilton House, gratefully acknowledging the many gifts bestowed upon him and the world by his birthplace. He was weak. He had trouble walking and even speaking. But Irene thought he was very happy.

The cause of Baker's death on March 8, 1985, was a spread of cancer, from stomach tumors. His stomach had bothered him off and on for decades, with flare-ups sending him a few times to St. Luke's Hospital in

Manhattan. By the time of his death, virtually all the judges and other attorneys and former members of his long-ago United Action club had moved out of Bedford-Stuyvesant, which had become undesirable to those looking for rising real estate values. Baker died in the bedroom of his Jefferson Avenue brownstone, his wife, Irene, nearby. In addition to a portion of his pension going to Irene (perhaps $10,000 annually), he left a bank account of about $50,000 (or about $110,000 in present-day dollars). The home might have sold for about $40,000 at that time. Baker left all his documents, photos, and books to the author.

There were those who would say that Bertram Baker, after he began to assert his power in the late 1940s, put his deepest trust in two people. One was J. Daniel Diggs, the City Councilman who died in 1968. The other was Albert R. Murray, the southern-born striver who thought of Baker as a surrogate father and was grateful for the judgeship that Baker maneuvered to get him back in the 1960s. It was also Murray who, quietly, helped acquire the Midwood Street rowhouse that was the home of Baker's mistress, Marie Smallwood. Being a man of conscience, Murray began to show signs of guilt about the treatment of Irene Baker. Though not well, Murray drove from his retirement home in the Poconos area of Pennsylvania to speak at the wake for Irene held at a funeral home in Brooklyn in 2001. Murray said it was Irene Baker who was the hero of the Baker family, and he recalled a time when she had spoken eloquently and with great effect on a sound truck during one of Bertram's campaigns for state Assembly in the 1950s. This was a time, Murray noted, when some were beginning to develop suspicions that Baker was not the best of husbands or family men.

Murray, who died in 2005, said in a chat with the author after Irene Baker's funeral, "If you write a book, you should say it was Mrs. Baker who held the family together. She's the one that really has the crown upstairs."

11
Author Commentary
Downtown Brooklyn: Soul of the Boss, Soul of a People

The image that stays most fixed in my mind from my grandfather's funeral in March 1985 is that of New York state Justice Franklin Morton. All of the several judges in attendance were wearing their robes during the ceremony. They had agreed to do so in honor of the Chief, whose self-declared job for most of his working life was opening the doors to civil service jobs, especially those jobs in the downtown courthouses, especially those on benches with nearby gavels. None of the judges spoke at the service. Bertram Baker said in his will that he wanted no eulogy. But, as I was the grandson raised in his home, my grandmother declared it my job to say at least a little something. Before a crowd of hundreds, I succinctly related his historic legacy. I kept it brief, out of fear, as I said, that thunder and lightning would descend from above us at St. Luke and St. Matthew, the Episcopal church there on the fringe of Downtown Brooklyn, between Fort Greene and Bed-Stuy.

Judge Morton had been sick with a heavy cold in the days leading up to the memorial gathering. He did his best to keep his discomfort to himself, and after the service he put on his gray coat to head to his car where his wife was waiting for him. Then, grasping the two sides of the coat with one hand, he stopped before the pallbearers as they were putting the casket into the hearse and raised his hat in a gesture that had the bell rings of *The Last Hurrah*.

Fifteen years had passed since Bertram Baker had retired from the state Assembly, and during that interval the city had all but forgotten who he was. When I'd called the *Times* several days before to inform them of his death, the black reporter with whom I spoke had no knowledge of who Baker was, and the reporter cautioned me that the paper might not run an obituary. But one of the paper's photographers, Chester Higgins Jr., came from a family that had deep connections to black history. (His father, the late Chester Higgins Sr., had been a writer for black newspapers around the country through the middle decades of the twentieth century.) And so Chester Jr. knew that the death of Bertram Baker was an event deserving of his paper's attention. The *Times* ran an article about the passing of the boss, and elected officials from around the city came to the funeral. Chester Higgins's photograph of Morton giving his gentlemanly tribute was published in the *Times* the day after the funeral.

In some ways it was poetic that it was Judge Morton whose visual farewell would be recorded for posterity. For it was his father who in 1920 suffered the humiliation of having won a race for state Assembly in the downtown section of Brooklyn, where blacks were concentrated at the time, only to have that victory challenged by the white power holders who winced at the idea of having a black Assemblyman. In a re-count, Franklin Morton Sr. lost by one vote and never recovered from the indignity of that episode, which many blacks attributed to crass racism. It was to be another twenty-eight years before a black person would win a race for elective office in Brooklyn, and that person was Bertram L. Baker, who engineered Franklin Jr.'s way onto the bench in the 1950s.

St. Luke and St. Matthew had something of a racist background in the early twentieth century, as mentioned in the chapter on Irene Baker's childhood. But it is located in the downtown area of Brooklyn; and Downtown Brooklyn is where the Morton and Baker families lived with so many other up-and-coming blacks in the early 1900s. Notably, it was where so many of the borough's first black churches got their start, before moving in the mid-1900s to Bedford Stuyvesant. It was where Bertram Baker's father (Rev. Alfred Baker) lived when he came from Nevis and, in 1905, became the founding pastor of Ebenezer Wesleyan Methodist Church. And it had been the home of St. Augustine Episcopal Church, which Bertram Baker adopted as his place of worship, rejecting his father's Methodist faith. The connection between downtown and black religiosity went back to antebellum decades, in fact.

And so I chose to place the cremated remains of Bertram Baker in the columbarium of Lafayette Presbyterian Church, located between Downtown Brooklyn and Fort Greene. It wasn't Episcopalian, as Bertram Baker perhaps would have wanted. But it was steeped in the history of black Brooklyn, and that is surely comforting to Bertram Baker's soul. Lafayette

Presbyterian was established in 1857 and earned a treasured place in the history of the Underground Railroad, which harbored blacks escaping slavery in the South. Sojourner Truth and Harriet Tubman spoke at Lafayette Presbyterian, the very same church structure where Bert Baker rests. Escaped slaves were sheltered in tunnels below the building.

When Irene Baker died in 2001, I placed her cremated remains there at Lafayette in an urn next to the one marked "The Chief." I chuckle when I recall an encounter outside Lafayette Presbyterian Church in 2001, several weeks after Irene Baker's passing.

I had taken my grandfather's urn from the church over to Green-Wood Cemetery, where my grandmother was being cremated. My grandfather's urn had been made of tin, and I wanted to upgrade it to one of the nicer-looking copper containers coming into use and into which I'd put my grandmother's ashes. When the two urns were ready, I put them both on the passenger seat of my gray Honda Civic and talked to them as I drove the three miles back to Lafayette Presbyterian.

I parked on Lafayette Avenue right across from the church and sat there in the car, tears welling in my eyes, spurting out parting words before I took them to their home. Then, walking right past me on the driver's side came a guy who had grown up with me on Jefferson Avenue. I hadn't seen Ronnie R. in years, not since he'd served several years in prison for selling cocaine to an undercover cop. I used to buy marijuana from him in his pre-prison days. He was always such a good guy, and it pained me that he had lived behind bars. We were two of three Ronnies on the block. He yelled, "Ronnie, how's it going?" After a minute of catching up, he asked, "How's your grandmother and grandfather?"

"Funny you should ask," I couldn't avoid saying and pointed to the urns. He chuckled. We chatted for several minutes more before he took off. The rest of the day was somber.

The religious devotion that had dominated Bertram Baker's life when he came to America in 1915, when he wanted to be a priest, had mostly given way to earthly pursuits, like political deal making. But the fervor came back modestly upon his retirement in 1970. He joined the Brotherhood of St. Andrew at St. George's Episcopal Church in Bed-Stuy. It was a fraternity of Episcopalians that traced its origins to the late 1800s in the United States and dedicated itself to encouraging men to engage themselves in their churches' activities. The few times Bertram Baker gave speeches in Brooklyn in the years after his retirement, his "brothers" from St. Andrew were involved, helping him publicize the events.

My religious impulses were so much different from my grandfather's.

As a kid who wanted to be a Catholic priest, I was self-flagellating.
I suffered from what Catholic religious scholars call scrupulosity, an
compulsive obsession with the notion of sin. It was my grandmother
who tried to caution me to be gentle with myself. When I was at Yale
I gave up religiosity for drugs and whatever else gave momentary pleasure. To the extent that I returned to a connection to the beyond, it came
through Eastern meditation and veganism. I seemed sometimes to be
skating toward the edges of a breakdown, but I was rescued always by
the attention of a wife, Marilyn—and by a resurgence of faith that there
was a loving power beyond. Religion fascinated me, even as I later in life
avoided joining a formal church. But there was one priest who stood out
far beyond all others for me, in his understanding of what it means to be
a seeker after Truth. That was an eighteenth-century Anglican priest in
England by the name of William Law, who in 1729 wrote *A Serious Call
to a Devout and Holy Life*. In his life he rejected the authority of the British
regents, entering a category of priests referred to as "non-jurors," who
were not allowed to perform services at churches in England. The mystical
quality of his ideas, and the science-like exploration of Christian traditions,
made him a progressive in an age of Biblical dictatorship. From William
Law came the Quakers and the Methodists. So, yes, had he been around
to converse with them, he might have been the link joining the lives of
the rigid Episcopalian Bertram Baker and his father, Rev. Alfred Baker, the
Wesleyan Methodist minister. Peace might have been found, and Freudian
anger might not have eaten at the ego of Brooklyn's first black boss.

William Law never directly affected Bertram Baker. But he did pro-
foundly touch Bertram's wife, Irene, who Judge Albert Murray said was
the one wearing the crown in heaven. Shortly after Bertram Baker's death,
I left a copy of *A Serious Call* at his Jefferson Avenue home. I was so
touched when I saw it soon afterward on my grandmother's bedtable. She
read it every night for years. She once said to me, "I wonder, How does
he come up with such thoughts, so many thoughts?"[1] James Boswell said
pretty much the same thing about William Law in Boswell's 1791 classic
book *The Life of Samuel Johnson*.

As I've tried to understand the impulses of my grandfather, the boss
of black Brooklyn, I've wandered here and there, along Bed-Stuy streets
and in archives. The past of black Brooklyn, visible in its churches, is so
captivating. And in seeking to learn more, I came to appreciate the significance of another man, who also lived on Jefferson Avenue—and who also
was a grandfather of mine. He was an Episcopal priest and writer whom I
hardly knew.

12

Author Commentary
My Other Grandfather, a Priest and Writer
I Hardly Knew

I think it now the oddest thing that my paternal grandfather, the Rev. Charles Garfield Howell, lived just one block away from us. We in the Baker household were at 399 Jefferson Avenue, and "Grandpop" and his wife, "Nana" (Beryl Howell), occupied the ground floor of 316 Jefferson, a four-minute walk from us.

(I called Grandpop's wife, Nana, my grandmother, but she was actually my step-grandmother. Grandpop's first wife, Edythe, had died in 1928.)

I did go to visit him a number of times on Jefferson, accompanied by my mother, or a few times with my father, when he was sober enough to pick me up at 399 and take me over there. Rev. Howell died in 1962 when I was thirteen years old. I recall vividly being taken to his bedside for him to smile at me the night before his passing.

The first thing that comes to mind as I reflect on Rev. Howell was that he was kind-hearted, so easy to be around. I came to learn also about his erudition. He was an Episcopal priest, the very position in life that my grandfather Baker had wanted when he came to America in 1915.

Rev. Howell had pastored a couple of churches in Brooklyn and Manhattan back in his glory days, the 1920s and '30s. (My dad, Wilfred, was born in 1922 in the rectory of St. Barnabas Episcopal Church in the East New York section of Brooklyn when Rev. Howell was the pastor there.) Rev. Howell also taught Latin and history in public junior high schools. My father once told me that he and his brothers, when they were boys sitting at the dinner table with their father and stepmother, would get grilled by the Latin teacher. He would hold up a shaker of salt and demand that one of the boys decline it in Latin. The victim was supposed to say without hesitation: "Sal, salis, sali, salem, sale." I don't think that the sisters, my Aunt Carrie and Aunt Beryl, had to go through that, because they, as the girls, went the commercial routes in school, to be secretaries, rather than having college in mind, because, hey, that's the way it was in those days with West Indians.

I have to think that Rev. Howell was proud of me when I was a kid, knowing that I was an altar boy who knew the Latin Mass. I don't believe that West Indian Episcopalians had problems with the Catholic Church— beyond the issue of priestly celibacy, that is—because the rituals and beliefs were so similar, the main prayer of both faiths being the Nicene Creed, with the final reference to "the one holy Catholic and apostolic Church." The Episcopalians were, at their root, the Catholic Church of England.

Charles Garfield Howell immigrated to the United States from Barbados in 1912, having had the advantage of an education at the very-well-regarded Codrington Divinity School in Barbados, where he was one of the first blacks to attend. The school through the 1800s had been the priestly training ground for Europeans serving in the English-speaking New World.

At some point, so my father had told me, his dad attended Harvard Divinity School also, but I have no idea how far he went or anything else about the experience—other than that a white student had once told him no black could ever finish the studies there.

Despite being a preacher, Charles G. Howell was a relatively quiet type. He loved to write—not fiction or poetry, but expository writing of the kind that . . . well, that I have done as a journalist.

In 1929, he traveled by ship to Europe and wrote about the experience in an unpublished manuscript of 159 pages that he titled "I Was a Stranger." (His new wife, Nana, in a fine West Indian tradition of male dominance, took care of the home and children in Brooklyn while he worked, explored, and wrote.)

Grandpop wrote that in Barbados even black folks spoke of England as "home." And he told of the effect that being in the United States for more than a decade had had on him:

> [I]n 1929, I had lived 17 of my 40 years in the United States, and had become completely identified with 12 million Negro Americans. I had become very conscious of my race, and had come to know the limitations and restraints, social, economic and political, which America imposes on its citizens of Negro blood. So, whatever

I might see in Europe, I shall view not merely as a man, but as a Negro. Was it true what they said about Europe, that color prejudice does not exist there? I plan to find out for myself. So, if in these pages, in the midst of a journey to Oxford, or a visit to some old-world Castle or Cathedral, the race question should crop out, please dear reader, do not attribute it to bitterness, or feel that I have introduced an inharmonious note into my story. Would God it were possible for us black men to forget this race question, to treat it as if it didn't exist!

On the first full day of his visit to England he came face to face with the racism he was hoping would be either nonexistent or under some gentlemanly control.

My walk brought me to . . . a less prosperous district, somewhere in the neighborhood of Tottenham court road. I have explained that it was a hot afternoon, so I walked into the nearest pub and ordered an ale. The stupid-looking bartender gaped at me as if I were a Gorgon's head, and there was an embarrassing moment of suspense which was broken by a woman who came forward with the announcement: "We don't serve colored men here." She was kind enough, however, to point out another pub across the street, where, she said, I would be served. Well, you could have knocked me down with a feather! So this was England, about which I had bragged so much! What a let-down! What is the difference between this and Alabama or Mississippi? And to be fair to the south, it might even happen in New Jersey, but who was expecting it in London? And yet I should not have been surprised, because the press had recently carried a report of the exclusion of Paul Robeson, distinguished Negro actor, from one of London's large hotels . . . .
    It is hard to say which emotion was stronger as I left that neighborhood—my feeling of anger for my own injury, or shame for England. At any rate I rose superior to the occasion, and walked out of that pub with my head up.

Over the years, I had wondered a couple of times if Grandpop was a womanizer like my maternal grandfather, Bertram Baker, was. They often say that black ministers attract women. There's something about the magnetism of preaching. But it turns out that everyone I ever put the question to—whether Grandpop was a chaser—said no, never, not that they knew of.
    Grandpop preached on the radio also. And sometimes he'd even write

about politics, in pamphlets that he would sell for 15 cents each. Even those political pieces had a spiritual twist.

Like the one he wrote called "The Wicked City," in which he imagined Jesus Christ's coming to New York City of the 1940s and roaming the streets and reading the newspapers.

> . . . Suppose Jesus were to come to New York City today, what would he find?
>
> . . . He would find a city of eight million people, a million and a quarter school children, seven hundred theaters, and fifteen hundred churches. That would please him, for surely a city with fifteen hundred churches must be a godly city. . . . And when he learns that New York is the financial center of the country, and indeed of the world, and that the Stock Exchange, the Curb[1] and Wall Street are there, he would think that here at last must be a city without poverty and starving people. . . . Perhaps he will stay in the city a few days, and he will read the newspapers and listen to the radio. And here his education will really begin. He will add new and strange words to his vocabulary—racketeers, mobsters, gangsters, G-men . . . . He will hear and read about corrupt judges and lawyers. He will see a lot of people out of work and read about commercialized vice and gambling. Perhaps he will visit the slum areas and see for himself what breeds crime and social disease and juvenile delinquency. . . .
>
> And being now quite disillusioned, he might ask, "What are my churches doing? There are fifteen hundred of them. Surely their influence is felt." But on investigation he will find that many of the trustees and vestrymen of the churches are big politicians and money changers and real estate operators, who are more interested in property rights than in human rights. They call the ministers to the churches and provide their salaries. So, although most of the ministers are good men, they can't afford to speak out. This might also explain why he had found "white" churches and "colored" churches. He could never understand that, and no amount of logic and reasoning on the part of theologians and bishops and high-powered executives would make him understand it. This is not the Church he had left less than two thousand years ago. . . . Then in disgust, and pity, Jesus would go off to some quiet spot overlooking the city, perhaps the Palisades or Washington Heights, and he would burst into tears . . . .

Rev. Howell wrote that in the 1940s. Perhaps it goes without saying that Bertram Baker would have referred to the political occurrences in a different way, in a more favorable light. I wondered if this divergence explained what I saw as the thick wall between them. I don't recall having ever seen my two grandfathers together.

If there was one of Grandpop's children who seemed to have special connections to Bertram Baker, it was my Uncle Charles. Charles Jr. was quick-witted and fast-talking. He even looked intellectual, wearing glasses as a teenager. By all accounts he was a facile writer and a voracious reader. After graduating in 1939 from St. Augustine College in North Carolina, a black institution of higher education that was affiliated with the Episcopal Church, Uncle Charles had planned to follow in his father's footsteps and become an Episcopal priest.

In the photo-filled book about midcentury Brooklyn *Brooklyn Is America*, Uncle Charles is pictured leading a discussion of literature at St. Philip's Episcopal Church in Bedford Stuyvesant. Furthermore, to my surprise, I recently found out that Uncle Charles, after World War II, had been president of Bertram Baker's United Action Democratic Association youth division.

In his teenage years, Charles Jr. had been a boyfriend of Lilian Baker—in other words, my mom's older sister. But it didn't work out. This would have been in the mid-1930s. I always assumed Aunt Lil dropped Charles because Aunt Lil figured out Charles was a womanizer. But in fact it was not until the 1950s that Charles's womanizing became a thing of gossip and shame.

I recently learned that Aunt Lil had been encouraged by her maternal grandmother, Sarah Huggins Baker, to dump Charles, because his complexion was too dark. This knowledge came from a conversation I had with Pat Morrissey, who was in her nineties and living in a nursing home in Manhattan when she told me. But she was possessed of a good memory. She had been a close Baker family friend since childhood.

I was obviously struck by this, that my great-grandmother didn't want Uncle Charles to date or marry her granddaughter because he was too black. But it did make some sense. Aunt Lil later would marry my Uncle John, who was from Vicksburg, Mississippi, and—had it not been for the insularity of the place, with everyone knowing everyone else—he could have passed for white there, or anywhere.

An obvious question arises for me. Did the Baker family have color concerns about their other daughter—my mom, Marian—marrying Charles's brother Wilfred? My dad was perhaps a shade lighter in complexion than Charles, but he was brown-skinned and more African than most of the Bakers.

Here's the explanation I came up with. I learned that my color-conscious great-grandmother was, yes, a significant influence on Aunt Lil; but my great-grandmother died in 1936. And so my mother, born in 1925, would not have had her around as an influence during Mom's dating years. I would say that most of my mom's boyfriends in the span of her life, including retirement years, were dark in complexion.

Color did affect me personally, though never in a crude way—as in, "You're too black to be around here" or anything like that. My cousin Jay, Aunt Lil's son, told me as a kid that girls couldn't run their fingers through my hair. That was an allusion to a popular television commercial pitching Brylcreem, a hair-styling product. "Brylcreem! The gals'll all pursue ya! They'll love to run their fingers through your hair!" My cousin Lynn told me that when she and her nuclear family moved to the Hollis section of Queens in the late 1950s, they did a pretty good job of passing for, well, something other than black. That is, until I arrived and started spending nights there. Wouldn't matter much now, because Hollis went from being virtually all-white to being all-black over the past two generations.

Growing up on Jefferson Avenue, I never heard my maternal grandfather, Bertram Baker, say a phrase or a single word reflecting Afrophobia or color bias. Maybe he just never had that tendency, or maybe he somehow saw what he was up against when he arrived in this new world and he decided to make his stand on the side of his black ancestors.

When I was around my paternal grandfather, Rev. Howell, I couldn't understand most of what he was saying. That is because, by the time I was born, he had had surgery for throat cancer and he spoke through a voice box. When talking, he would pull off the cloth that covered the hole over his throat. The words that he managed to say came out raspy. I assume the cancer had to do with Grandpop's love of cigars. Incredible as it may seem nowadays, he smoked cigars even in his post-cancer condition. That's the way it was back then, I suppose.

I remember especially well an occasion when my mom left me over at Grandpop's for an afternoon. He took me out into the small back yard behind his apartment. We began picking some of the grapes that grew there. Then we brought the grapes into the house and began squeezing them into a pot. I was helping him make his own wine.

At that time, I was an altar boy in the Roman Catholic Church, in which the most solemn ritual—indeed, the miracle that defined the

Roman Catholic faith—was that part of the Mass in which the altar boy would pour wine into the priest's chalice. The priest would then take it and consecrate it, turning it—literally, in the beliefs of the Church at the time—into the blood of Christ.

And so I think of that momentary bond between me and my paternal grandfather as a manifestation of the "communion of saints," the pledging of oneself to sacrifice in the interests of another, via a simple act of love.

Rev. Howell's three sons were well educated, and their fine backgrounds had everything to do with their firm and rigid upbringing under his hands and eyes. This tough love was handed down legitimately. Grandpop's own dad, James Howell, was also very strict. He had been an administrator at Dodds Reform School for wayward boys in Barbados in the late 1800s. Grandpop seems to have loved him. On the first page of his 1929 manuscript *I Was a Stranger*, he wrote:

To the Memory of James N. Howell
This book is dedicated
As an expression of respect and affection.
By His Son
   The Author

And so it's fair to expect that Rev. Howell's three sons were on their way to successful lives. All three went to Boys High School, which prided itself on attracting ambitious students from around the city. Charles would have been there at the same time as Isaac Asimov, who went on to become a biochemist and great science fiction writer. After high school, Charles attended and graduated from St. Augustine's College in North Carolina. Frank, the middle son, completed his studies at Brooklyn College and became a pharmacist. And Wilfred, my dad, the youngest, went to Lincoln University and then to Brooklyn Law School.

Grandpop must have been painfully disappointed in the way things turned out for his sons. My father began in the early 1950s to succumb to alcohol, dropping out of law school and leaving me and Mom in the Fort Greene projects, even as mom was stricken with polio. Grandpop would have been pained that his second son, Frank, also began drinking heavily and even disruptively—although at least Frank was able to open his own pharmacy and live at home with his wife and daughter.

But Grandpop must have been absolutely devastated that his oldest son, Charles, eventually abandoned the eleven children he had fathered with two women in Brooklyn. Charles, in the year or so before Grandpop's death, took off for Detroit, never to be heard from again by his abandoned children. The wife he left behind, a lovely, proud, and strong-willed woman, raised her six kids as a single mom living in a public housing project in the Brownsville section of Brooklyn. And then there was yet another lady in Brooklyn with whom Charles had had a secret relationship; and Charles also ran away from that lady, leaving her alone also to raise those five children.

I'm told that Grandpop, weak as he was, would take some of the young Howell kids to Coney Island and did his best to stay in touch with them.

Once, in the early 1990s, thirty-five years after his brother Charles had disappeared, I asked my father what he thought had happened to Charles. "I just assume he's dead," he told me.

My dad went to a peaceful death in 1996. I was there with him, free of resentments about the abandonment of four decades before. I wrote about the heavy obligations of fatherhood in an *Essence* magazine article after my father's death:

> I remember a day back in the late 1950s when my father came to visit and play a round of catch with me in the backyard. It was a rare treat. My parents had split up when I was a tot, and my mother and I went to live in the brownstone home of her parents. It was a lovely house and my grandparents doted on me, but I felt the absence of my father like a dull ache that surges and recedes but never goes away. I greeted this day of his visit with nervous anticipation. I must have been about 9 years old.
>
> I don't believe we had tossed the ball back and forth three times when my dad announced he needed something in the kitchen. He went inside, found a bottle of my grandfather's favorite stash, and poured himself a drink. He washed it down with water. He poured himself another. I don't recall much about the rest of the day, and it's possible my father, wherever he woke up, remembered nothing.
>
> There were times, even as an adult, when I clenched a fist in anger over this and other episodes like it. Still, I write these words now not bitterly, but gratefully. There eventually came a day when my father was freed from the chains of his alcoholism and when I, as a grown man, received the gift I had longed for in my youth: a father.
>
> For 25 years, until his death a year ago, I shared men's secrets with my father and listened to the words of his accumulated wisdom. I learned about his stint as one of the first Blacks in the U.S. Marine Corps; about the wandering years during which he drank

his way out of law school and out of a marriage; and about how he ended up in a dead-end job he despised. I came to respect the gray-flannel dignity, the stoically tragic air that he used to good effect late in life as an actor with the Black Spectrum Theatre Company in Queens, New York.

I don't mind acknowledging that the Ghost of Christmas Past would rear its ugly head from time to time. Where was my father in those old photos? Oh, yes, he certainly knew I harbored resentments that I couldn't wash away completely. He wanted me to become close to the son he had by another woman, but I never did. In my mind there were priorities of commitment to be respected—like to my mother, who suffered through two years of crippling polio when she and my father broke up, but who recovered and worked nine-to-five for many years, raising me without the help of a husband.

Despite all this, I owe my father a debt of gratitude for many spiritual, if not tangible, things he gave me over the years. I knew this beyond a doubt when I returned from a trip abroad last summer and learned he had been hospitalized. I soon got word that it was a galloping cancer from which there was no hope of recovery. I'm not easily given to tears—a trait that my own son has described as one of my faults—but that night love and sorrow suddenly welled up within me in a way I could not conceal, and I wept for what my old man was going through.

In the end, my father taught me how to die a brave death. During the remaining two weeks of his life he prayed without tears and tried to make sure he left something of value to those he'd loved or hurt. To my surprise, he exhibited a dry wit he had previously kept under wraps.

At his funeral I felt little of the guilt and remorse that sometimes follow a loved one's death. I vowed to express my affection for my own son, who has lived with me and his mom through fat years and lean, fun times and rough times, here and abroad, and who is now venturing into the world of work with a recent degree from Amherst College.

Dads: When the wayward spirit tugs at you, or the desire to escape the burdens of being a Black man in a hostile world beckons you from afar, let the primal voice of your paternal instinct sound clear in your mind.

And sons: When the heat of your anger and righteous resentment [boils] up in your chest, think hard before you burn the mys-
tic bridges to the ancestor who looks so much like you. Sometimes
those bridges should be burned, but often they are burned too
quickly.

They say it takes a village to raise a child, but I believe that deep
down inside, as quiet as the proud lad may keep it, every little boy
wants a father.[2]

Two years after that article appeared, I was working as a professor of
journalism at the Brooklyn campus of Long Island University. It was a
time of preparing lectures and doing freelance articles. Then, on March
3, 1999, in one of my more frantic moments, I headed home from the
university to sit at my computer and begin transcribing notes for a book
I was working on, *One Hundred Jobs: A Panorama of Work in the American
City*. Before beginning to type, I called my university phone number to
retrieve telephone messages. There was only one message. It was from a
woman who said, "My name is Linda Mahome. I'm calling to tell you that
your Uncle Charles Howell died yesterday. You can call me at . . ."

The pressure of impending deadlines dropped like metal from a tall
building. I sat for a few moments trying to absorb the words of this Linda
Mahome and their implications, which were loaded like the clip of an
M-16. I dialed the number in Detroit, Michigan, and spoke with Linda.

Linda identified herself as Uncle Charles's wife and said he had
"crossed over" peacefully the day before at their home in Detroit. He'd
had leukemia. It turned out that Linda subscribed to *Essence* magazine and
had read my piece about my father's death.

Because my article carried my name and also featured my picture—
with a graying beard that made me look like a younger version of Uncle
Charles—Linda immediately saw the relationship.

"This is your brother who died!" Linda told me she exclaimed to
Uncle Charles.

Charles took the magazine from her and read the article intently. She
said to him, "Look, it says your nephew teaches at Long Island University. We can call him there." But he said it would be wrong for him to
contact me after all these years of never reaching out to see how his
brother or others in the family were doing. He told her to promise not
to call. Linda—loquacious, a college graduate, thoughtful, a registered
nurse—was, nonetheless, like other susceptible women before her, blindly
enamored of the dashing Charles Howell; and so she complied with his

wishes, waiting until he died before she retrieved the article, obtained my number at LIU, and called me.

Not only had I not seen Uncle Charles in forty years (when I was about eleven years old), but to my lasting disappointment and shame, I did not get to know his kids right here in Brooklyn.

And, in the coming weeks and months, learning especially about the two boys he had left behind taught me lessons about the plight of the black male in urban America, a lesson that pertained to the sons of black immigrants as well to as the sons of parents from the southern states of old slavery.

Uncle Charles's children were from two households, one headed by his wife, Barbara, who bore him six children from 1945 through early 1950, and the other by Agnes, with whom he lived through the 1950s and had five children. Aunt Barbara's clan grew up in a public housing project in Brooklyn. She had only one boy, Peter, known as Peetie. Aunt Agnes moved from Brooklyn to Queens, where she raised her children, among them one boy, whose name was Alexandre. (Please note, dear reader, that Aunt Agnes was of Haitian descent and gave her son a French name. Please note further that I have changed the names, as given here, of Uncle Charles's children and mothers. I do this hopefully to diminish the pain of the still-living ones, as they hear Uncle Charles's breathtaking story of infidelity.)

Because I grew up in the all-black Bedford Stuyvesant section of Brooklyn, where black boys often fell victim to gang violence in the 1950s and then, over the next two decades, to the scourge of narcotics, I have always been sensitive to the difficulties of being a black male. I cannot help but believe that absent fathers are a big part—if not the biggest part—of the crisis of black males in America.

Uncle Charles's two sons—Peetie and Alexandre—were my only male first cousins on my father's side. After Peetie was murdered on the streets of Brownsville in 1985, not much was done in the way of follow-up police work, and the once-silent pain of a woman who had been left alone with six children intensified. As for Alexandre, he became a drug addict. Alexandre's mom, my Aunt Agnes, once told me she believed Uncle Charles's sudden departure was the principal cause of Alexandre's descent into instability and then into drugs. Family members were vague as to Alexandre's current whereabouts.

Needless to say, the revelation that Uncle Charles had been living in the open as an activist and supporter of black arts was a shock to everyone who had known him in Brooklyn.

Those who knew him in Detroit were astounded when I visited there and told them that the man they loved and respected so much had abandoned children in Brooklyn. I had gone to learn about this man of Shakespearean deviousness. His reason for fleeing his former hometown and his families was, I concluded, very simple. He had turned his back on Brooklyn because he could not support so many children while living the life he wanted, writing poems and essays, advising those who wanted to start black arts groups, and charming the ladies. He never fathered any more children, it seems.

Those he had left behind back East, the children and their mothers, felt a resurgence of anger, knowing for sure they would never have a chance to unleash their anger at the man who had done the unthinkable to them. I got the impression some of them were suspicious of me, perhaps thinking I might have known all along what was going on and had agreed to keep silent until Uncle Charles died. For some of his children, it was a heavy emotional blow to know their dad had been living a quick plane ride away in a comfortable home with another woman—a nurse, no less—who could comfort him in times of illness.

The story of Uncle Charles is an exposure of fragility of black fatherhood in America.

In the late 1990s Harvard sociologist Mary C. Waters published a book titled *Black Identities: West Indian Immigrant Dreams and American Realities*, in which she said that—despite all the bragging about West Indians' being so much more successful than their native-born black American counterparts—all it takes is one generation for offspring of black immigrants to become African Americans, with all the baggage that the designation carries. The effect of this is especially harsh on the males. They are disproportionately in the prisons. They are disproportionately in the morgues as murder victims. I now believe that my father and his brothers showed evidence of this reality described by Mary Waters. Even their dad, Grandpop, realized this in 1945 when he wrote a pamphlet, *It Could Happen Here: The Menace of Native Fascism After World War II*, in which he noted the indignity of his three sons' serving in a war-time army and marine corps that were racially segregated. The psychic effects of midcentury urban life for a black man in America were life-threatening. All three of Grandpop's boys showed its destructive results—my dad and Uncle Frank in their fierce addiction to alcohol, Uncle Charles in the sinful lack of self-discipline and introspection.

My grandfather Bertram Baker must have intuitively known that we black boys in the rising ghetto of Bedford Stuyvesant were facing dangers unknown to his generation, dangers from a resentment and anger turned inward. Coupled with the increasing density of post–World War II New York, it was all a recipe for the riots of 1964, the heroin and crack epidemics of the later decades, and the horrific gang violence that lasted through the turn of the next century in black neighborhoods throughout the city.

Irene and Bertram Baker were so protective of me that, initially, they didn't want me to participate in the boys' baseball leagues affiliated with my grandfather's political club. Many of the boys were gangsters from the Albany Projects and other rough parts of Bed-Stuy. But my grandparents ultimately saw that I very much needed to be with those guys. I was not yet calling them "my brothers," as I would when I reached Yale, but I knew I had a deep bond with them.

In the end, color issues aside, I'm so happy for Aunt Lil that she chose Uncle John over Uncle Charles, the only issue being character.

If I'd had more time with my grandfather Bertram Baker in the mid-1980s, I'd surely have wanted to ask him about Uncle Charles. More than anything else, I suppose, I'd want to let him know how much it meant to me that he and his wife, Irene, let me live in their Jefferson Avenue home as if it were mine. After they died, my mom lived and died right there. Now I own it and am renting one floor to the young lady who cared for my mother and the rest of the house to one of my son Damani's closest friends, a young man named Jamal Murphy, who's there with his wife, Monique, and their son, Kareem. Jamal's father was one of my best friends at Yale, Clyde Murphy, who died too young. Jamal's late grandfather was the Rev. Henson Jacobs, an immigrant from the Caribbean island of Grenada, who in Brooklyn became pastor of St. Augustine Episcopal Church, the very church that Bertram Baker's long-ago radical hero, the Rector George Miller, pastored in the years during and after World War I. I can never repay what Bertram Baker gave me, but I'll try to show gratitude in ways that are within my means.

Conclusion
Century of Promise, Century of Hope

Bertram Baker, though mostly forgotten after his retirement, was honored before his death in a way that lit a spark in his soul and helped make his death a happy one. The event was the conferring of an honorary doctorate in 1983 by St. John's University. On the stage, Baker stood and bowed with an elegance that could have been the ending scene in a movie about an old-time Democratic boss. Leaning over and whispering to Baker's daughter, Marian Baker Howell, family friend Shirley Tempro said, "They don't make them like your father anymore." A new Brooklyn was emerging at that moment, a Brooklyn with more black elected officials than one could name in ten minutes, a Brooklyn that was becoming known as the capital of the African diaspora. In the process, the past was forgotten. Today there is a growing appreciation of black Brooklyn's history. This is true in part because of the consciousness of gentrification, and the speed with which it is displacing black and brown residents who can't afford to remain in the place they called home for so long. History is practical, in that it can tell us about people and issues in ways that help us plan for a better future. But history is also simply tender. In recent years, as I've attended graduation ceremonies at Brooklyn College, where I've been teaching journalism, I wear the same red St. John's robe that my grandfather wore in 1983. As I do, I hope that somehow he is accepting my apologies for the disrespect he thought I displayed almost half a century ago. That was in 1970 when I refused to wear a cap and gown at my graduation from Yale. I would never have been accepted to Yale had it not been for him. He was outraged at what he felt was my contempt for tradition and for him. He refused to attend.

I thank him here for the brownstone that kept me warm and safe, for the jobs that came from the education he provided, and for the mother who birthed me. But high on my list of acknowledged gifts is this: that I was given Brooklyn as the place of my birth and rearing. The curious monkey in me has made me search endlessly to better understand Brooklyn. (Please don't be offended, black brothers and sisters, by my reference to "the monkey in me." My grandmother Irene Baker, as well as many other West Indians, would call each other monkey with affection. My grandmother always called my mother her "little monk.")

What I have been absorbing about Brooklyn leaves me with a trio of feelings: pride, disappointment, and hope. Let's start with the middle one, disappointment.

Twenty years before this book was published, I wrote a cover article for the highly regarded public policy magazine *City Limits*. I was attempting to look at the black political scene in Brooklyn a decade after Bertram Baker's death. The year was 1997, and the article focused on then-Assemblyman Al Vann. The article was titled "What Ever Happened to Al Vann? The Dream of Black Power in Brooklyn Fades to Gray."[1]

Vann had been a hero of mine. He came to the public eye in the late 1960s and, as head of the African-American Teachers Association, he outspokenly opposed the go-along–get-along policies of old-fashioned machine bosses (ummm, like Bertram Baker). Vann and other black folks were feeling freer to express anger about decades of abuses by police officers, by banks, by school administrators. The black activists grew in number and volume.

In 1974, Vann won the state Assembly seat representing Bedford Stuyvesant. That was four years after Baker's retirement. Soon after that he was able to win the election to become Bed-Stuy's Democratic district leader. Baker had always considered the holding of those two positions to be the pinnacle of achievement for a local politician. It meant you could help pass laws doing good for your community (as an Assemblyman). And you could wield political influence (as the Democratic district leader), helping local lawyers become judges. Thus armed at both hips, Vann became the new boss of black Brooklyn. He shed his *dashikis* for suits and ties, and he began to accustom himself to the ways of the Democratic machine, all while maintaining a progressive profile.

Vann's ambitions were big. He wanted growing black Brooklyn to become the center of power in New York City.[2] In 1984 he, along with the late Congressman Major Owens, formed the Coalition for Community Empowerment and tried to harness the power of the minority vote in Brooklyn and throughout the city. Eyes on the prize, he joined Reverend Jesse Jackson's strenuous bid for the presidency of the United States of America. It was a precursor of the future presidential candidate Barack Obama's call for hope, action, and change. With Vann in the forefront of Jesse Jackson's presidential campaign in New York state in 1984, hope was high. Jackson did well in New York City, and black politicians saw themselves as the avant-garde of a larger campaign to right the wrongs of America's racial past. It seemed that a new era was dawning on local politics. With Vann as coordinator of ideas, a band of black progressives hoped to run a slate of candidates across the city in the 1985 elections and then pump their fists in victory.

But it turned out that Vann's brightest political days were already behind him.

The 1985 election was supposed to have been black Brooklyn's moment of triumph. It was a bold grasp at power by progressive black politicians led by Vann and backed by a multi-ethnic coalition. They were trying to forge an alliance with Puerto Rican mayoral aspirant Herman Badillo, who wanted to unseat the increasingly conservative incumbent, Edward I. Koch.

But in a move that shocked Vann, the so-called "Gang of Four" from Harlem—Charles Rangel, David Dinkins, Basil Paterson, and Percy Sutton—broke ranks and put forth their own candidate for mayor, Harlem Assemblyman Herman "Denny" Farrell, a dark horse if ever there was one. "The coup that the Gang of Four was able to pull off basically diminished Al's power as leader of black Brooklyn," said Esmeralda Simmons, Executive Director of the Center for Law and Social Justice at Medgar Evers College, part of the City University of New York.

"And it diminished Brooklyn's emergence as the locus of political power for black folks in New York City," Simmons added.

It didn't just diminish it. It ended it.

The dominance of the entrenched old-line Harlem leadership continued, culminating in Dinkins's election as Mayor in 1989. In Brooklyn, on the other hand, black leaders became increasingly parochial in their concerns, even as the number of black elected officials soared. Today, the borough has scores of black elected officials, far more than any other borough. And all around Brooklyn today, people of African descent feel despair. As real estate developers have asserted control over elected officials, gentrification has intensified, bringing in new groups, largely whites and East Asians, and struggling black residents are forced to move to find affordable housing.

Data show that in Community Board Three, the city-administered local planning office covering Bedford Stuyvesant, the percentage of whites in Bed-Stuy between 2000 and 2015 increased by 1,235 percent, from 3,087 to 41,203. The portion of blacks dropped by 17 percent, going from 90,732 to 75,237. (Hispanics went up by 16 percent, from 23,457 to 27,112, and Asians were up by 552 percent, from 562 to 3,664.)

Historical Perspective

As of the writing of this book, black Brooklyn is in a crisis state like never before in recent memory. In the last years of the 1700s and early years of the 1800s, Brooklyn was 34 percent black. Blacks were concentrated in the section known as Crow Hill, after the many black crows in the area. There was a huge jail there, the Crow Hill Penitentiary, all the better to house the black men who wouldn't happily take meager-paying jobs. But by late 1800s, realtors looked at newly arriving Irish and Italian families and saw opportunity. They began building beautiful homes and parkways. They tore down the Crow Hill Penitentiary and changed the name of the neighborhood to Crown Heights.[3] Thus we witnessed our first explosion of Brooklyn gentrification, way before the term came into popular use.[4] The portion of African Americans in Brooklyn dropped from the one-third it was at the beginning of the nineteenth century to the 1 percent it was when my great-grandparents came from Nevis in 1897.

This story of early Crown Heights should be scary to struggling black New Yorkers today.

History seems to be repeating itself. By the year 2000, following the Great Migration of blacks from the South and immigration from the Caribbean, the black portion of Kings County's population zoomed up to one-third, roughly where it was at the beginning of the nineteenth century. Now a hypothetical question can be asked: Will blacks in Brooklyn all but disappear again, their numbers dropping precipitously to zero or thereabouts, as they did one hundred years ago?

Shamefully, rather than examining the past and trying to learn, many of our leaders are showing stunning disregard for history and its relics. Old buildings, even churches, are being torn down. Workers can no longer easily commute to their jobs because of the construction projects underway, and especially in Brooklyn. Elected officials have handed the future of the city over to developers. They have put many dark-complexioned central Brooklyn residents onto a trail of tears, like the one taken by Native Americans out of their homelands a century-and-a-half ago.

This descendant of Bertram Baker sometimes weeps. Reflecting on the early 1900s, when the first cohort of West Indians came to Brooklyn, I sometimes think of their century as the "century of promise." They left their descendants feeling proud of their accomplishments. Yes, they faced high obstacles, but they also saw the hills in the distance as sun-lit. No one better captured the personality of the collective black immigrant in the early to mid–twentieth century than that goddess of story-telling Paule Marshall. My mother loved Paule Marshall and read her classic tale of being a second-generation Caribbean girl, growing up in pre–World War II black Brooklyn, the moment it came off the printing presses in 1959. *Brown Girl, Brownstones* made real the inner conflicts suffered by those dark immigrants as they tried to make it in America while suffering the same insults and assumptions of inferiority that native-born black Americans faced. Paule Marshall was born in the 1920s, as my mother was. She attended Girls High School, as my mother did. But my mother, reader and lover of foreign languages though she was, stopped short of earning a college degree. Marshall attended Brooklyn College and Hunter College, where my mother's sister, Lilian, earned her bachelor's degree. While I have no evidence that Marshall knew of or studied Bertram Baker, I assume she knew of him. I was struck by sections of her book in which she writes of the tragic struggles between the mother and father of Selina Boyce, the main character. The tensions spoke of class differences between West Indians, a tension often based on skin color but also on ancestry. The divergent backgrounds came with a common preoccupation—a strong desire for property ownership and expectations of high education and mobility for offspring. West Indians, notably the ones referred to as Bajans (from the island of Barbados, sometimes referred to in those days as Little England), were known for putting copious amounts of energy, and the sacrificing of egos, into menial jobs, all so that they could one day purchase a home. They were New York's first day laborers, those West Indian women in Brooklyn. They walked the streets hoping white wives desiring help in the home would offer them a job.

> Sometimes the white children on their way to school laughed at their blackness and shouted, "nigger," but the Barbadian women sucked their teeth, dismissing them. Their only thought was of the "few raw-mout' pennies" at the end of the day which would eventually "buy house."[5]

The scenes presented themselves as recognizable to me. Perhaps it had to do with my paternal family's having come here from Barbados. It must have had roots also in the conversations my grandmother Irene Baker had had on the phone with her friends over the years. I would listen. Her own accent was pure Brooklyn, but her heart was always in the islands.

In my first reading of *Brown Girl*, I drew my head back in surprise as I read the following:

> "You hear Ena Roacheford finally buying house she been leasing since the year one? . . . Look Eulise Bourne. She buying another one despite the wuthless husband . . . I butt on Vi Dash on Fulton Street crying poor but she buying the second house, best proof. . . . [And] you did know a girl name Eloisee Gittens? . . . Well, soul, she and all buying house."[6]

My grandmother Irene Baker's sister was named Vi Dash. Aunt Vi was born in Brooklyn in 1902 with the birth-name Baker, a first cousin of Bertram Baker's. I had never in my life known of another Vi Dash. I assume somehow Paule Marshall recalled my aunt and felt comfortable using the name. Aunt Vi in fact had sold her Dash family home in Bedford Stuyvesant and moved to Crown Heights, as many up-and-coming blacks in those days were doing.

The story of the generation of Vi, Irene, and Bertram Baker was the story of the century of promise. It was a story of the victories of so many blacks like them, including the Carrington family, which had roots in Barbados and included the most successful real estate owners in old black Brooklyn. William Carrington immigrated to Brooklyn in 1904, and twenty years later, with his brother Ethelbert McDonald Carrington, formed an investment company that quietly backed Bertram Baker and was also one of his behind-the-scenes social buddies. William Carrington's daughter Carmel (Carrington Marr) attended Hunter College along with my mother's sister, Lilian, and later became a United States delegate to the United Nations and a member of the New York state Public Service Commission. Carrington family members played tennis in Bertram Baker's American Tennis Association. At the time of William Carrington's death in 1983, the *New York Times* ran an article quoting Bertram Baker saying, "Everything he touched brought success financially. He purchased properties in Bedford Stuyvesant and Brownsville and Williamsburg and after he took them over they were owned or tenanted by Negroes and that opened up a field of opportunity for Negroes." Oh, and William Carrington's nephew, Dr. Ethelbert Carrington (son of the Ethelbert Carrington who started the real estate business with William

Carrington), was the pediatrician who delivered me in 1949 at the now-shuttered Unity Hospital in Bed-Stuy. Goodness.

The stories of that generation of the first West Indian cohort are many and rich. There was the wealthy Barbadian immigrant in early-1900s Harlem, by the name of Adolph Howell. Imagine that—a Howell, and from the then-British island of Barbados that my paternal grandparents came from. Not only was he a wealthy funeral director, but in the early 1920s he purchased a five-story Y.W.C.A. dormitory on the corner of West 135th Street and Seventh Avenue for $72,000. That was according to James Weldon Johnson, the great Harlem Renaissance writer, in his classic article titled *Harlem: The Cultural Capital*. (I have no idea how many millions of dollars that would be in today's out-of-control New York real estate market.) Adolph Howell furthermore, by the way, ran at various times to represent Harlem in the New York state Assembly, in the U.S. Congress, and the New York City Board of Aldermen (precursor to the New York City Council). He lost each time, even as he continued filling his bank accounts. Howell also took out ads in annual journals of the American Tennis Association, the national organization that Bertram Baker was heavily involved with from the 1920s through 1966.

I may be in trouble if I don't add to this roster of successful early Caribbean immigrants the name of Adella Butts, my wife Marilyn's maternal grandmother. Adella Butts arrived in 1924 from Guyana with $24. She worked cleaning homes and began buying homes, accruing more than a dozen and turning herself into a relatively wealthy black New Yorker in the mid-1900s. Adella was named one of the "100 black millionaires" in the country in *Ebony* magazine in the 1960s. She passed along her real estate business to her daughter Mazie Butts Henry and son-in-law George Henry, the deceased parents of Marilyn.

But the century of promise that boosted the spirits of our first cohort of West Indians turned into an unsettling fog. Selina experienced this in Marshall's *Brown Girl, Brownstones*. She goes to college in the years just before World War II, joins clubs, and takes delight in dancing and writing. Selina's white friend's mother was present at a dance performance the two young ladies were giving. The mother learns that Selina is the child of Caribbean immigrants and proceeds to offer the type of congratulations that so many second-generation black immigrants have heard:

> The woman sat back, triumphant. "Ah, I thought so. We once had a girl who did our cleaning who was from there . . ." She caught herself and smiled apologetically. "Oh, she wasn't a girl, of course.

We just call them that. It's a terrible habit. . . . Anyway, I always told my husband there was something different about her—about Negroes from the West Indies in general. . . . I don't know what, but I can always spot it. When you came in tonight, for instance . . . ."[7]

Selina then looked at the mother and saw a truth that most black immigrants knew in their hearts but resisted in the hope that the dream that sang to the Italian and eastern European immigrants was singing to her and her parents.

But when she looked up and saw her reflection in those pale eyes, she knew that the woman saw one thing above all else. Those eyes were a well-lighted mirror in which, for the first time, Selina truly saw—with a sharp and shattering clarity—the full meaning of her black skin.[8]

The wisest of those early West Indian arrivals quickly learned that the native-born black scholar W. E. B. Du Bois knew of what he spoke when he asserted that the problem of the twentieth century was the problem of the color line. Du Bois appeared to know that the color-line problem would last beyond 1999, and, indeed, it did. There is today, as I write, a New York City Mayor who styles himself progressive and has a black wife. That couple is Mayor Bill de Blasio and First Lady Chirlane McCray. But many blacks in Brooklyn and the rest of New York City feel that not enough is being done to counter the effects of the real estate development that is out of control and ruining the lives of hundreds of thousands of people of color, especially in central Brooklyn. Discrimination in the construction industry persists and by some accounts is worse than it was in the 1960s. The U.S. Equal Employment Opportunity Commission in 2017 found that a large contractor with offices in black Brooklyn (the part now called East Flatbush) had a foreman who called black workers "niggers" and made them use separate bathrooms. When a black employee complained, he was fired. The E.E.O.C. arranged to have the contractor, the Laquila Group, with reported ties to organized crime, pay more than $600,000 to black former workers. Despite this outrageous pattern of behavior, no elected official in Brooklyn stepped forward to publicly denounce the Laquila Group after details were published in the New York Daily News. The Rev. Al Sharpton, known for his muscular protests against racism in the 1990s, expressed dismay at the lack of a response to the racist policies of Laquila. Rev. Sharpton wondered in a conversation with me if perhaps Laquila has been paying off elected officials. Al Sharpton, if he were younger and on the streets like before, would be all over television with that Laquila story. And elected officials would have to join with him. That's what happened after the outrageous police killing of African immigrant Amadou Diallo in 1991. Diallo was shot 19 times by white cops as he tried to put a key into the door leading to his apartment building in the Bronx. Sharpton led protests outside police headquarters. One politician after another joined and subjected themselves to arrest in the growing outrage. The white officers were acquitted, as almost always in America, but the city police department's notorious Street Crimes Unit was ultimately disbanded.

In December 2006 I attended an event at which David Paterson showed up. It was before Paterson became New York state's first black Governor. When I introduced myself to Paterson and began speaking to him about Bertram Baker, his eyes seemed to me to open wide. Legally blind, he turned his head toward me and left the group he had been with. He recalled with tenderness his childhood years visiting Albany in the 1960s. That was when his father, the late Basil Paterson of Harlem, was in the state Senate. He told me that Bertram Baker had made himself a role model for David's dad, Basil; for Charlie Rangel, who would go on to defeat the legendary Harlem Congressman Adam Clayton Powell Jr. and be Harlem's representative in Washington for half a century; and for David Dinkins, who would go on to become New York's first black mayor. The fondness in David Paterson's face made it clear that Bert Baker had also affected him.

Born in 1954 (in Brooklyn), David Paterson is a rare intergenerational link to New York's black political past. His late father Basil was the son of West Indian immigrants. In a 2013 radio interview with the public radio WNYC host Brian Lehrer, David Paterson spoke of elected officials today. He said they don't compare with those who preceded them, decades ago. "I think that the caliber of legislators, of state senators and assembly members, has diminished considerably in New York State. And it's not just character. People don't prepare as much. They don't know the issues. They don't spend time with their colleagues of opposing points of view to try to learn something."[9]

I myself could never have gone into politics. I'm not that good at giving quick answers to tough questions on television. Even so, I'll have to say that I've had my good times with politicians. I worked in cousin Deval Patrick's campaign when he made his historic run to be the first black Governor of Massachusetts. Then there's Letitia James, the New

York City Public Advocate. I'm impressed with how she seems to attend almost every community meeting having to do with housing needs or police issues. She's poised to be the first black and first woman ever to serve as elected Attorney General of New York state. And I can't forget Hakeem Jeffries, the black Congressman representing parts of Brooklyn and Queens. He told me once that my 1997 *City Limits* article on Al Vann made him decide to go into politics.

Some have said we need "tree shakers" in this day and age. One tree shaker is Brooklyn Assemblyman Charles Barron, who once demanded that the city get rid of Thomas Jefferson's portrait at City Hall. The reason, Barron said, was that Jefferson was a slaveholding pedophile. I'd have to go along with Charles on that one, as well as others. But here's the thing. Once one of my articles so angered Barron that he called me up and yelled at me for five minutes, hanging up before I could say a word. That's what I mean. I just don't think I was made to make it in politics.

But I do love Brooklyn, and I want to find ways to fight for its people, especially those with roots here, struggling to survive. When I'm not griping about elected officials or evil realtors, I do know how to chill. I walk central Brooklyn streets, with their low-lying brownstones to my left and right, the sky easily visible. Sights and sounds from the past sometimes tease my mind, like those of kids playing stickball, or guys on the corner singing Doo-wop songs. Brownstones offer a feeling of refuge that a parent can't always muster. You walk the streets, you walk away. You come back and fight another day.

Acknowledgments

I thank first of all my wife, Marilyn Henry Howell, who has long been encouraging me to write this book about my grandfather Bertram L. Baker. Over the years she has been a fountain of strength that she passed on to me at times when I very much needed it. I thank her for our son, Damani Howell, or Dr. Damani Howell as Marilyn insists on calling our only child, who's an orthopedic surgeon. He has shown singular devotion to his wife, Brittny, also a surgeon, and to his three children, Xavier, Oliver, and Ella. My extended family has meant much to me in the writing of this book, especially Sharon Bourke, an artist and writer who went through recent versions, editing and offering valuable thoughts. Sharon, like me, is a descendant of the Bakers who came to this land of opportunity from the island of Nevis more than 115 years ago. She shared with me that wonderful diary she kept from her visit to the island in the late 1950s.

I so appreciate that my cousin by marriage, former Massachusetts Governor Deval Patrick, was willing to share his memories of his grandfather-in-law Bertram Baker in the foreword to this book. Deval is married to my first cousin Diane, my baby cousin who's had a distinguished career as a lawyer and as the First Lady of Massachusetts. Diane's sister is Lynn, a retired Delta flight attendant whom I call my twin cousin. She and I spent our first days of life in the same room of Unity Hospital, with our respective mothers, Lilian Baker Bemus and Marian Baker Howell. Diane and Lynn's brother Jay, the oldest of us, is a retired electrician who, as a youngster, was always willing to step in and intercede if someone was trying to bully me. We've shared memories of the past as only boys always determined to overcome fear can do.

I'd also like to express gratitude to the late Constance Baker Motley, the great civil rights attorney and New York City political pioneer. She was the first black woman to be the President of a New York City borough and the first to sit as a federal judge. It was also she who introduced me to the island of Nevis. That was when in her retirement years in the mid-1990s she welcomed me into her home on the island of Nevis and encouraged me to become a citizen and hold onto the property that my ancestors had owned going back to the 1800s. I did become a citizen of St. Kitts and Nevis, and I did so by showing my blood links to my late grandfather Bertram L. Baker. As for my paternal family, the Howells, who hailed from the Caribbean island of Barbados more than a hundred years ago, I want to express appreciation to my first cousin, Joan King, for all the photos and documents she saved over the decades, helping me to better understand the flavor of that era when the first cohort of West Indians came to Brooklyn.

I'm perhaps going to risk alienating some whose names are not mentioned here, but I do want to thank that gem of an archivist Victoria O'Flaherty, the Director of Archives for the government of St. Kitts and Nevis. Over the past year or so, I joyfully spent money on phone calls from Brooklyn to her home and her office on the island of St. Kitts. I learned about her and about the history of the old British Caribbean. She would kindly find and send me images of newspaper clippings from the 1800s and early 1900s.

And then there are friends and colleagues here in Brooklyn who inspired me and offered valuable wisdom. One dispenser of such gifts was Paul Moses. Paul and I spent years working together as journalists at *Newsday* and then later as professors teaching journalism in the English Department at Brooklyn College. His beautiful and scholarly book, *An Unlikely Union: The Love-Hate Story of New York's Irish and Italians*, reflected impulses that were similar to mine in writing *Boss of Black Brooklyn*.

Calling the great historian William S. McFeely my colleague feels presumptuous. McFeely was the advisor on my Yale senior thesis back in 1970, the months when I was toting guns and risking jail time in the name of a black revolution that never happened. McFeely went on to write the Pulitzer Prize–winning biography of Ulysses S. Grant, as well as other books. All the while he displayed the generosity that makes teaching a cherished craft. Over the years, as I bounced from newspaper to newspaper and sought fellowships, he wrote recommendations every time

I asked for one. He read and commented upon the manuscript for this book. And I thank him.

I am compelled to pay a tribute to someone who was like a brother, an uncle, and a hero to me in my journalism career. That would be the Pulitzer Prize-winning journalist and former *Newsday* top editor Les Payne, who died of a sudden and strong heart attack as I was finishing *Boss of Black Brooklyn*. The day he died, in March 2018, Les was putting the finishing touches on his long-awaited biography of Malcolm X. I am expecting one day to see that book in print. Meanwhile, I caution all with whom I exchange greetings to live one day at a time. If I have more time with them I encourage them to identify, and then seek to live out, their dreams.

I cannot take my leave from you, dear reader, without saying what an honor and pleasure it was to work with the Director of Fordham University Press, Fredric Nachbaur. The patience and generosity he has shown make me feel special. I can't imagine being in a more productive relationship with someone who's directing one's work on a project as engrossing as a book about one's grandparent. Fred understands the issues that are hyperlocal and philosophical. With him all the way has been Will Cerbone, Editorial Associate, who finds and gives me full answers to the questions I ask. Then there is Ann-Christine Racette, whose work as an artist left me speechless when I first saw the cover of this book. And I thank Managing Editor Eric Newman, who supervised the tedious work of copy editing this book, so that many readers will go from one page to the next, all the way to the end. I hope that many do.

Peace to all.

Notes

Introduction: An Ancestor Speaks from Beyond

1. The article was published in the March, 1925, issue of the New York–based *Survey Graphic* magazine. That issue of the magazine was edited by Alaine Locke, known as the dean of the Harlem Renaissance. The issue was dedicated to the topic "Harlem, the Mecca of the New Negro."

2. Now called the Brooklyn Historical Society.

3. An encyclopedia published by Oxford University Press in conjunction with the W. E. B. Du Bois Research Institute of Harvard University. The Institute is now known as Hutchins Center.

4. Diane was the third and youngest child of Lilian Baker Bemus and John Bemus. Her siblings were John II and Lynn. The Bemuses moved from Jefferson Avenue to the Hollis section of Queens in 1959.

1. The Lasting Anger of an Abandoned Son

1. This account of Nevis is uniformly accepted by the few authors who have written about the nineteenth century and the island, including, notably, Vincent K. Hubbard, author of the 1996 book *Swords, Ships & Sugar: A History of Nevis to 1900* (Corvallis, Ore.: Premiere Editions International, 1996).

2. This is referred to in Hubbard's *Swords, Ships & Sugar* but also underlies descriptions in the writings of Sir Probyn Innis, who was the Governor of St. Kitts–Nevis until 1981 (two years before its independence from Great Britain) and who thereafter began practicing law while also writing histories of the islands, including the self-published *Forty Years of Struggle*, which covers 1896 to 1935 but also lays historical groundwork for the period.

3. "Phthis" is the term used in the British records that give the cause of her death.

4. A June 7, 1882, baptismal record at St. George's Parish shows that Lilian de Grasse was baptized in that Anglican church.

5. Some of the details about Bertram's early life come from a penciled diary that he kept from December 1914 through August 1915, totaling about 500 words. Also, Baker was interviewed about his life four times on tape in the six months before his death in March 1985. Irene Baker, his wife, was also interviewed from 1994 through 1996.

6. Rupert Byron was interviewed by the author during a visit to Nevis in the summer of 1996 and again by telephone in December 2014.

7. Details about Rev. Baker's marriage were in archives kept by the government of St. Kitts–Nevis.

8. These dates are in the records of the Ebenezer Wesleyan Methodist Church, now located on Dean Street in Brooklyn. It celebrated its 110th anniversary in the summer of 2015.

9. Victoria O'Flaherty, Director of Archives for St. Kitts–Nevis, says she knows of only one Nevisian newspaper, the *Somnambulo*, that was published on Nevis between 1880 and 1930; and she knows of only one copy of that paper, from 1883. In December 1938 and January 1939, *The St. Kitts–Nevis Daily Bulletin* published articles about Bertram's maternal uncle Willie de Grasse's role in receiving King George VI's official representative to the island.

10. Vernon L. Farmer and Evelyn Shepherd-Wynn, *Voices of Historical and Contemporary Black American Pioneers* (New York: Praeger, 2012), p. 304.

11. From interviews in the 1990s with Irene Baker.

12. Details about St. Kitts Grammar are based on interviews with Baker but also with Sir Probyn, mentioned above, during a 2006 visit to his office in Basseterre, St. Kitts, and in phone interviews in 2014. Sir Probyn also attended the school.

13. This deduction is made after many conversations with Nevisians such as Eustace Huggins, M.D., who said Frances and Sarah were descended from the "white" Hugginses of Nevis, as opposed to those blacks whose ancestors adopted the name but did not have blood ties to the Britishers. Some of the information about the Brooklyn Hugginses comes from a grandniece and granddaughter of the clan. That was my cousin Sharon Bourke, who kept notes written by her Huggins and Baker ancestors and retained many memories of them from childhood. Born in 1929 in Brooklyn, she was, in 2018, a writer and artist living in Central Islip, New York.

14. These are recollections from interviews with Irene Baker in 1995.

15. Ira De A. Reid, *The Negro Immigrant: His Background, Characteristics and Social Adjustment, 1899–1937* (New York: Columbia University Press, 1939).

16. This and other information about Rev. Baker and Eva Baker's home are in the 1910 U.S. Census records.

17. These details are in copies of a 1935 Ebenezer Church journal that was among the Bertram Baker possessions passed on to the author.

18. The doctor's statement was conveyed by Bertram Baker in a January 5, 1985, tape-recorded interview.

19. This fact was noted in the penciled diary.

20. Bertram Baker noted this repeatedly during the interviews in the months before his death.

21. Handwritten entries about the Baker and de Grasse ancestors were in papers left by Bertram Baker at his death and recovered by the author.

22. In the Statue of Liberty–Ellis Island database.

23. That was the designation for both Bertram and his father.

24. This aspect of Nevisian religiosity, its closeness to and difference from Anglicanism, is mentioned in chapters of Karen Fog Olwig's *Global Culture, Island Identity: Continuity and Change in the Afro-Caribbean Community of Nevis* (Reading, U.K.: Harwood Academic Publishers, 1993; Abingdon, U.K.: Taylor & Francis [e-book], 2005). The relevant chapters are "In Pursuit of Respectability: Toward an Egalitarian Order" and "The Methodist Society."

25. This was related by Irene Baker in the recorded interviews in 1995 with the author.

26. The salary is mentioned in Bertram Baker's diary. Abraham & Straus was commonly referred to as A&S. Later in the century, A&S closed, and Macy's opened in that same Fulton Street location.

27. This is from an October 7, 1995, interview with the then-101-year-old Jessie Warner at her home on Decatur Street in the Bedford Stuyvesant section of Brooklyn. Warner died at the age of 108.

28. In the early 1940s, when Bertram's older daughter, Lilian, was attending Hunter College, the elite public institution of higher learning in Manhattan for women, she met another student whose surname was also Baker and said her father came from Nevis. The young lady said her paternal grandfather was a Methodist minister who turned out to be Lilian's very own grandfather Rev. Alfred Baker, the father of Bertram Baker. So it's possible that an extramarital relationship gone bad was a reason for Rev. Baker's departure. The reverend spent his years immediately following 1917 with his wife, Eva, on the ministering circuit in the British Caribbean, especially the island of Anguilla, sixty miles north of Nevis. The story of the outside-marriage son, called the "off-child" by Nevisians, was kept hushed. In the 1990s, after Bertram's 1985 death, Irene told of the time in the 1940s when the half-brother, whose name is still not known, came from his home in New Jersey and rang the bell at the Bakers' brownstone in Bedford Stuyvesant, only to have Bertram answer, listen, and then slam the gate in the face of the man, who was never heard from again.

29. Recorded interview with the author in the months before Baker's death.

30. The depth of Bertram Baker's involvement with the Garvey movement is not clear. Baker served during the late 1920s as treasurer of the Brooklyn branch of the African Orthodox Church, a West Indian group with Garvey

and Episcopal affiliations. This is detailed in Chapter 3 ("Searching for a Band of Brothers").

31. This was published in *Marcus Garvey and United Negro Improvement Association Papers*, edited by Robert Hill, Volume II, page 222. It contains reports filed by an undercover agent (Berkeley: University of California Press, 1983).

32. Julie A. Gallagher mentions that West Indian immigrants were active in the Garvey movement and more likely than native-born blacks to be Democrats. This is in the chapter "The Political Geography of New York City in the Progressive Era," in her *Black Women and Politics in New York City* (Champaign: University of Illinois Press, 2012).

33. This is from the 1985 interviews with Irene Baker.

34. The Jefferson Avenue brownstone was purchased with a loan in the name of Bertram's older daughter, who was in college. The reason for putting it in her name, it seems, was that Bertram's credit was tarnished from the foreclosure on the Throop Avenue home.

35. From the July 26, 1935, flier titled "Testimonial Supper in Honor of Reverend A. B. B. Baker, Founder of Wesleyan Methodist in New York City," in the possession of the author.

36. This letter and others are now in the possession of the author.

37. This was part of an entry in the diary Sharon Bourke kept from that trip and turned over to the author.

2. Irene: Baker Forever, but Never a Boss

1. Irene Baker's handwritten notes, booklets, and sketches are in the possession of the author.

2. Irene Baker, interviewed by the author in 1995.

3. P.S. 93 was (and is) located at 31 New York Avenue, several blocks from the Dean Street home of Irene's father, Edwin, who worked in the 1910s as the janitor, even as he went during the weekdays to his job as a clerk-typist with a shipping company.

4. The connection here was made based on obituaries of McCooey family members after 1930 in the *New York Times*.

5. Sarah's maiden name was Huggins, and her lineage reaches back to the white slave- and plantation-owning Hugginses of the early 1800s. Sarah's mulatto Huggins family considered itself to be Anglican (American Episcopalian) by birth and tradition.

6. This incident experienced by Sarah Baker is recounted, with Irene Baker as the source, in a booklet published by St. Luke and St. Matthew Episcopal Church in 1991. It was titled "The Sesquicentennial Celebration of The Episcopal Church of St. Luke and St. Matthew: 1841–1991."

7. Irene's parents moved from place to place in Brooklyn, looking for the cheapest rents. They did not own a home until the mid-1920s, when they purchased their Bedford Stuyvesant brownstone on Throop Avenue near

Putnam Avenue. But Ned Baker owned the 38 Lawrence Street home that was the meeting hall of the wide Baker coterie. Ned had been given the house at a bargain price that was pretty much like a gift, from a previous owner who was a seaman of Italian descent.

8. The only boy among the Bakers Dozen, Eddie Baker, was called up to serve and entered the segregated army as part of the 369th Regiment, which was known as the Harlem Hellfighters who saw action in Europe during the war.

9. From the 1995 interview with Irene Baker.

10. Irene Baker in previously cited 1995 interview.

11. They married December 10, 1919; the Amendment was ratified August 18, 1920.

12. Found on a slip of paper in a drawer of Irene Baker's home nine years after her death in 2001.

13. From interviews during the late 1990s with Marian Baker Howell, younger daughter of Bertram and Irene Baker.

14. Quoted by Keith S. Henry, writing in *Journal of Black Studies*, June 1977, "The Black Political Tradition in New York: A Conjunction of Political Cultures."

15. In Constance Baker Motley, *Equal Justice Under Law: An Autobiography* (New York: Macmillan, 1999).

16. Detailed in the *Amsterdam News*' coverage of that race during the summer and fall of 1968.

17. Tape-recorded 1995 interview with Irene Baker.

18. The Bishop Henry B. Hucles Nursing Home became the Brooklyn Gardens Nursing Home and is no longer affiliated with the Episcopal Church.

3. Searching for a Band of Brothers

1. The churches were nomadic in the early 1900s, but by the 1930s both St. Augustine's and St. Phillip's would be based in what would be called Bedford Stuyvesant. After a devastating fire in the early 1970s, St. Augustine's moved to the Flatbush neighborhood, where it is located still. St. Barnabas was, and is today, in the East New York section of Brooklyn. The author's paternal grandfather, the Rev. Charles G. Howell, was named pastor of St. Barnabas just after World War I. A 1912 immigrant from Barbados, he had graduated from Codrington Divinity School in Barbados, the oldest theological academy for the training of Anglican priests in the Caribbean. He was one of the first blacks to attend and graduate from there.

2. "The Origins of the African Orthodox Church," in *Black Power and Black Religion: Essays and Reviews*, edited by Richard Newman (West Cornwall, Conn.: Locust Hill Press, 1987).

3. "Archbishop Faces Deportation: Court Orders Cops to Hunt for Minister," by Wesley McD. Holder, the *New York Amsterdam News*, October 4, 1933.

4. Clarence Taylor mentions the African Orthodox Church as an outlet for frustrated blacks in those years. Chapter titled "The Failure to Make Things Better," in *The Black Churches of Brooklyn* (New York: Columbia University Press, 1994).

5. It was published in the form of a classified-type ad in the *Amsterdam News*, November 23, 1927.

6. Garvey returned to the Caribbean after his 1927 release from a U.S. penitentiary. In the following years, blacks in New York and elsewhere continued to show allegiance to Garvey, but their numbers were greatly reduced. Garvey died in London in 1940 at the age of fifty-two.

7. Hall said this during a telephone interview in 2013.

8. Much of the following information was gathered from the copious letters and other documents in the Harry Williamson Collection at the Schomburg Center for Research in Black Culture.

9. Fort Greene is located between the Bedford section and Downtown Brooklyn.

10. In her January 1958 article in the *Journal of Negro History*, Emma L. Thornbrough published "More Light on Booker T. Washington and the New York Age." The article details the involvement in the purchase of noted black journalist, T. Thomas Fortune, who relinquished his shares, and Fred R. Moore, a businessman–*cum*–political player who retained his interest through the time of his death in 1934, as Baker was writing articles.

11. It appeared in the October 29, 1932, edition of the *New York Age*.

12. The *New York Age*, October 29, 1932.

13. The *New York Age*, February 4, 1933.

14. That was on page 260 of Muraskin's *Middle-Class Blacks in a White Society: Prince Hall Freemasonry in America* (Berkeley: University of California Press, 1975).

15. The *New York Age*, June 3, 1933.

16. Dr. Roscoe Giles was a member of the Alpha Phi Alpha black fraternity, the oldest in the nation (started at Cornell in 1907). The fraternity has published biographies of its prominent graduates. Roscoe Giles's can be found at http://rmc.library.cornell.edu/alpha/earlyalpha/earlyalpha_3.html.

17. The *New York Age*, June 24, 1933.

18. That address was around the corner from 523 Throop Avenue, where the Baker family was living at the time.

19. The *New York Age*, March 17, 1934.

20. The *New York Age*, March 24, 1934.

21. The *New York Age*, April 14, 1934.

22. The *New York Age*, June 2, 1934.

23. In the Schomburg's Williamson Collection.

24. This occurred on May 22, 1942, and the petition is in the Williamson files at the Schomburg Center.

25. In Elinor Des Verney Sinnette's *Arthur Alfonso Schomburg: Black Bibliophile and Collector* (Detroit: Wayne State University Press, 1989), pp. 186–187.

26. In the Williamson Collection at the Schomburg Center.

27. Details in the italicized section of this chapter come from: Emma Lou Thornbrough's biography, *T. Thomas Fortune: Militant Journalist* (Chicago: University of Chicago Press, 1972) and *The Colored American*, November, 1907.

4. A "Coloured" West Indian in the Realm of the Irish and the Jews

1. Scholar Craig Steven Wilder, in his book *A Covenant with Color* (New York: Columbia University Press, 2000), has a chapter, "Irish Over Black," that outlines the great hold that the Irish had on politics in New York City, and a recurring hostility to blacks, especially in the 1800s.

2. Interview with Baker, by the author, January 5, 1982.

3. Everett Williams, interviewed at his home in Brooklyn in March 1995.

4. The *Amsterdam News*, November 5, 1930.

5. January 6, 1992, interview of Holder by the author.

6. Author's note: My conversion to Roman Catholicism in the 1950s, my hours spent studying the Latin that I used as an altar boy, my desire in the mid-1960s to become a priest, were an outgrowth of our family roots in the Episcopal Church.

7. Regarding the information about Minnie Abel in this paragraph up to this point: Ancestral research on Abel and background research on the Hagen family were done by librarian Laura Mann, M.L.S., for the author.

8. The *Amsterdam News*, April 11, 1936.

9. The *Amsterdam News*, March 28, 1936.

10. Harold X. Connolly, *A Ghetto Grows in Brooklyn* (New York: New York University Press, 1977), p. 65.

11. The *Amsterdam News*, September 18, 1937.

12. From interview with Moritt's daughter, Rabbi Leana Moritt, on June 12, 2015.

13. The *New York Age*, Oct. 1, 1938.

14. Connolly, op. cit., p. 108.

15. Connolly, op. cit.

16. John G. Van Deusen, "The Negro in Politics," in the *Journal of Negro History*, July 1936, p. 267.

17. Spring 2001 report by Joseph J. Thorndike, in the *Administrative Law Review*, Vol. 53, No. 2, Spring 2001, pp. 717–780.

18. In Johnson's obituary in the *New York Times*, October 3, 1981.

19. W. E. B. Du Bois coined the "Talented Tenth" to refer to those educated blacks who would seek and find power and respect during the coming years of the twentieth century.

5. The American Tennis Association as a Brotherhood/Sisterhood

1. The first big wave was during World War I.

2. Blacks in Brooklyn were actively involved in tennis from at least the early

1920s. Among Baker's possessions were notebooks of meetings of central Brooklyn black tennis enthusiasts, with the first meeting having occurred on February 20, 1920.

3. Norman remained close to Bertram Baker over the years, and Baker kept biographical sketches of friends such as Norman who he felt were "breaking down barriers." Those notes are in the possession of the author.

4. Such as the *Amsterdam News*, April 7, 1973, "Gerald Norman, ATA Founder, Dead at 91."

5. It was published in the *Brooklyn Daily Eagle*, December 30, 1929.

6. That one and dozens of other American Tennis Association bulletins and newsletters were passed on by Bertram Baker to the author.

7. Based on discussions in the 1990s with Bertram and Irene Baker's daughter Marian.

8. The *Amsterdam News*, October 4, 1941, p. 11.

6. Climbing the Ladder to Elective Office

1. Julie A. Gallagher, *Black Women and Politics in New York City* (Champaign: University of Illinois Press, 2012).

2. Baker at the Brooklyn Historical Society in 1976.

3. Verina Morton married again after the death of Dr. Walter Morton and assumed the surname of her new spouse, Emory Jones, a musician.

7. On a Mission in the 1950s: Desegregation of Housing

1. "East Side Housing Project Will Bar Negro Tenants," *New York Post*, May 20, 1943.

2. "'Wall Town' Housing OK'd Over Protests." *New York Post*, June 4, 1943.

3. "New York Is Called 'Segregated Town,'" *New York Times*, March 6, 1955.

4. Interviews with Metcalf conducted by phone in 1992 and later in the 1990s.

5. This and other such quotes from Metcalf are from a forty-five-page synopsis given by George Metcalf to the author in the late 1990s. Decades ago he said he had hoped to include it in a chapter about housing but found no publishing interest and said I was free to use it.

6. From Metcalf's synopsis.

7. Early 2000s interview.

8. Metcalf synopsis.

9. Ibid.

10. The Bemuses stayed on Jefferson Avenue with us and the Bakers for two years and then moved to the Hollis section of Queens, in those days considered a social step upward for blacks.

8. Master of Black Compromise

1. "Carlton Avenue YMCA shatters all-time record in drive," *New York Age*, October 16, 1848.

2. Booker T. Washington, *Up from Slavery: An Autobiography* (New York: Doubleday, Page & Co., 1905).

3. Interview by the author with Holder, January 13, 1992.

4. The vote results and other details were cited from saved notes by Baker at his 1976 talk at the Brooklyn Historical Society.

5. Some interviewees, including James Shaw, said Schor took a room on Madison Avenue. Connolly also mentions the residency issues in *A Ghetto Grows in Brooklyn*.

6. Interview with Albert R. Murray, July 30, 1992.

7. Interview with Josephine Bravo, December 22, 2006.

8. From author's December 1995 interview with Lawrence Pierce.

9. Ibid.

10. "Baker First AD Head Here; Defeats Holder in 6th: Won 'Decisive' Victory to be leader," *Brooklyn Eagle*, September 15, 1954.

11. Connolly, op. cit., chapter, "The Politics of Success."

12. Daphne Sheppard, "Marie Flagg Defies Baker; Splits Democratic Ranks; Bert Baker Has Woman Trouble," The *Amsterdam News*, August 31, 1957.

13. The *Amsterdam News*, June 29, 1957.

14. Pierce interview.

15. From the 1962 *"29th Anniversary Ball" Journal of the United Action Democratic Association.*

16. P.O.N.Y. stood for Protect Our Nation's Youth. It was for boys, thirteen and fourteen. The Little League was for boys nine to twelve.

17. Connolly, *A Ghetto Grows in Brooklyn*, p. 47.

9. The 1960s, Political Reform, and Personal Tragedy

1. From a Thomas Russell Jones interview with the author, October 26, 1995. The author spoke with Jones numerous times through the 1990s and early 2000s.

2. Ibid.

3. Ibid.

4. The request was denied July 5, 1955, by the U.S. Court of Appeals, Second Circuit. Court records show that Jones represented defendant Chin You.

5. Walter, John C. *The Harlem Fox: J. Raymond Jones and Tammany, 1920–1970* (Albany: SUNY Press, 1989).

6. *Fifty Years a Democrat: The Autobiography of Hulan E. Jack* (Leesburg, Va.: New Benjamin Publishing House, 1983).

7. See Robert F. Pecorella and Jeffrey M. Stonecash, *Governing New York State* (Albany: SUNY Press, 2006); Alan G. Hevesi, *Legislative Politics in New York* (New York: Praeger, 1975).

8. For the Jewish advance in Brooklyn politics, see Jeffrey Gerson, "Building the Brooklyn Machine: Irish, Jewish and black political succession in central Brooklyn, 1919–1964," City University of New York doctoral thesis.

9. Interview with retired U.S. Court of Appeals Judge Lawrence Pierce.

10. Nineteen-ninety-five Jones interview with the author.

11. Ronald Sullivan, "Deadlock Continues in Albany," *New York Times*, January 8, 1965.

12. The *Amsterdam News*, January 30, 1965.

13. R.W. Apple, "Travia Elected Speaker; Steingut Is Defeated," *New York Times*, February 4, 1965.

14. "Wagner Denies Pressure," *New York Times*, January 19, 1965.

15. "'I Took No Bribe'!—Baker." The *Amsterdam News*, January 30, 1965.

16. "Shelve Neighborhood School Bill." *Newsday*, Albany Bureau dateline, March 16, 1966.

17. In a 1985 interview with the author.

18. Jeffrey Nathan Gerson. "Building the Brooklyn Machine: Irish, Jewish and black political succession in central Brooklyn, 1919–1964," CUNY Doctoral Thesis, 1990, p. 336.

19. From a biographical note sent by Archibald to Bertram Baker and kept by Baker.

20. "R. Risley Dent, Jr., Brooklyn Lawyer: Democratic Primary Victor for State Senator Dies," *New York Times*, June 8, 1964.

21. Diggs left his maroon-colored Cadillac in his will to me. I sold it to purchase a Volvo, the car I used to transport rifles and shotguns during the May Day disturbances at Yale in 1970.

22. Loretta Smallwood Dehaney was interviewed at her residence in Weschester County, N.Y., on December 12, 1995.

23. The *Amsterdam News*, December 18, 1965.

24. Sydney H. Schanberg, "Assembly, in a Quick Shift, Votes for Quarter-Horse Pari-Mutuels," *New York Times*, April 23, 1969.

25. The *Amsterdam News*, February 28, 1970.

10. Irene, in the End, Became His Connection to Home and Mother

1. From notes and booklets left in the home of Irene Baker.

11. Author Commentary. Downtown Brooklyn: Soul of the Boss, Soul of a People

1. Unable by British law to obtain work as a clergyman, William Law devoted his life to working as a tutor, living in the home of the Gibbon family. His student was Edward Gibbon, father of the Edward Gibbon who wrote *The Decline and Fall of the Roman Empire*.

12. Author Commentary. My Other Grandfather, a Priest and Writer I Hardly Knew

1. Brokers used to call the main trading room on Wall Street "The Curb Exchange," according to Business Insider and other sources. This was before it became known as the American Stock Exchange, in 1953.

2. *Essence*, December 1997. Used with permission.

Conclusion: Century of Promise, Century of Hope

1. *City Limits: New York's Urban Affairs News Magazine*, November 1997. Note: Al Vann is retired from active politics, while Esmeralda Simmons is still Executive Director of the Center for Law and Social Justice at Medgar Evers College.

2. In 1915 when Baker arrived from the island of Nevis, blacks made up 1.4 percent of the population of Brooklyn; in the 1940s, when he finally won the backing of Democratic bosses and began running for office, blacks were 4 percent of the population. By 1960, blacks constituted 14.1 percent. The 1965 Hart–Celler Act widened the entry doors for non-Europeans, and Caribbean immigrants began coming in numbers never before seen. By 1990, an astounding 38 percent of Brooklyn's residents were black.

3. On the grounds of the old penitentiary they built a school for the Irish and the Italian boys flooding into the neighborhood. Oh how teasing time can be. The new school was run by Jesuit priests and named Brooklyn Preparatory College, the very school that my grandfather Bertram Baker used his clout to get me into in 1962.)

4. The British sociologist Ruth Glass coined the term "gentrification" in 1964. She used it to describe population shifts occurring when well-off residents, i.e., the gentry, moved into neighborhoods and displaced poorer, working class ones.

5. Paule Marshall, *Brown Girl, Brownstones*. (Mineola, New York: Dover Publications, Inc. 2009). Rights to publish these sections were granted by the Faith Childs Literary Agency, on behalf of Paule Marshall.

6. Ibid., p. 61.

7. Ibid, p. 248.

8. Ibid, p. 250.

9. David Paterson became New York's first black governor in 2008, after former Gov. Eliot Spitzer resigned following a prostitution scandal. Thereafter Paterson also took media hits, notably after he and his wife, Michelle, admitted to having had extramarital affairs. It was also alleged that members of his administration had been involved in witness tampering. David was too idiosyncratic to be in politics and bowed out after the expiration of his term in December 2010.

Bibliography

The sources for this book were primary and secondary; they were people I listened to and things I read. They are, together, too numerous to list here. Among the significant places housing materials that were helpful to me are: the Schomburg Center for Research in Black Culture; the Brooklyn Collection room of the Central Branch of the Brooklyn Public Library; the St. Kitts and Nevis Archives located on the Caribbean island of St. Kitts; the Nevis Heritage Center located on the island of Nevis, which with St. Kitts forms the smallest nation in the Western Hemisphere; the Municipal Archives of the City of New York; the old Family Life Center of the Mormons in New York City; the Brooklyn Historical Society; the New York Public Library; and the various homes of those who searched for and shared relevant materials with me.

Notable among those who have written about Brooklyn and its twentieth-century history are Jeffrey Gerson, who's in the list that follows. In the late 1980s and early 1990s he did a tremendous amount of research into the foundations of twentieth-century Brooklyn politics. In the years just after Bertram Baker's death in 1985, Gerson was the only person to have written significantly about him and his legacy. In more recent times, black scholars such as Craig Steven Wilder of MIT, Clarence Taylor of Baruch College (CUNY), and Brian Purnell of Bowdoin College have set the path toward meaningful discovery of black Brooklyn's past. The burden now will fall on those whose job it must be to write about black Brooklyn's present and its future, as it faces challenges at least as strong as when Bertram Baker began his life in local politics in the 1920s.

Following are some books and articles that might be helpful and/or interesting to students and others delving into topics discussed in *Boss of Black Brooklyn*. It goes without saying that I will cringe later upon learning I left out meaningful works. So be it.

Selected Publications

Andreassi, Anthony D. *Teach Me to Be Generous: The First Century of Regis High School in New York City.* New York: Fordham University Press, 2014.

Arian, Asher; Goldberg, Arthur S.; Mollenkopf, John H.; and Rogowsky, Edward T. *Changing New York City Politics.* New York and London: Routledge, 1991.

Barron, James; Quindlen, Anna; and Levitas, Mitchel. *Book of New York: 549 Stories of the People, the Events and the Life of the City—Past and Present.* New York: Black Dog and Leventhal, 2009.

Benardo, Leonard, and Weiss, Jennifer. *Brooklyn by Name: How the Neighborhoods, Streets, Parks, Bridges, and More Got Their Names.* New York: NYU Press, 2006.

Brown, Elaine. *A Taste of Power: A Black Woman's Story.* New York: Pantheon Books, 1992.

Browne, Arthur. *"One Righteous Man: Samuel Battle and the Shattering of the Color Line in New York."* Boston: Beacon Press, 2016.

Byron, Rupert McDonald. *The Dawn of Statehood in St. Kitts–Nevis–Anguilla.* AuthorHouse, 2005

Caro, Robert A. *The Power Broker: Robert Moses and the Fall of New York.* New York: Vintage, 1975.

———. *The Years of Lyndon Johnson: The Path to Power.* New York: Vintage, 1982.

———. *The Years of Lyndon Johnson: Means of Ascent.* New York: Vintage, 1990.

———. *The Years of Lyndon Johnson: Master of the Senate.* New York: Vintage, 2003.

———. *The Years of Lyndon Johnson: The Passage of Power.* New York: Vintage, 2013.

Chernow, Ron. *Alexander Hamilton.* New York: Penguin, 2005

Connolly, Harold X. *A Ghetto Grows in Brooklyn.* New York: NYU Press, 1977.

Dawkins, Wayne. *City Son: Andrew W. Cooper's Impact on Modern-Day Brooklyn.* Jackson: University Press of Mississippi, 2012.

Donaldson, Greg. *The Ville: Cops and Kids in Urban America,* Updated Edition. New York: Fordham University Press, 2015.

Dyde, Brian. *Out of Crowded Vagueness: A History of the Islands of St. Kitts, Nevis and Anguilla.* New York: Macmillan, 2006.

Flateau, John Louis. *Black Brooklyn: The Politics of Ethnicity, Class and Gender.* AuthorHouse, 2016.

Ford, F. Donnie. *Caribbean Americans in New York City, 1895–1975.* Mount Pleasant, S.C.: Arcadia, 2002.

Furman, Robert, and Merlis, Brian. *Brooklyn Heights: The Rise, Fall and Rebirth of America's First Suburb.* Charleston, S.C.: The History Press, 2015.

Gallagher, Julie A. *Black Women and Politics in New York City.* Champaign: University of Illinois Press, 2012.

Gerson, Jeffrey, "Bertram L. Baker, the United Action Democratic Association, and the First Black Democratic Succession in Brooklyn, 1933–1954." In *Afro-Americans in New York Life and History*, Vol. 16, No. 2, July 1992.

———. "Building the Brooklyn Machine: Irish, Jewish and Black Political Succession in Central Brooklyn, 1919–1964." Doctoral thesis, City University of New York, 1990.

Glazer, Nathan, and Moynihan, Daniel. *Beyond the Melting Pot: The Negroes, Puerto Ricans, Jews, Italians, and Irish of New York City*. Cambridge, Mass.: MIT Press, 1967.

Glueck, Grace, and Gardner, Paul. *Brooklyn: People and Places, Past and Present*. New York: Abrams, 1991.

Golway, Terry. *Machine Made: Tammany Hall and the Creation of Modern American Politics*. New York: Norton, 2014.

Gray, Frances Clayton, and Rice Lamb, Yanick. *Born to Win: The Authorized Biography of Althea Gibson*. Hoboken, N.J.: Wiley, 2004.

Greer, Christina M. *Black Ethnics: Race, Immigration, and the Pursuit of the American Dream*. New York: Oxford University Press, 2013.

Hamm, Theodore, and Cole, Williams. *Pieces of a Decade: Brooklyn Rail Nonfiction, 2000–2020*. Brooklyn: The Brooklyn Rail & Black Square Editions, 2010.

Harris, Brandon. *Making Rent in Bed-Stuy*. New York: HarperCollins, 2017.

Helmreich, William B. *The Brooklyn Nobody Knows: An Urban Walking Guide*. Princeton, N.J.: Princeton University Press, 2016.

Hill, Robert A. (ed.). *The Marcus Garvey and Universal Negro Improvement Association Papers, Vol. 1 (1826–Aug. 1919)*. Berkeley: University of California Press, 1983.

Hill, Robert A. (ed.). *The Marcus Garvey and Universal Negro Improvement Association Papers, Vol. 1I (Aug. 1919–Aug. 1920)*. Berkeley: University of California Press, 1983.

Hoetink, H. *Caribbean Race Relations: A Study of Two Variants*. London and New York: Oxford University Press, 1971.

Holder, Calvin. "The Rise and Fall of West Indian Politicians." In *Political Behavior and Social Interaction: Caribbean & African American Residents in New York*, ed. George A. Irish and E. W. Rivier. Brooklyn, N.Y.: Caribbean Research Center, Medgar Evers College, 1970.

Hubbard, Vincent K. *Swords, Ships & Sugar: History of Nevis to 1900*. Corvallis, Ore.: Premiere Editions, 1992.

Hymowitz, Kay S. *The New Brooklyn: What It Takes to Bring a City Back*. New York: Rowman & Littlefield, 2017.

Ignatiev, Noel. *How the Irish Became White*. New York: Routledge, 1995.

Jack, Hulan. *Fifty Years a Democrat: The Autobiography of Hulan E. Jack*. New York: The New Benjamin Franklin House, 1983.

Jackson, Kenneth. *The Ku Klux Klan in the City, 1915–1930*. New York: Oxford University Press, 1967.

Johnson, John B. *Governors of New York*. Watertown, N.Y.: Watertown Daily Times, 1958.

Jonnes, Jill. *Conquering Gotham, A Gilded Age Epic: The Construction of Penn Station and Its Tunnels*. New York: Viking Press, 2007.

Kasinitz, Philip. *Caribbean New York: Black Immigrants and the Politics of Race*. Ithaca, N.Y.: Cornell University Press, 1992.

Krase, Jerome, and LaCerra, Charles. *Ethnicity and Machine Politics*. New York and London: University Press of America, 1991.

Lankevich, George J. *New York City: A Short History*. New York and London: NYU Press, 2002.

Lardner, James, and Reppetto, Thomas. *NYPD: A City and Its Police*. New York: Holt, 2000.

Levine, Naomi. *Ocean Hill-Brownsville: A Case History of Schools in Crisis*. New York: Popular Library, 1969.

Lewinson, Edwin R. *Black Politics in New York City*. New York: Twayne, 1974.

Lewis, David Levering. *When Harlem Was in Vogue*. New York: Oxford University Press, 1989.

———. *W. E. B. Du Bois: Biography of a Race, 1868–1919*. New York: Holt, 1994.

———. *W. E. B. Du Bois: The Fight for Equality and the American Century, 1919–1963*. New York: Holt, 2000.

Lockwood, Charles. *Bricks and Brownstone: The New York Row House 1783–1929*. Classical America Series in Art and Architecture. New York: Rizzoli, 2003.

Manoni, Mary H. *Bedford-Stuyvesant: The Anatomy of a Central City Community*. New York: Quadrangle, 1973.

McInnis, Bryant. *Glory in a Snapshot (Photos of Bed-Stuy)*. Brooklyn: Word for Word, 1999.

Merlis, Brian. *Brooklyn: The Way It Was*. Brooklyn: Israelowitz, 1995.

Morrone, Francis. *An Architectural Guide to Brooklyn*. Kaysville, Utah: Gibbs Smith, 2001.

Moses, Robert. *Public Works: A Dangerous Trade*. New York: McGraw-Hill, 1970.

Muhammad, Khalil Gibran. *The Condemnation of Blackness: Race, Crime, and the Making of Modern Urban America*. Cambridge, Mass.: Harvard University Press, 2011.

Muraski, William A. *Middle-Class Blacks in a White Society: Prince Hall Freemasonry in America*. Berkeley: University of California Press, 1975.

Naison, Mark. *White Boy: A Memoir*. Philadelphia: Temple University Press, 2002.

Newman, Richard. *Black Power and Black Religion: Essays and Reviews*. West Cornwall, Ct.: Locust Hill Press, 1987.

Osman, Suleiman. *The Invention of Brownstone Brooklyn: Gentrification and the Search for Authenticity in Postwar New York*. New York and London: Oxford University Press, 2011.

Osofsky, Gilbert. *Harlem, The Making of a Ghetto: Negro New York, 1890–1930*. New York: Harper & Row, 1968.

Otis, Ginger Adams. *Firefight: The Century-Long Battle to Integrate New York's Bravest*. New York: St. Martin's Press, 2015.

Peterson, Carla L. *Black Gotham: A Family History of African Americans in Nineteenth-Century New York City*. New Haven, Conn., and London: Yale University Press, 2011.

Platzer, Brian. *Bed-Stuy Is Burning*. New York: Atria, 2017.

Powell, Adam Clayton, Jr. *Adam by Adam: The Autobiography of Adam Clayton Powell, Jr*. New York: The Dial Press, 1971.

Purnell, Brian. *Fighting Jim Crow in the County of Kings: The Congress of Racial Equality in Brooklyn*. Lexington: University Press of Kentucky, 2013.

Rampersad, Arnold. *Jackie Robinson: A Biography*. New York: Ballantine, 1998.

Rangel, Charles B. *And I Haven't Had a Bad Day Since: From the Streets of Harlem to the Halls of Congress*. New York: Thomas Dunne Books, an Imprint of St. Martin's Press, 2007.

Reid, Ira De A. *The Negro Immigrant: His Background, Characteristics, and Social Adjustment, 1899–1937*. New York: Arno, 1939.

Rhodes, Jane. *Framing the Black Panthers: The Spectacular Rise of a Black Power Icon*. Champaign: University of Illinois Press, 2007.

Rhodes Kelly, Wilhelmena. *Bedford Stuyvesant: Images of America, of New York*. Mount Pleasant, S.C.: Arcadia, 2007.

Sacks, Marcy S. *Before Harlem: The Black Experience in New York City Before World War I*. Philadelphia: University of Pennsylvania Press, 2006.

Sayre, Wallace S., and Kaufman, Herbert. *Governing New York City: Politics in the Metropolis*. New York: Norton, 1965.

Schroth, Raymond A., S.J. *The Eagle and Brooklyn: A Community Newspaper, 1874–1955*. Westport, Conn.: Greenwood, 1974.

Shapiro, Milton. *Jackie Robinson of the Brooklyn Dodgers*. New York: Archway and Washington Square Press, 1969.

Sinnette, Elinor Des Verney. *Arthur Alfonso Schomburg: Black Bibliophile & Collector*. Detroit: Wayne State University Press, 1989.

Smorkaloff, Pamela Maria. *If I Could Write This in Fire: An Anthology of Literature from the Caribbean*, New York: The New Press, 1994.

Sokol, Jason. *All Eyes Are Upon Us: Race and Politics from Boston to Brooklyn*. New York: Basic Books, a Member of the Perseus Books Group, 2014.

Swan, Robert. *Thomas McCants Stewart and the Failure of the Mission of the Talented Tenth in Black America, 1880–1923*. Doctoral thesis, New York University, 1990.

Taylor, Clarence. *The Black Churches of Brooklyn*. New York: Columbia University Press, 1994.

———. *Knocking at Our Own Door: Milton A. Galamison and the Struggle to Integrate New York City Schools*. Lanham, Md.: Lexington, 2001.

Thornbrough, Emma Lou. *T. Thomas Fortune: Militant Journalist.* Chicago: University of Chicago Press, 1972.

United States of America. *The WPA Guide to New York City: The Federal Writers Project Guide to 1930s New York.* New York: The New Press, 1995.

Vanderbilt, Gertrude Lefferts. *The Social History of Flatbush, and Manners and Customs of the Dutch Settlers in Kings County.* Frederick Loeser and Company, 1881; Bowie, Md.: Heritage Books, 2003.

Vickerman, Milton. *Crosscurrents: West Indian Immigrants and Race.* London: Oxford University Press, 1999.

Walter, John C. *The Harlem Fox: J. Raymond Jones and Tammany, 1920–1970.* Albany: SUNY Press, 1989.

Watkins-Owens, Irma. *Blood Relations: Caribbean Immigrants and the Harlem Community, 1900–1930.* Bloomington: Indiana University Press, 1996.

Weld, Ralph Foster. *Brooklyn Is America.* New York: Columbia University Press, 1950.

Wellman, Judith. *Brooklyn's Promised Land: The Free Black Community of Weeksville, New York.* New York: NYU Press, 2014.

Wesser, Robert F. *Charles Evans Hughes: Politics and Reform in New York 1905–1910.* Ithaca, N.Y.: Cornell University Press, 1967.

Whitehead, Colson. *The Colossus of New York.* New York: Anchor, 2003.

Wilder, Craig Steven. *A Covenant with Color: Race and Social Power in Brooklyn.* New York: Columbia University Press, 2001.

Wilkerson, Isabel. *The Warmth of Other Suns: The Epic Story of America's Great Migration.* New York: Knopf Doubleday, 2010.

Willensky, Elliot. *When Brooklyn Was the World.* New York: Harmony, 1986.

Williams, Mason B. *City of Ambition: FDR, La Guardia, and the Making of Modern New York.* New York: Norton, 2013.

Winslow, Barbara. *Shirley Chisholm: Catalyst for Change.* Florence, Ky., and New York: Westview, 2014.

Woodsworth, Michael. *Battle for Bed-Stuy: The Long War on Poverty in New York City.* Cambridge, Mass.: Harvard University Press, 2016.

Yans-McLaughlin, Virginia, and Lightman, Marjorie. *Ellis Island and the Peopling of America: The Official Guide.* New York: The New Press, 1997.

Younger, William Lee. *Old Brooklyn in Early Photographs, 1865–1929.* New York: Dover, 1978.

Zukin, Sharon. *Global Cities, Local Streets: Everyday Diversity from New York to Shanghai.* New York: Routledge, 2015.

A Selection of Books from the Several Hundred That Were in the Library of Bertram L. Baker

Allen, James Egert. *The Negro in New York.* New York: Exposition Press, 1964.

Balkin, Harry H. *The New Science of Analysing Character.* Philadelphia: Harry H. Balkin, 1922.

Berry, Jean. *Finding Oneself in the Universe*. New York: Putnam, 1923.

Brown, B. H. *Plane Trigonometry and Logarithms*. Boston: Houghton Mifflin, 1925.

Burns, Sir Alan. *History of the British West Indies*. London: Allen & Unwin, 1954.

Cannons, Harry George Turner. *The Executive and His Control of Men*. New York: Macmillan, 1915.

De Fontenoy, the Marquis. *Revelation of High Life Within Royal Palaces: The Private Life of Emperors, Kings, Queens, Princes, and Princesses*. Edgewood Publishing Company (no locale given), 1892.

Douglass, Frederick. *Oration Delivered by Frederick Douglass at the Unveiling of the Freedman's Monument, In Memory of Abraham Lincoln*. New York: Pathway, 1940.

Du Bois, W. E. B. *Encyclopedia of the Negro*. New York: Phelps–Stokes Fund, 1945.

Halsey, Francis W. *Seeing Europe with Famous Authors*. New York and London: Funk and Wagnalls, 1914.

Hendrickson, Robert, *Hamilton* I and II. New York: Mason/Charter, 1976.

Hillis, Newell Dwight. *Right Living as a Fine Art*. New York, Chicago, and Toronto: Revell, 1899.

Kerr, John H., D. D. *An Introduction to the Study of the Books of the New Testament*. New York, Chicago, and Toronto: Revell, 1892.

Levine, Donald N. *Wax and Gold: Tradition and Innovation in Ethiopian Culture*. Chicago and London: University of Chicago Press, 1965.

Lindsey, Judge Ben B. *The Companionate Marriage*, New York: Garden City Publishing, 1929.

March, the Rev. Daniel, D. D. *Night Scenes in the Bible*. Zeigler, McCurdy & Co., Philadelphia, PA, Cincinnati, OH, Chicago, IL, St. Louis, MO., Springfield, MA.,1869. No name given as author or publisher, "The Garland or Token of Friendship," perhaps circa 1900.

Poe, Edgar Allan. *Little Masterpieces*. New York: Doubleday & McClure, 1898.

Reed, Thomas B. *Modern Eloquence*. Philadelphia: John D. Morris, 1900.

Richardson, J. D. *A Compilation of the Messages and Papers of the Presidents, 1789–1897*. Washington, D.C.: United States Congress, 1899.

Schuyler Baxter, Katharine. *In Beautiful Japan: A Story of Bamboo Lands*. New York: Hobart, 1904.

Smart, James D. *Promise to Keep*. Philadelphia: The Westminster Press, n.d.

Spofford's Library of Choice Literature and Encyclopaedia of Universal Authorship. *The Masterpieces of the Standard Writers of All Nations and All Time*. Philadelphia: Gebbie, 1890.

State University of New York. *Functions of a Modern University*. Proceedings of the First Symposium. Albany: State University of New York, 1950.

Syrett, Harold C. *The Papers of Alexander Hamilton*. New York: Columbia University Press, 1962.

Index

ESE SELECT TITLES FROM EMPIRE STATE EDITIONS

Allen Jones with Mark Naison, *The Rat That Got Away: A Bronx Memoir*

Edward Rohs and Judith Estrine, *Raised by the Church: Growing up in New York City's Catholic Orphanages*

Janet Grossbach Mayer, *As Bad as They Say? Three Decades of Teaching in the Bronx*

William Seraile, *Angels of Mercy: White Women and the History of New York's Colored Orphan Asylum*

Andrew J. Sparberg, *From a Nickel to a Token: The Journey from Board of Transportation to MTA*

Daniel Campo, *The Accidental Playground: Brooklyn Waterfront Narratives of the Undesigned and Unplanned*

Howard Eugene Johnson with Wendy Johnson, *A Dancer in the Revolution: Stretch Johnson, Harlem Communist at the Cotton Club*. Foreword by Mark D. Naison

Joseph B. Raskin, *The Routes Not Taken: A Trip Through New York City's Unbuilt Subway System*

Phillip Deery, *Red Apple: Communism and McCarthyism in Cold War New York*

Stephen Miller, *Walking New York: Reflections of American Writers from Walt Whitman to Teju Cole*

Tom Glynn, *Reading Publics: New York City's Public Libraries, 1754–1911*

Greg Donaldson, *The Ville: Cops and Kids in Urban America, Updated Edition*. With a new epilogue by the author, Foreword by Mark D. Naison

R. Scott Hanson, *City of Gods: Religious Freedom, Immigration, and Pluralism in Flushing, Queens*. Foreword by Martin E. Marty

Dorothy Day and the Catholic Worker: The Miracle of Our Continuance. Edited, with an Introduction and Additional Text by Kate Hennessy, Photographs by Vivian Cherry, Text by Dorothy Day

Pamela Lewis, *Teaching While Black: A New Voice on Race and Education in New York City*

Mark Naison and Bob Gumbs, *Before the Fires: An Oral History of African American Life in the Bronx from the 1930s to the 1960s*

Robert Weldon Whalen, *Murder, Inc., and the Moral Life: Gangsters and Gangbusters in La Guardia's New York*

Joanne Witty and Henrik Krogius, *Brooklyn Bridge Park: A Dying Waterfront Transformed*

Sharon Egretta Sutton, *When Ivory Towers Were Black: A Story about Race in America's Cities and Universities*

Pamela Hanlon, *A Wordly Affair: New York, the United Nations, and the Story Behind Their Unlikely Bond*

Britt Haas, *Fighting Authoritarianism: American Youth Activism in the 1930s*

David J. Goodwin, *Left Bank of the Hudson: Jersey City and the Artists of 111 1st Street*. Foreword by DW Gibson

Nandini Bagchee, *Counter Institution: Activist Estates of the Lower East Side*

Carol Lamberg, *Neighborhood Success Stories: Creating and Sustaining Affordable Housing in New York*

Barbara G. Mensch, *In the Shadow of Genius: The Brooklyn Bridge and Its Creators*

Susan Celia Greenfield (ed.), *Sacred Shelter: Thirteen Journeys of Homelessness and Healing*

Andrew Feffer, *Bad Faith: Teachers, Liberalism, and the Origins of McCarthyism*

Susan Opotow and Zachary Baron Shemtob (eds.), *New York After 9/11*

Elizabeth Macaulay-Lewis and Matthew McGowan (eds.), *Classical New York: Discovering Greece and Rome in Gotham*

For a complete list, visit www.empirestateeditions.com.